A HISTORY OF AFRICA
1840–1914

Michael Tidy
with
Donald Leeming

Volume Two 1880–1914

AFRICANA PUBLISHING COMPANY

A division of Holmes & Meier Publishers, Inc.

NEW YORK

TO

my wife Anastasia Obuya
(whose loving spirit and
practical assistance have
sustained me in the writing
of this book, and who has
given my life a new dimension)

M.T.

First published in the United States of America 1981 by
Africana Publishing Company
a division of Holmes and Meier Publishers Inc.
30 Irving Place, New York, N.Y. 10003

Copyright © 1981 Michael Tidy and Donald Leeming

Library of Congress Catalog Card Number: 81-68515
ISBN 0-8419-0662-9

Printed in Great Britain

Contents

List of maps

Preface

This two volume history aims to supply a need for a readily available survey of the whole African continent during the critical periods before, during and immediately after the European Partition. The writing of the book owes an immense debt to the work of innumerable historians of Africa. However, much of their work has been unavailable to the general reader while other material has been published in regional, national or local histories. *A History of Africa 1840–1914* attempts to bring together much of this material in one history and to make it more readily accessible. Inevitably a history such as this has to be selective, but it is believed that the selections of material will give the reader a good overall picture of Africa between 1840 and 1914.

Volume 1 covers the period from about 1840 to the beginning of the Scramble. It examines the considerable African achievement in the pre-colonial era by looking at a number of diverse societies, and surveys their response to European penetration throughout the continent. The increasing European interest of the nineteenth century, including the work of traders, missionaries and explorers, is dealt with. The Volume ends at the point where the European powers are poised for the Scramble. Volume 2 deals with the period of the Scramble and the African response to the loss of independence.

We are both deeply grateful to our Kenyan students, fellow-teachers, historians and other friends and colleagues, all of whom have made our work in Kenya so meaningful and our lives there so enjoyable.

M.T./D.L.
October, 1979

1
The Scramble for Africa: background and overview

The European background to the partition of Africa

Europeans had established some colonies in Africa in the first half of the nineteenth century and before, but the last quarter of the century saw an unprecedented expansion of European colonization. By 1914 all of the African continent, except Ethiopia and Liberia, had been partitioned. The suddenness of this movement has led to its being known as the 'Scramble' for Africa.

Why did this partition of Africa by European countries take place? Why did the partition occur in the last quarter of the nineteenth century and not before? What were the factors in Africa which encouraged the Europeans to make colonies there? Changing conditions in Africa as well as in Europe help to answer these questions.

Amongst the changes in Europe was the formation in 1870–1 of two new large nation-states, Germany and Italy. These states, especially Germany, had considerable economic and military resources and so were capable of making colonies in other continents. National prestige was a powerful factor in European imperialism. France and Britain were already 'Great Powers' and already had colonies. Nationalists in both Germany and Italy felt that their own countries should have colonies and so increase their status and influence in international affairs. France also felt the need to maintain her prestige by making colonies. In 1870–1, her armies had been completely defeated in the Franco-Prussian War. While France was not strong enough for many years to regain lost provinces and prestige by launching a new war against Prussia, the dominant state in Germany, she hoped to recover the latter by making colonies in Africa.

It was particularly important at international conferences and at times of treaty-making in Europe. European countries needed to have sufficient prestige to be represented at an international conference. It explains why the Italians attempted to establish colonies in North-east Africa.

Strategy was another key factor in the partition. The French fear that Italy might occupy the North African coast and gain increasing

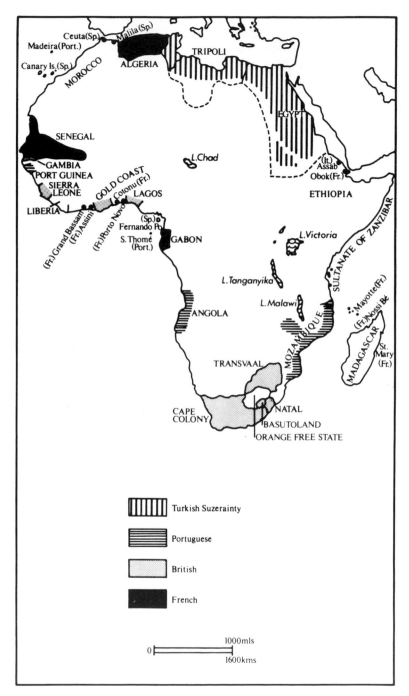

Map 1.   Africa, 1880.

control of the Mediterranean led to the French occupation of Tunis. Strategic reasons particularly influenced British policy in North and East Africa. The most important part of the British empire was India: in 1869 the Suez Canal was opened, and this became the shortest and most important route between Britain and India. Britain wished to make certain that the rulers of Egypt, who could easily interfere with the Canal, remained friendly to her. In 1881 there was a nationalist revolt in Egypt led by Arabi Pasha, an army colonel, against the control of the country's finances by a European financial commission. Arabi established himself as the real ruler of Egypt. The British, afraid that Arabi would interfere with shipping in the Suez Canal and so endanger their trade route to India, decided to invade Egypt. At the Battle of Tel-el-Kebir in 1882, Arabi was defeated and Britain took control of Egypt. Further considerations of strategy caused Britain to stay there. She feared the growing power of Russia and was afraid that the Russian fleet might enter the Mediterranean from the Black Sea. In response Britain developed the Egyptian port of Alexandria as a major base for the Royal Navy. As Egypt was dependent on the waters of the Nile, it became an aim of British policy to prevent any other European country from making colonies along the Nile banks. To achieve this, Britain eventually occupied the Sudan, Uganda and Kenya.

The increasing importance of public opinion in European countries was another important factor in the partition of Africa. The extension of the vote in most European countries meant that governments had to pay more attention to their electorates than earlier in the century. Voters generally had little knowledge of colonial matters but were strongly in favour of their country acquiring colonies. In 1882 the French Assembly agreed to ratify De Brazza's treaty with Chief Makoko, chiefly because of the pressure from public opinion.

British public opinion had some influence with the establishment of a British protectorate in Uganda. The German Chancellor Bismarck was influenced by increasing public support for colonies. In 1884 there were elections to the German *Reichstag* (parliament). Bismarck realized that if his supporters were going to be elected he would have to change his previous policy of opposition to colonization. He created German protectorates in South West Africa, Togo, the Cameroons and Tanganyika. The influence of the press and colonial societies led many Europeans to favour imperial policies. In England *The Daily Mail* was becoming the most popular paper and it was strongly imperialistic. *The Times* was widely read by the British ruling class and one of its journalists was Flora Shaw, who later married Lugard: she strongly favoured the expansion of the British empire in Africa and wrote articles supporting such men as Goldie, Rhodes, Johnston and Lugard. A society called the Primrose League encouraged the Conservative Party to support imperial policies. The most active colonial society in Germany was the Society for German

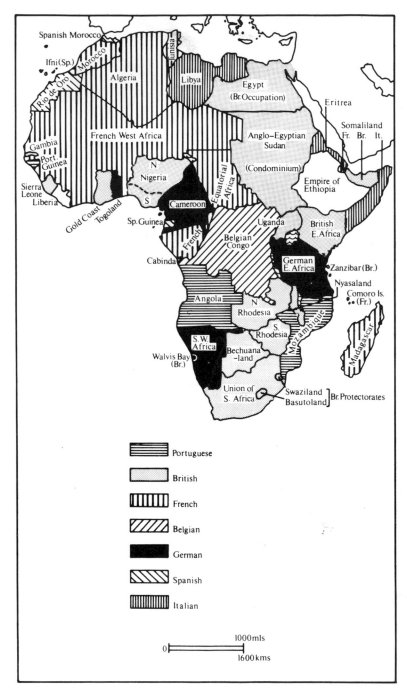

Map 2. Africa, 1914: after the European Scramble.

Colonization founded in 1884 by Karl Peters. In France and Italy various geographical societies and newspapers supported imperialism in Africa.

During the Great Depression in the economy of Europe from 1875 to 1900, investment of capital in Europe was becoming less profitable. Many European businessmen came to believe that investment in Africa would bring greater profit. In some areas of Africa this proved to be true. King Leopold was able to get wide support from Belgian and British businessmen for his ventures in the Congo (Zaire), and an investment of 40 million francs brought a profit of 28 million between 1878 and 1908. In South Africa, highly lucrative investments in the Rand gold mines after 1886 was a powerful factor in the events that led to war between Britain and the Afrikaner Republics in 1899. However, many European business activities in Africa were unsuccessful. The Pioneer Column of Rhodes' British South Africa Company entered Mashonaland confidently expecting to find a gold mine for every member of the column, but it found no gold. Mackinnon began building a road to develop trade from Dar-es-Salaam to Lake Malawi, but after a few miles the attempt had to be abandoned. However, European economic imperialism often thrived without political imperialism. Before 1800, Britain had a far greater investment in the railways of the USA and Argentina than she had in any of her African colonies. Why, then, did many European businessmen favour the establishment of colonies in Africa after 1875?

In many cases, they exerted pressure on their governments to colonize, because they were failing to make adequate profits and needed European government action against trading rivals. There are clear examples of this in West Africa. In the Niger delta in the 1870s and 1880s, rivalries intensified between African producers and European firms, and between African middlemen firms and the Europeans, as these groups competed desperately for a share of reduced profits in the palm-oil trade. In some parts of West Africa Europeans were unable to compete with efficient African economic and commercial organizations, like Jaja's trading house in Opobo. Jaja's skill in cornering the interior Igbo market for palm oil, and his plans to ship oil direct to Europe, were too much for the British traders in the Niger delta who put pressure on the British consul, Harry Johnston, to overthrow him. Similarly, Goldie's Royal Niger Company could not compete with the trading houses of Brass until it had political powers and military resources to deploy against the Brassmen. When African trading societies deliberately interrupted the supply of oil to the Europeans because of disputes over prices, as in the case of both the Itsekiri of the western delta and the Yoruba in the 1880s, European traders called for their governments to take action against African states. European administrators on the West African coast were now more willing to act against African traders. Their main task was to protect European trade, but they could not do so in trade war conditions; if they failed to end the trade wars their careers would be in jeopardy. Moreover, colonies' incomes were seriously affected. Destruction of African middleman trade and the consequent domination by European traders would push up prices and bring increased revenue from customers, thus helping to balance colonial budgets.

European businessmen were also increasingly concerned at the possibility of serious rivalry with each other. When French and German traders began to compete with the British, especially in the late 1870s, British traders began to favour customs duties to keep out the goods of their European rivals. In order to collect customs duties it was necessary to have political control, which meant establishing colonies. Both British and French firms feared that German commercial expansion would result in their exclusion from unclaimed areas of Africa, and so put pressure on their governments to forestall the Germans before they could take over too many new markets. In their turn German merchants feared possible British annexations in their areas of trading interest such as Togo and the Cameroons.

European militarism and humanitarianism both played roles in the partition. There was not enough fighting in Europe in the nineteenth centry for European military officers aspiring to glory and rapid promotion, and consequently they sought it in colonial wars. Moreover, because of the lack of modern weapons among Africans and other colonial peoples, it was less dangerous than in Europe.

In France, Bugeaud, Faidherbe, De Brazza and Gallieni were all military men who actively expanded the French empire in Africa. In the western Sudan from 1879 the military officers on the spot rather than the French government decided the direction and extent of French colonization. British soldiers such as Wolseley, Kitchener and Lugard supported and carried out the expansion of the British empire in Africa. By 1880, acute commercial rivalry had developed in West Africa between Britain and France. Each thought the other wanted to establish protectorates to guarantee trade for her own traders, and decided to establish them to forestall the rival Great Power.

Missionaries usually encouraged the establishment of European rule in Africa. They wanted their governments to put a stop to wars between African states, to end the slave trade in the interior, to protect them from attacks by Muslims in places like Malawi and Uganda, and to destroy the authority of traditionalist rulers like Jaja and Nana. All these things would make evangelization easier. Missionary societies had considerable influence in Europe and so governments, particularly the British, could not afford to ignore their views. The 'civilizing mission' and anti-slavery provided both an ideology and moral justification for political invasion. Lugard had such deep faith in the Protestant belief of Britain that he considered it to be his duty to spread it by almost any means. Harry Johnston was an unbeliever but at the same time a passionate supporter of Christian missionary work as a 'civilizing influence'.

Many Europeans believed in their 'civilizing mission' because they thought they were superior to other races. They based their assumption on the fact that European industry was more advanced than the industry of any other continent.

Cecil Rhodes remarked about Englishmen, 'We are the first race in the world and . . . the more of the world we inhabit the better it is for the human race'. In 1899 the English poet Rudyard Kipling wrote a poem *The White Man's Burden* about the duty of the European to rule other peoples in order to 'civilize' them. These erroneous but sincerely held views encouraged Europeans to make more colonies in Africa.

The beginning of the European Partition of Africa, 1875–85

Which event was most responsible for the flare-up of international rivalry known as the Scramble for Africa. King Leopold II's launching of his activities in Zaire, then known as the Congo, De Brazza's treaty with Makoko, Gladstone's occupation of Egypt or Bismarck's sudden declaration of German protectorates?

Leopold

Leopold II was King of Belgium from 1865 to 1909. Belgium was a small country, and Leopold was a constitutional monarch with limited power and income. In the tropics he sought absolute power and wealth. In 1875 the British explorer Lovett Cameron crossed Africa from Zanzibar to Luanda, and his journey stimulated Leopold's interest in Central Africa.

In 1876 Leopold hosted an international conference on Africa in Brussels. Ostensibly it was a geographical conference. The delegates agreed to set up a chain of European trading stations across Africa from the Congo (Zaire) mouth to Zanzibar. These stations would be bases for the suppression of the slave trade and slavery, and would be used to introduce Africa to civilization. No annexation of territory would take place. The stations would be organized by an International Association, in order to prevent European national rivalries bedevilling this humanitarian exercise. These were the declared aims of the Brussels conference. However, Leopold's real aims were to make massive trading profits for himself and to establish a political empire in the Congo region.

In 1877 Stanley crossed the continent from east to west and mapped the Congo river, most of which he found navigable. The next year Leopold recruited Stanley for an expedition to the lower Congo to set up trading stations and to make trade treaties with local rulers. Stanley was to amalgamate the trading stations he established, and set up a Free State with Leopold at the head. In 1879 Stanley arrived in the Congo and began to set up trading settlements. Leopold cannot be blamed entirely for starting the Scramble for Africa, but Stanley's activities certainly stimulated De Brazza's march into the interior.

De Brazza

Between 1875 and 1878 De Brazza, a French naval officer, explored the Ogoue river from the small French colony of Gabon. He discovered a route along the Ogoue valley to Stanley Pool and the vast navigable Congo basin. In 1879 he was sent to the Congo by the French government and the French committee of the International Association with instructions to make trade treaties with African rulers and so draw the future trade of the Congo basin to French Gabon. De Brazza arrived on the north bank of Stanley Pool in 1880. He made a political treaty with Makoko, ruler of some of the Bateke, and established a French post at Makoko's home. Makoko ceded territory to France for a number of reasons. A vast area of land was not ruled by him, and he hoped to impress De Brazza with his imaginary power. Secondly, he required De Brazza's presence as a boost to his position in the internal Bateke power struggle. Thirdly, he hoped to make profits from trade with the French. In 1882, De Brazza returned to France in order to try to get his treaty ratified by the French government, but the government was not interested in the Congo, which it regarded as the International Association's affair. It was opposed to a political treaty and it had enough colonial preoccupations elsewhere, especially as it had recently embarked on expansion from Senegal towards the upper Niger at the expense of the Tokolor empire. De Brazza launched a press campaign in Paris to try to get public opinion and the Chamber of Deputies, behind his treaty. At first the campaign was unsuccessful, but the whole situation was changed by the unexpected British occupation of Egypt. French public opinion changed almost overnight. France, which had looked on Egypt as its sphere of influence, sought compensation in the Congo; and the French parliament and government ratified the De Brazza-Makoko Treaty.

Gladstone

One of the great paradoxes of history is that William Ewart Gladstone, the British Liberal leader, and the champion of Irish, Boer and Afghan freedom from British imperialism probably did more than any other European leader to spark off the Scramble for

Africa. When Gladstone despatched Wolseley in 1882 to defeat Arabi and safeguard the Suez Canal, and sent Lord Cromer to administer Egypt until Egyptian debts to Europe had been paid, he unwittingly accelerated European imperial activities all over Africa. Robinson and Gallagher, in their book *Africa and the Victorians* (1961), wrote, 'Without the occupation of Egypt, there is no reason to suppose that any international scrambles for Africa, either east or west, would have begun when they did'. This is probably overestimating the impact of the British occupation of Egypt. Various factors in Europe and Africa were building up pressure towards a European scramble for African territory in the 1880s and 1890s. However, Britain's occupation of Egypt certainly helped to precipitate the Scramble. Originally, France had intended to participate in the expedition against Egypt, but when plans for a joint Anglo-French invasion were advanced, the French Chamber, owing to an internal political crisis, voted to withdraw. The French were chagrined when the British succeeded in defeating Arabi on their own. For some time France had regarded Egypt as its sphere of influence. French businessmen had dominated European enterprise in Egypt since the days of Muhammad Ali. A Frenchman supervised the building of the Suez Canal. Now Britain had plucked Egypt from France's hand.

The immediate result of Britain's occupation of Egypt without French help was that France ratified the De Brazza-Makoko treaty and sent De Brazza back to the Congo as Governor of a new French colony. In turn the ratification of the De Brazza-Makoko had radical effects. Leopold and Stanley had an excuse for stepping up their activities on the south bank of the Congo and many more stations were set up. In 1884 the Congo Free State was openly constituted, and recognized by the USA. In turn this stimulated the making of the Anglo-Portuguese Treaty of 1884, in which Britain supported Portuguese control of the Congo estuary in return for Portugal promising free trade on the Congo. The Treaty was not ratified by the British parliament because of missionary society protests that the Portuguese in Angola were lax abolishing slavery. Also, Germany's support for the French annexation of the north Congo was a further discouragement to the British. But Portugal then gained Britain's support by suggesting an international conference to settle the question of the lower Congo. The idea was taken up by Bismarck, who as part of his new foreign policy in Europe, wanted a better opportunity to show that Germany was friendly to France. The Berlin West Africa Conference met in Berlin at the end of 1884.

Bismarck

If Britain's occupation of Egypt was one factor that set off the Scramble in Central Africa, another was Bismarck's declaration of

German protectorates in 1884–5, and the decisions made by the Conference he hosted in the German capital.

Until 1884 the German Chancellor was opposed to colonization. A number of factors caused him to change his policy in that year, including the growing public demand for colonies and the election of 1884. Bismarck wished to unite a variety of political parties against the Social Democrats, who opposed colonial ventures. He also wanted to weaken the pro-British Liberal opposition in Germany who wanted more powers for the Reichstag. German colonial expansion would arouse national feeling against the British and against pro-British Germans. But in Bismarck's mind, considerations of foreign policy were uppermost. The key to his European policy was to keep France isolated from other Great Powers: to prevent her making alliances and fighting a war of revenge to recover Alsace and Lorraine, the two French provinces annexed by Germany in 1871. Bismarck hoped to divert France's attention to Africa, where she might not only concentrate on colonial expansion but also quarrel with Britain. If France quarrelled with Britain in Africa, then he could repair Franco-German relations. Therefore, in 1884–5 Bismarck not only supported France in the Congo but also upset and alarmed Britain by establishing German protectorates in areas adjacent to British colonies or spheres of influence: Togo next to the Gold Coast, the Cameroons next to the Niger delta, South-West Africa next to Cape Colony, and Tanganyika territory claimed by Britain's puppet Sultan of Zanzibar.

Britain's reaction was to form more colonies of her own. In order to forestall a possible German advance from the Cameroons, or French occupation of the lower Niger with the support of Germany, the British Consul Hewett speeded up his making of protection treaties in the Niger delta, and Goldie made similar treaties with the Muslim emirs of the interior. In 1885 Britain set up the Niger Coast Protectorate. Britain was also alarmed by the creation of a German protectorate in East Africa under Karl Peters. The upshot was the Anglo-German Agreement of 1886, which split East Africa from the coast as far as Lake Victoria into two 'spheres of influence'. Germany got the lion's share, because Salisbury, the then British prime minister, was not very interested in East Africa at this time, and wanted German diplomatic support against France for the British position in Egypt. If the partition of East Africa gave Britain at least a reasonable share it was because Bismarck wanted her support in Europe. In 1886 there was a crisis in the Balkans and the possibility of a war between Germany, Austria and Italy on the one side, and France and Russia on the other. Germany wanted the British Navy to protect Italy against the French Navy.

Thus lines were drawn across Africa to suit the convenience of the European diplomatic power game. The line that divided Kenya and Tanzania ran from the Umba River at the coast to its terminal point at Lake Victoria. It was originally straight, but it was later bent a little when Queen Victoria of Britain was allowed by her government to give Mount Kilimanjaro to her grandson, the German Kaiser Wilhelm II, as a Christmas present.

Bismarck did not therefore start the Scramble for Africa. It had already begun in the Congo. But he accelerated it in Africa as a whole, and started regional scrambles in West and East Africa. He also accelerated the scramble in Central Africa. German annexation of South West Africa in 1884 made the British fear a link up between the Boer republics and the Germans, which would block Cape Colony's expansion to the north. Therefore in 1885 Britain set up the Protectorate of Bechuanaland (Botswana) between the Germans and the Boers and thus safeguarded their 'road to the north' into Central Africa.

The Berlin West Africa Conference, though called by Bismarck as part of his plan to foster conflict between Britain and France, was more important for the impetus it gave to European occupation of Africa. The Conference laid down the doctrine for the effective occupation of Africa. Under this doctrine a European power could only claim African territory if it could prove first that it actually administered it. Further, the great river basins of western Africa were partitioned on paper: the Congo basin was divided between Portugal, France and the Congo Free State and the division was recognized by all the powers; the Niger basin was split between Britain and France; the occupying powers were to allow free trade on the rivers; the slave trade in the interior was to be suppressed. The Berlin Conference did not partition Africa along exact boundary lines. Rather, it defined spheres of influence near the coast and left vast areas of the interior unallocated to any European power. However, later colonial treaties between European powers enabled precise boundaries to be drawn. The doctrine of effective occupation was a powerful stimulus to actual European invasion on the ground in order to make good the claims made on maps. Between 1885 and 1912 all the continent, except Ethiopia and Liberia, was overrun by European-led military forces and brought under European colonial rule.

The African background to the Partition of Africa

European actions during the Partition of Africa cannot be explained entirely in terms of European motives. They were also influenced by African conditions.

African political weakness

One feature of Africa in the nineteenth century was the small size of most states. All African states were smaller than the states of South America and bore no comparison to the vast Chinese empire. Indeed for many African peoples the largest political unit was the clan. These small states were frequently at war with their neighbours, often as a result of the spread of the slave trade. Thus while in South America European businessmen could make agreements with a government which would enable them to exploit the economic wealth of quite a large area, this was less easy in Africa. An agreement with one ruler might automatically mean that a neighbouring ruler was hostile. Consequently, European merchants and administrators often urged their governments to make colonies or enlarge existing ones, which would end wars between small states and thus make possible trade on a larger scale. An example of this was the British annexation of Yorubaland to stop the wars there, thus enabling British merchants to trade freely. A further factor in Britain's conquests of the small Yoruba states was the fear that, if she did not, they would be taken over by France. The small size of most African states increased European competition for colonies.

African political weakness was also apparent in divisions of various kinds. There were frequent civil wars caused by succession disputes, and examples can be seen in Itsekiriland. Trade rivalries gave rise to many conflicts, and wars often broke out because of cultural and religious fervour between such states as Ethiopia and the Mahdist Sudan. European invaders were able to take advantage of these political divisions to play off one side against another and establish their own rule. The policy of 'divide and conquer' was followed by that of 'divide and rule'. There were hardly any alliances between African states against the European invaders, though a few abortive attempts were made, for instance by Samori Toure in West Africa, and Mkwawa of the Hehe in East Africa. Though some alliances came about, they were too late to offer effective resistance, as both Samori and Kabalega of Bunyoro found. Co-ordinated resistance was out of the question so long as resistance was under the direction of rulers trying to defend particular interests, and whilst there was no common ideology that could have united separate communities. Islam might have provided a unifying force in Northern Africa or in the West African savanna, but divisions within and between Islamic states, based on regional animosities or rivalries between Brotherhoods, proved to be more important than what held them together.

African military weakness

European countries were encouraged to make colonies in Africa and able to defeat African states in war, because of their vastly

superior military technology. The Industrial Revolution in Europe
ensured that by 1880 European armaments were vastly superior to
those of Africa. The decisive weapon was the machine gun.
European armies widely used the Gatling gun in the 1870s and the
Maxim gun in the late 1880s. The Maxim could fire eleven shots a
second continuously for two or three minutes before reloading.
Machine guns were also lighter than cannon and could easily be
carried. Their effect was devastating against African soldiers armed
with spears, bows and arrows or slow-firing muzzle-loading
muskets. As one English poet, Hilaire Belloc remarked,

'Whatever happens we have got
The Maxim gun, and they have not.'

Apart from machine guns, European armies of conquest had a whole
array of other powerful weapons. There were heavy artillery guns,
ideal for demolishing African city walls and defensive stockades.
From the 1860s European soldiers had breech-loading rifles, which
enabled a more rapid rate of fire than the old muzzle-loaders which
many Africans were equipped with. From the 1880s a number of
African armies began to obtain breech-loaders, but these were now
relatively obsolete as the Europeans progressively abandoned them
for magazine rifles, which made possible an even faster rate of fire. A
further disadvantage for African armies was that they were usually
armed with a multitude of weapons obtained from different sources
at different times; it was therefore very difficult to obtain replacement parts and compatible ammunition. There was also a shortage in
most areas of skilled repairmen or gunsmiths. African soldiers
generally lacked training in gun handling, marksmanship and
tactics, partly because the severe shortage of ammunition left them
little to train with. Ammunition also ran short during wars of
resistance, as during the Asante Rebellion of 1900.

Another advantage European armies had was their superior
discipline and organization. There were few African standing
armies, and even these were usually deficient in drill and training.
Superior weapons, better discipline and training helped European
armies to compensate for their inferiority in numbers. At Sokoto,
Lugard's force of 600 well-trained men routed the caliph's army of
30,000. Samori showed that Africans were quite capable of matching
European armies in discipline and organization if given sufficient
training. However, such training was rarely possible.

Another factor in African military weakness during the European
invasion was tactics. There were numerous examples of African
armies refusing to abandon outmoded traditional tactics and suffer-
ing the consequences. The Tokolor persisted in cavalry charges
against French machine guns and defence of mud-walled towns
against French artillery. The Ijebu of Yorubaland fired their rifles at
the British while standing up instead of from cover.

A final factor in European military success was that the 'European' armies which occupied Africa were primarily European-led armies of *African* soldiers, who were better able than European soldiers to live and survive in tropical conditions.

Although Europe had several military advantages over Africa, it should not be overlooked that African armies were sometimes able to inflict heavy defeats on European armies, for instance the Zulu victory over the British at Isandhlwana in 1879 (see Volume One) and Ethiopia's defeat of the Italians at Adowa (see Chapter 5).

Types of African response to colonial rule

The work of Terence Ranger, John Iliffe and others has led to the classification of African resistance to colonialism into the following categories: primary resistance, secondary resistance and modern mass nationalism. In this book we are concerned only with the first of these categories. Primary resistance took place before 1914 and consisted of armed struggles against the establishment of colonial rule. It can conveniently be sub-divided into two categories: initial primary resistance and post-pacification revolts. The former was essentially armed struggle against the imposition of colonial rule and was generally carried on by local community armies under traditional political and military leadership. An example would be Nandi resistance to British invasion in Kenya. Post-pacification revolts were rebellions against the immediate short-term effects of the imposition of colonial rule. They generally involved the masses and cut across ethnic boundaries; new types of leadership often emerged, particularly important were religious leaders including millenarian priests and spirit mediums. Examples can be seen in the Ndebele-Shona risings of 1896–7 and the Maji Maji risings of 1905–7.

Secondary resistance which does not concern us occured between the two World Wars and was usually peaceful. It involved welfare associations, trade unions, independent churches and elite organizations. These movements tended to be local rather than national in character. Modern mass nationalism emerged after 1945. Its aim was the regaining of independence. Modern political parties which were national rather than local were formed. The movement was usually peaceful but sometimes armed struggles developed as was the case in Kenya, Algeria, Angola, Mozambique and Zimbabwe.

This classification is not exhaustive. It does not take account of the response of Africans who accommodated themselves to colonial rule and largely accepted it. However, it is not meant to. It does provide a useful guide to armed resistance, which is covered in Chapters 2 to 5 and 10, and also in Chapters 7, 9 and 10 of Volume One.

Most Africans became subjects of one European empire or another without being aware of it. There were usually too few Europeans in the early days to occupy large areas of territory, and consequently most Africans lived in their villages without seeing a white man. To take two examples from Kenya: the Nandi between 1895 and 1906 and the Gusii in 1905 and 1908 resisted British attempts to replace 'paper' colonial rule with actual rule. They were not in revolt, as European colonial officers thought. Rather, they were attempting to prevent the actual establishment of colonial rule.

Armed resistance was only one type of African response to colonialism. There were in fact four main types of primary response to the establishment of colonial rule.

Active or armed resistance This is well documented by European colonial writers, and well-remembered in African oral tradition.

Passive resistance Unarmed non-co-operation. It is not well documented or so clearly remembered; consequently there are huge gaps in present-day knowledge of passive resistance.

Adaptation This is sometimes called 'diplomacy'. It took various forms. Two of the most common were alliance with European invaders against dangerous local enemies, and treaties with the Europeans in order to buy time.

The mercenary technique This involved alliance with the invaders for trading profits or loot.

Adaptation and the mercenary technique have often been referred to as collaboration.

The two commonest forms of response were armed resistance and adaptation. It is remarkable that Africans maintained determined resistance for so long against such overwhelming odds. The courage of their soldiers and their determination to preserve independence partly explains this. Equally important is the fact that a number of states and societies adopted guerilla tactics against the European invaders.

Traditional methods of warfare such as pitched battles and frontal assaults were hopelessly ineffective against European guns. But the forces of Samori's Mandinka empire and Kabalega's Bunyoro were considerably more successful when they changed to guerilla warfare. Similarly, the Ndebele were heavily defeated in 1893 when they charged in Zulu fashion into the disciplined and accurate rifle fire of the British, but their resistance was more effective in 1896 when they resorted to hit-and-run tactics. There were many examples of strong resistance by segmented societies like the Baoule of the Ivory Coast, the Igbo of Nigeria, the Turkana of Kenya and the Acholi of Uganda. In these communities each small political unit offered its separate guerilla resistance; thus there was no identifiable army for the Europeans to defeat in a decisive battle, as was possible, for example, with states like Sokoto or the Mahdist Sudan. European armies found it difficult to fight guerillas. The guerillas were on home ground whereas the Europeans were not only fighting in unfamiliar territory, but were at the end of extended lines of communication and often forced to march single file through forest in which they could easily be ambushed.

Sometimes stiff resistance was put up because a measure of inter-ethnic co-operation was achieved. The Ndebele were far more effective in 1896 when they allied with the Shona than in 1893 when they fought alone. Tanzanian resistance—Abushiri in 1888–9 and Maji Maji—owed much of its impact to its lack of ethnicism.

It has often been stated or implied that armed resistance was backward-looking rather than forward-looking. However, some of the primary resistance movements may have been attempts to enlarge the scale of African political behaviour. The post-pacification revolts were often regional or national rather than local, involving masses of people, not just warrior elites. The emergence of a charismatic and revolutionary religious leadership, frequently with prophets of witchcraft eradication cults, overcame some of the problems of small-scale societies in their response to the Europeans.

A fairly common opinion is that armed resistance achieved nothing. This is not true in all cases. As a result of the 1880–1 Gun War with Cape Colony the Basuto were allowed to keep their guns and secured protection against white settlement. The Ndebele achieved a negotiated settlement to their 1896 rising and many of the indunas' powers were restored to them. Hehe resistance from 1891 to 1898 ended in total defeat with no concessions won, but the Hehe preserved their self-respect.

Various explanations to the phenomenon of one African group helping Europeans to conquer another African group have been given. One explanation for African adaptation or diplomacy of this kind is that there was a lack of racial consciousness among Africans. One society was not prepared to help another simply because they both happened to be black. Certain African societies had traditionally been hostile to one another. The arrival of white men did not alter this. European rule was sometimes considered a lighter burden than the rule of a hated local enemy; this helps to explain the Fante alliance with the British against Asante.

'Christian Revolutions' in Buganda, Bulozi, Botswana and southern Nigeria have often been discussed within the context of collaboration between Christian Africans and colonial officials. It is true that in Buganda and southern Nigeria a minority group like the Christians might assist colonialism for the group's advantage, but in all these societies Christianity was just one among several factors leading to co-operation between local Christians and the British. Christianity did not of necessity mean co-operation with the colonialists. The Ganda Catholics actually fought against colonialism.

2
European Scramble and African response: West Africa

European Partition: a summary

The Berlin West Africa Conference, as we have seen, had its origins in Bismarck's attempt to turn France away from thoughts of revenge for her defeat in 1870–1. At the same time, he intended to dislodge Britain's influence in the Congo and the Niger. At the Conference Britain could do little to safeguard her interests on the Congo as she had abandoned her support of Portuguese claims there before the Conference had even begun. King Leopold of Belgium conducted a careful propaganda campaign in Britain and the United States stressing the humanitarian nature of the regime he hoped to establish: the Congo Free State. At the Berlin Conference he was supported by France and the United States. Thwarted in the Congo, Britain determined to spend her energies defending her interests on the Niger.

During the period from 1884 to 1900 a series of agreements were signed between Germany, France and Britain which effectively divided West Africa up between them. As early as December 1885 a Convention was signed which recognized Germany's claim to Togoland. Britain and France also negotiated a boundary settlement which restricted German claims in the Cameroons. Britain and France signed a comprehensive frontier settlement in August 1889 which settled the boundaries at the coast of The Gambia, Sierra Leone and the Gold Coast. It also fixed the boundaries for a short distance inland. Rivalry between the powers at the coast thus came to a rather tame end. However, the race into the interior now began in earnest, with control of the Niger the biggest prize to be won.

On the Niger Britain's interests were largely salvaged by Sir George Goldie. By 1879 Goldie had united all the British traders on the Niger into the National African Company. In a ruthless price war he drove out the French traders and so obtained a monopoly of the palm-oil trade. The Berlin Conference granted to Britain the responsibility for the administration of navigation on the Niger. Britain was, however, reluctant to saddle herself with the cost for this, and in 1886 negotiated a charter with Goldie whereby his Royal Niger Company was given both the task and expense of the administration. Meanwhile, Goldie had been signing treaties of protection with numerous African rulers. Britain's claims to the lower Niger were thus relatively secure.

While Britain had been consolidating her hold on the lower Niger the French had not been idle. The expansion from Senegal, which had begun before the Scramble, continued. France also established herself on the Ivory Coast and at Porto Novo and Cotonou on the coast of Dahomey. In 1893 France finally attacked and conquered Dahomey. However, her expansion along the upper Niger was hindered by African resistance, especially by Samori Toure.

After the French conquest of Dahomey the threat of conflict between Britain and France arose over Borgu. Goldie wished to have this area under the control of his Royal Niger Company. France was determined that she should control the area and thus gain access to the lower part of the Niger which was navigable. Encouraged by the British government Goldie sent his forces to Borgu. During this expedition the emirates of Nupe and Ilorin were conquered. For a while British and French troops faced each other at Bussa on the Niger but the dispute was settled by diplomacy in Europe. In 1898 Britain and France finally settled the boundaries of their spheres of influence in West Africa.

African response: an overview

It has been said that West African resistance to the French was stronger than West African resistance to the British, and that Islam was the main reason for the strength of resistance to the French. It is doubtful whether either part of this statement can stand up to detailed examination. Whereas states like Samori Toure's Mandinka empire put up a prolonged struggle against France, with notable resistance by Cayor, the Sarrakole, the Tokolor and Bornu, a number of Muslim states not only failed to resist the French but openly allied with them. Examples are the upper Senegal states which fought alongside the French against Tokolor, and Sikasso and Kong which allied with France against Samori. Resistance to the British was often very determined. Wars were fought by Bai Bureh in Sierra Leone and the Asante in Ghana; there was a heroic last-ditch stand by Sultan Attahiru of Sokoto, and Igbo resistance continued until 1917. Islam was not always a strong factor in this resistance. Neither the Asante nor the Igbo were Muslim societies. It seems that the safest generalization that can be made about West

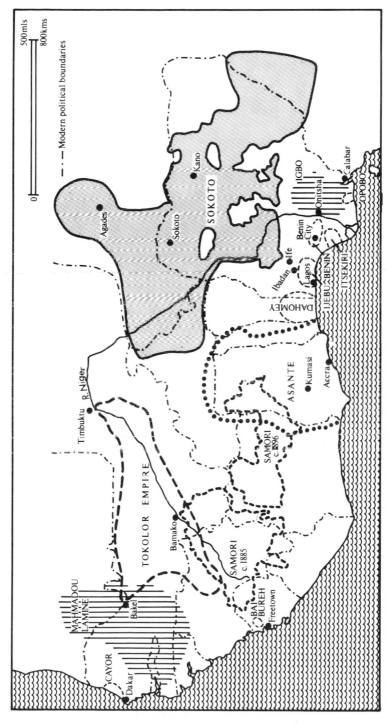

Map 3. Some West African states and peoples on the eve of the European Partition.

African resistance is that some states and societies, regardless of religious background, fought strongly to preserve their political, economic and religious independence; whereas others, again regardless of religion but largely because of the local balance of power, linked themselves to the European invaders.

The motives for acceptance of European rule by West African societies varied considerably. It was sometimes considered a lighter burden than the rule of certain African leaders. The Fante preferred British to Asante rule. Sometimes the society concerned was aware of European military power and consequently regarded resistance to it as futile. The Asante thought this way in 1896. Certain Africans welcomed the peace that European rule brought in some areas. This was true of some of the Yoruba.

The Western-educated black Creole elite generally welcomed the extension of colonial rule. The Creoles believed that European protectorates would open up vast fields for trade, would help to spread Christianity, and would provide an opportunity to Creoles to help govern the new protectorates. On the first two of these three points, the Creoles were proved correct; but on the last one they were disappointed. The more farsighted envisaged a period of temporary European colonial rule followed by the emergence of a vastly expanded western-educated African 'elite' which would re-assert West Africa's political independence.

Senegal

In the late 1870s France resumed her expansionist policies in the Senegal. In 1878 she began to build the St Louis-Dakar railway but in the beginning the railway was almost not built. This was largely because of the resistance of Lat-Dior Diop, the *Damel* (Ruler) of Cayor, a state in the immediate hinterland of the coastal colony of Senegal. Lat-Dior was born in about 1842 and became damel in 1862 but was obliged to spend four years in exile from 1864 to 1868. Although challenged by a number of claimants to the throne Lat-Dior consolidated his position by expanding agricultural production and supporting the farmers against the warrior class. Initially the French found the damel a useful ally who exported large quantities of groundnuts through French-controlled ports. In 1871 they recognized him as damel and a decade of mutually advantageous but uneasy co-operation followed.

However, when the French decided to build their railway through his territory Lat-Dior realized the dangers. For some time there had been growing distrust of the French, since they had been encouraging the royal slaves to desert their master. Lat-Dior believed correctly that the advent of the railway would be followed by permanent French settlements which would ultimately take away his territory and authority. After his refusal to co-operate with the

French he was declared deposed by them in 1882 but embarked on a campaign of resistance which was to last until 1886.

At first, the economic effects of Lat-Dior's resistance were considerable. The export of groundnuts from Senegal dropped in 1883 to about a quarter of the usual figure. Lat-Dior allied with Ali Bouri of Djollof and Abdul Bubakar of Futa Toro against the French but in January 1883 the French attacked Cayor before the damel's allies could come to his assistance. Cayor was invaded from several directions and Lat-Dior fled. The French then placed one of his relations, Samba Yaye, who had collaborated with them, on the throne. Lat-Dior continued guerilla activities until 1886 when he was defeated and killed at Dyaqlé. His two allies continued their resistance by joining forces with Ahmadu of the Tokolor empire.

Although Lat-Dior had lost the fight against the French his rule had a major impact on the Wolof people of Cayor. During his period of exile from 1864 when he had been in Saloum he had been converted to Islam. On his return to Cayor he assisted in the spread of Islam. The new faith was particularly welcomed by the downtrodden farmers. Islam united them with the damel against the soldiers who exploited them. Lat-Dior managed to suppress much of the looting of the soldiers and so persuaded many to accept Islam. However, his policy alienated many powerful elements in society and helped to pave the way for his defeat by the French.

Another Senegalese resister was the Sarrakole *marabout* (religious teacher) Mahmadou Lamine who had been born between 1835 and 1840. He had gone on the pilgrimage to Mecca in about 1868 but did not return home until 1885. He had spent seven years in Mecca and a further seven as a captive of Ahmadu, the Tokolor ruler at Segu. In 1885 he began to amass many thousands of followers for a purifying jihad and, in 1886, proclaimed himself the Mahdi. Mahmadou wished ultimately to reform the world; but his immediate practical aim was to establish a great Sarrakole empire in the upper Senegal valley, at the expense of both the French in Senegal and the Tokolor empire under Ahmadu. In the early 1880s the Sarrakole had refused to be recruited either as guides and porters in the French army or as labourers on the Senegal railway. Mahmadou added religion to their grievances and built on this existing pattern of resistance. As a Muslim jihadist he was implacably opposed to French imperialism. As a Sarrakole, he was opposed to Tokolor imperialism. There was thus a strong tradition of Sarrakole anti-Tokolor nationalism for Mahmadou to work upon.

In late 1885 and early 1886 he rapidly gained support and built up a state which included Bambuk, Bondu, Guoy, Khasso and the emirates of Diafounou and Guidimaka which had formerly been part of the Tokolor empire. In 1886–7 he attacked French posts at Bakel and Senedoubou, from which his forces were repulsed after long sieges. Early encounters with the French ended in Lamine's favour. A clash at Kounguel in March 1886 resulted in a rout of French forces and the loss of quantities of weapons. However, his attacks on the French posts at Bakel and Senedoubou were repulsed after long sieges. In the end Mahmadou was defeated and his state destroyed by a combination of diplomatic and military factors. France, the Tokolor empire and the Kingdom of Futa Toro allied against him. Samori Toure's peace treaty with the French in 1886 enabled them to release troops to fight Mahmadou. The weapons of the Sarrakole were old-fashioned guns and bows and arrows. In December 1887 they were defeated at Toubakouta by Joseph Gallieni, the French commander of Upper Senegal. Mahmadou was killed in battle and his eighteen-year old son was executed.

Ali Bouri Ndiaye who was born in 1842 and became King of Djollof in Senegal in 1875 is a symbol of both inter-ethnic and pan-Islamic co-operation against European invasion. In the 1880s he attempted, without success, to link up with Samori against the French. In 1890 his state was occupied by the French, but he escaped to the Tokolor empire and assisted Ahmadu in his final resistance to the French. Ali Bouri fled with Ahmadu to Sokoto, where he joined the caliph Attahiru in his resistance to the British.

The Tokolor empire

In 1880 the French demanded a protectorate over the Tokolor empire. The emperor Ahmadu refused to grant this, but he made a trade treaty with them in 1881 in which he allowed France 'most favoured nation' trading status. The French immediately took advantage of this treaty and established two trading forts deep inside the Tokolor empire: Fort Kita on the Senegal in 1881 and Fort Bamako on the Niger in 1883. Ahmadu was both unable and unwilling to offer armed resistance to France in the 1880s. He was unable to because of internal rebellions and his earlier reduction in the size of his mutinous army. He was unwilling, because he wanted French weapons for use against internal rebels, and in 1886–7 he made an alliance with France against Mahmadou Lamine. Therefore, Ahmadu made no attempt to unite with Muslim resistance leaders, like Lat-Dior in Cayor, Abdul Bubakar, a Tokolor leader in lower Senegal, and Samori. In 1886 the French had crushed revolts in Senegal and Samori had signed a peace treaty with them. The chance of saving the Tokolor empire had been lost.

The French, of course, did not want merely an entente with Ahmadu; they wanted to take over his empire completely. In 1889 Ahmadu signed a protection treaty with France without realizing its implications. However, he woke up to reality in 1890 when the French, under Major Archinard, invaded in force and captured the city of Segu, at the heart of the empire. Ahmadu belatedly resorted to armed resistance; but Jenne fell to the French and Timbuktu was

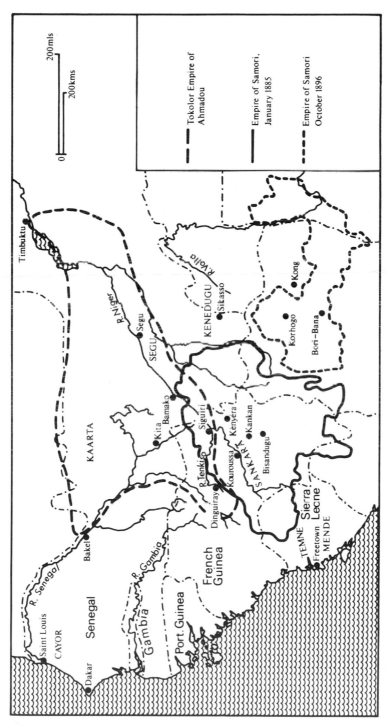

Map 4.   The Tokolor and Mandinka empires.

captured in 1894. Ahmadu fled to Sokoto, his mother's homeland, where in 1898 he died.

A number of factors explain the failure of Tokolor resistance. In the first place there was a great disparity in weapons. The French troops, mainly black Senegalese, were highly trained and superb in the use of their modern weapons. The French also had the advantage of numerous African allies. They were able to deploy many auxiliary soldiers from the anti-Tokolor communities in the Senegal valley, who hated Tokolor rule and wanted loot. Even Ahmadu's younger brother, Aguibou, Emir of Dinguiray, fought on Archinard's side. The non-Muslim Bambara of Segu and Kaarta at the heart of the Tokolor empire welcomed the French as liberators from Tokolor rule. A third factor was Tokolor tactics. Unlike more successful resisters such as Samori Toure and Bai Bureh, Ahmadu did not resort to guerilla warfare. Instead, the Tokolor relied on their traditional tactics of cavalry charges in open savanna or the defence of walled towns and fortresses. Both tactics were disastrous against French field guns, machine-guns and modern rifle fire.

The Mandinka empire

Samori Toure, who had spent 20 years building up his Mandinka empire, fought his first war against France from 1882 to 1886. The French thought they were advancing into the Tokolor empire when they invaded the northern part of Samori's empire, north of the Niger and Tenkiso rivers, in 1882. The result was an indecisive four-year war. Samori repulsed the invasion of his northern domains at the Battle of Kenyera (1882), but he failed in competition with the French to take the town of Bamako from the Tokolor (1883). It was at this time that Samori proposed an anti-French alliance to Ahmadu who turned the proposal down. In 1886 the Franco-Mandinka peace treaty was a result of Samori's desire for peace with France so that he could continue the campaign he had already begun against Tieba of Sikasso. Samori wished to secure his northern front by peace treaty in order to concentrate on the eastern front against Sikasso. Under the terms of the treaty Samori gave up a small part of his empire, north of the Niger, to France.

The period from 1886 to 1891 was, at least officially, one of peace between France and the Mandinka empire, but France used it to weaken and undermine Samori. The French contributed to Samori's defeat at Sikasso by sending military supplies to Tieba, and to the Great Revolt of 1888–90 by invading Samori's northern provinces and inciting an already disaffected people to revolt. Samori was forced to abandon the siege of Sikasso in order to crush the revolt. A large part of his empire was ruined and deserted. Incredibly he managed to replace the men and horses he had lost and even to improve his army. However, he was forced to abandon his dream of building a new society, based on Islam, in order to concentrate on the struggle against advancing French colonialism.

In the late 1880s Samori hoped to stave off a French invasion with help from Britain. At first he proposed an alliance with Britain against France, through the Governor of Sierra Leone. Britain rejected the proposal because, at the Berlin West Africa Conference of 1884–5, Samori's empire had been declared to be a French 'sphere of influence'. In the early 1890s Samori even offered to put his empire under British rule. He believed that the British, on the evidence of their rule in Sierra Leone and Gambia, would not interfere with Islam whereas the French would, and also that under British rule he would keep his position of 'almami'. However, the British refused a protectorate for the same reason as they had turned down an alliance. Although Britain would not ally with Samori, British traders in Sierra Leone were allowed to supply him with six thousand modern repeater rifles and a vast quantity of ammunition.

Samori's second war against the French was fought from 1891 to 1898. By 1891 the resistance of the Tokolor empire was collapsing and the French could safely divert forces to fight Samori. The French sent forces against Samori south from Senegal and the Niger valley, north from the Ivory Coast and east from Guinea. The war was fought ruthlessly on both sides. The French committed numerous atrocities against civilians. Samori waged total war by employing a scorched earth policy, destroying crops and buildings and evacuating people from areas about to be occupied by the enemy. There was enormous destruction of property and loss of life. In 1894 the French overran the Mandinka empire. Samori therefore abandoned it, escaped with a remnant of his army, and conquered and founded an entirely new empire to the east, in the present north-east Ivory Coast and north-west Ghana. In 1897 Samori captured and destroyed the Muslim city of Kong, and defeated two powerful French columns. A British column was also defeated at the Battle of Wa. In 1895–6 Samori began negotiations with Prempeh, the asantehene, for an anti-European alliance; but an alliance was forstalled by Britain's occupation of Asante in 1896.

By 1896 Samori was very much on the defensive. The French captured Sikasso in 1898. Finally, Samori himself was captured by the French in 1898, in the Liberian hinterland. The almami had 100,000 followers with him but their food and flocks had gone. Thousands had died and thousands more were dying of starvation, and even his soldiers were deserting to the French to get food. Samori was deported to Gabon where he died in 1900.

Although Samori was finally defeated, he had been able to resist the French for a considerable length of time. Samori's army was unusually strong for one in a pre-industrial society—in organization, in weapons and in tactics. Modern weapons were bought from European traders. The soldiers were intensely loyal, partly because they shared their almami's Mandinka nationalism and Islamic zeal, partly because they were well looked after, well-equipped and trained, and partly because there was no ethnicism in appointments or promotions in the army. Samori was a successful trader and used his experience and resources to build up an excellent supply organization for the army. He established state control of agriculture and markets to ensure a regular food supply for the army. He employed the highly skilled Mandinka smiths in government workshops to make ammunition and replacement parts for rifles. He reorganized his *sofa*, or infantry, along European lines in small units of riflemen trained to shoot accurately, firing volleys in response to bugle calls. Some of his soldiers were sent as spies to enlist in the French army to learn French drill and tactics. He abandoned traditional cavalry charges and defence of walled fortresses; horses were used as transport, to carry packs or to move soldiers quickly, but not in attacks on the enemy. He employed with devastating effect the guerilla or commando tactics of surprise ambushes and night raids by small, highly mobile forces on the extended enemy lines of communication. He thus avoided direct confrontation with superior French weapons. Finally, Samori had the support of many elements of the Mandinka people in a national war of defence. Unlike most leaders of resistance to the initial imposition of colonial rule, he was able to mobilize the masses against the invaders; in supplying food to the army, in manufacturing ammunition and in applying scorched earth methods and mass evacuation to deny supplies and workers to the invaders. In their war of resistance Samori and his people demonstrated their capacity for organization and modernization. However, the resistance finally failed in the face of vastly superior armaments.

Dahomey

France's main motive for occupying Dahomey was the desire to control the palm-oil trade. In 1883 the French occupied the coastal Popo Kingdom of Porto Novo to tap the Yoruba palm-oil trade, and French firms moved from Whydah to Porto Novo. Since Whydah was under Dahomeyan administration, Dahomey lost revenue from customs duties as a result of this shift in trade. In 1887 Dahomey's exports fell to less than £100,000 worth whereas they had totalled over £500,000 worth in the late 1870s. This loss of wealth meant that King Glele found it very difficult to buy sufficient arms and ammunition to defend Dahomey against French encroachment. In any case, Glele was unwilling to fight France, believing that, 'He who makes the powder must win the battle.' He allowed France to strengthen its position at the coast unchallenged. In 1889 he even conceded his kingdom's claims to the port of Cotonou after the French had sent a threatening mission to Abomey, his capital. Glele was so ashamed of his weakness that he committed suicide by poisoning.

Behanzin, Glele's son and successor, refused to accept French rule at Cotonou. He crushed a revolt of Dahomeyan chiefs who wanted to follow his father's policy of surrender and sent his army to attack Cotonou in 1890. However, the French defended Cotonou successfully, and came to the conclusion that Cotonou would only be safe if Dahomey itself were conquered.

Behanzin tried to get allies against France. His agents held unsuccessful talks with Portuguese traders, the British in Lagos and the Germans in Togo. He did not try to get African allies against France. The Yoruba states to the east were traditionally hostile to Dahomey, and in any case absorbed in war against each other. Dahomey had little contact with Asante to the west.

In 1892–3 a French army advanced from the coast and captured Dahomey after encountering very strong resistance. The French army was commanded by General Dodds, a Senegalese Eurafrican. Behanzin was captured, deposed and deported to the West Indies. French forces numbered only 2,000 against Dahomey's 16,000. However, the French were far superior in both weapons and tactics. Dahomey had many guns including 1,700 rapid-firing repeater rifles, six cannon or field guns and five machine-guns bought from the German traders. The rest of the army was armed with old flint-lock rifles which were very slow to load and fire. The Dahomeyan soldiers did not know how to use their modern German weapons properly. They fired the repeater rifles from the hip not the shoulder, so their fire was inaccurate. The machine-guns jammed or overheated through improper use and bad maintenance. In contrast, the French soldiers, who were nearly all Senegalese, were highly trained and experienced. The French never divided their small force and so were able to use superior firepower on all occasions. They also avoided possible ambushes. The Dahomeyan soldiers were only trained in dawn attacks on towns and did not know how to stop a French advance.

African divisions also helped the French against Dahomey. The coastal Popo Kingdoms like Porto Novo, Whydah and Allada aided the French. The French invasion also encouraged the many thousands of Yoruba slaves on Dahomeyan palm-oil plantations to revolt in the rear of Dahomey's army. Many Yoruba ran home but many went on the rampage in Dahomey, killing Dahomeyans and destroying crops and property. Moreover, when the slaves destroyed farms and crops, Dahomey's army starved.

Behanzin was captured by the French, deported to the West Indies and replaced by a French Governor. The capital was moved from Abomey to Porto Novo. French middleman firms could now sell palm oil in France at a price ten times higher than what they had paid the producers.

Bornu

In the Lake Chad region, the French were able to play upon African divisions in order to overcome armed resistance. On the eve of the European conquest Bornu had become a part of a large new state created by Rabeh, a Mahdist from the eastern Sudan. Rabeh, a son of slave parents, had risen to be commander of the forces of Zubair Pasha, the slave-trader Governor of Darfur in the Egyptian Sudan. When Zubair was deposed and imprisoned in Egypt, Rabeh had taken his army westward to seek a new future there, and later he accepted a Mahdist flag. Rabeh defeated the Kingdom of Wadai and seized the province of Bagarimi. In 1893 he conquered Bornu, destroyed the old capital at Kukawa, and established a new one at Kikwa. There was much devastation of land and property and selling of people. However, Rabeh did begin to modernize the administration of Bornu, although he was not given time to complete the task.

In 1899 and 1900 three French forces converged on Bornu: one across the Sahel from the Western Sudan, one across the Sahara from Algeria, and one northwards through the forest from Gabon. The French wished to complete their overall plan of linking their North, West and Central African territories at Lake Chad. Rabeh naturally chose armed resistance and called for a jihad and an alliance against the Europeans. But he was not supported either by Sokoto or the Sanusiyya. The caliphate was upset because Rabeh had given refuge to a pretender to the throne of Sokoto. The Sanusi could not forgive him for taking Bagirimi from Wadai. Bagirimi itself went over to the French. First Rabeh and then his son Fad el-Allah were killed in battle by the French. Most of his empire went to Britain, in accordance with the agreements reached at the Berlin Conference.

Sierra Leone

In the mid-1880s, British West African policy was to forestall French or German occupation of coastal states which traded with her and to achieve this by treaty-making rather than by resort to force of arms. From 1895 to 1903, when Joseph Chamberlain was Colonial Secretary, British policy was more active. Britain's strategy was now to forestall French and German occupation of areas in the hinterland of British coastal interests, and to achieve this by a forward policy of military occupation. Hence the British wars of conquest in Asante in 1896, northern Ghana in 1897, most of Yorubaland after 1895, Benin in 1897, northern Nigeria between 1900 and 1903, and the Sierra Leone hinterland in the 1890s.

The Creole merchants of the Sierra Leone coast had long requested the British government to extend its authority to the interior, to protect their trade there, especially when the French began to expand into the hinterland. In 1896 Governor Cardew paid heed to them and declared a protectorate over the Sierra Leone hinterland. The British government did not wish to pay large subsidies to new protectorates and Cardew was forced to impose a five shillings house tax in order to raise revenue. This provoked war. In January 1898 the Temne and Mende rose in armed rebellion. Their grievances were wider than the house tax. They resented the humiliation of their traditional rulers by the new government police, price-fixing by Creole traders, and—if they were Muslims—Christian missionary activity.

The Mende side of the revolt was led by the Poro, a religious, educational and trading society. The Poro declared total war against the government and all who associated with it, especially the Creoles. Over a thousand Creoles were killed, including many women and children. Temne resistance was led by Bai Bureh, the ruler of the small state of Kassah in northern Sierra Leone. Bai Bureh adhered to traditional religion, though he was influenced by Islam, employed an Arabic writing clerk and traded with Muslims. From January to November 1898 he conducted a relatively successful guerilla war against Britain. He had waged war almost continuously since 1865; there had been no period of peace in which his military skills could decay. The son of a professional warrior, Bai Bureh had followed his father's profession, being hired by rulers to fight in return for the rights of plunder. Therefore, he had a regular army to use against the British. Temne country was very thickly wooded, so the British columns, already slowed down by carriers, could only advance in single file and were thus easily ambushed. Bai Bureh's marksmen picked off the carriers and the officers, depriving the British forces of both food and leadership. His soldiers were well supplied with rifles and ammunition bought at the coast. Bai Bureh also built huge defensive stockades, barricaded forest paths, and used bushfires to cut off the British forces. Britain was unable to defeat him without reinforcing the Sierra Leone contingents with troops from Nigeria and even Britain.

The Creoles had opposed the house tax, even though they had welcomed the extension of British rule. They suffered badly in the war of 1898, but they also suffered most in the peace that followed the capture of Bai Bureh. If the Creoles were seen by the Africans of the interior as agents of the white man and his colonialism, they were regarded by Cardew, because of their opposition to his tax, as disloyal Africans, not loyal black British. Cardew and his successors began to discriminate systematically against Creoles, forcing them out of the Sierra Leone civil service, and so undermining the multi-racial achievement and Creole-white partnership that had so greatly distinguished British colonialism in the colony.

Asante

Surprisingly, Asante did not resist British occupation in 1896. Why did the British invade and why did the Asante not resist?

Britain had weakened Asante in the war of 1873–4 (see Volume One), but the Kingdom revived under Asantehene Agyeman Prempeh I, who was enstooled in 1888. Prempeh reunited the weakened Asante Confederacy by defeating rebel Asante states like Nsuta, Kokofu and Mampong. Nsuta returned to Asante rule but British threats prevented Kokofu and Mampong from rejoining the Confederacy. However Prempeh was not content with trying merely to revive the Confederacy, he also hoped to revive the Asante empire. He alarmed the British on several occasions. In 1889 Prempeh sent a letter to the British Governor of the Gold Coast, objecting to the British protectorate over Kwahu which had formerly belonged to Asante. He sent a letter the following year demanding the restoration to Asante of all the former southern vassal states and refugees in Gold Coast Colony. In 1892–3 Prempeh actually conquered the Boron states to the north-west. Naturally, the British feared an Asante revival. What upset the British most was the asantehene's refusal to accept British rule, and his insistence on being treated on equal terms as a fully sovereign ruler. In 1891 Prempeh rejected the suggestion that Asante should become a British protectorate. He temporized over a British request in 1895–6 to station a Resident in Kumasi to direct Asante government policy. An Asante delegation was sent to London in 1895 to try to persuade the British government to accept the complete independence of Asante, but this was rejected.

Britain occupied Asante in 1896 partly because she wanted to forestall French expansion from the Ivory Coast and German expansion from Togo. Moreover, British traders on the Gold Coast wanted Asante and other areas of the interior to be opened up to them. Since Asante refused free trade, a war of conquest would be necessary to achieve it. Britain also wished to abolish the slave trade and human sacrifice and to spread Christianity. However, the fundamental reason for the invasion was that the British government felt it ought to respond to Asante political initiative. Prempeh was too bold for London's liking. In 1895–6 the asantehene's ambassadors negotiated a treaty of friendship between Asante and Samori's second Mandinka empire. The British were determined to forestall a possible African grand alliance against expanding European colonialism.

In 1896 a powerful British force under General Sir Francis Scott, the conqueror of the Ijebu Yoruba in 1892 marched on Kumasi. The casus belli was ostensibly the non-payment of most of the 1874 indemnity, which Prempeh regarded not as his responsibility but as that of Kofi Karikari, an earlier asantehene. Prempeh's response to Scott's advance was to offer no resistance. The asantehene hoped for a treaty which would leave him in power. As soon as he heard of preparations for an expedition he gave way on the issue of a British Residency and said he would accept one, believing that this would both avoid war and leave him with the substance of power. However, it was too late. The British continued their invasion, and, on reaching Kumasi, arrested Prempeh, his family and chief counsellors, and deported them to Sierra Leone. A British protectorate was declared, and the Asante now had no king. They felt deeply resentful at what they regarded as the treachery of the British in deporting Prempeh after he had accepted a British Residency. Without the presence of Prempeh's restraining hand, the Asante turned to armed resistance. There were disturbances in 1898 and 1899, and a full-scale rebellion broke out in 1900.

Yorubaland

The British takeover of Lagos in 1861 had been followed by the expansion of Lagos Colony along the coast in the 1860s and 1870s. The British occupied the Yoruba interior in the 1890s. Most of Yorubaland accepted British 'protection' soon after the British invasion and conquest of Ijebu in 1892.

Ijebu was in southern Yorubaland. It lay between Lagos and the

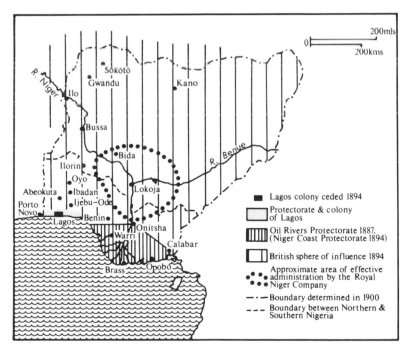

Map 5. Imperial advance in Nigeria.

palm-oil producing regions of the interior, such as the powerful state of Ibadan on its northern border. Thus Ijebu occupied a middleman position between Ibadan and Lagos. By 1892 Britain had several reasons for conquering Ijebu. Britain feared French expansion into Yorubaland from Dahomey. The *Awujale* (King) of Ijebu was a strong traditionalist who had refused to allow Christian missionaries to enter his country; the missionaries put strong pressure on the Lagos administration to send a military expedition to attack Ijebu. However, the most important reasons were economic. In general, Britain wanted to establish control over all Yorubaland in order to end the endemic warfare of the region and thus ensure a steady flow of palm oil to Lagos. Britain also wished to conquer Ijebu because the awujale charged tolls on Lagos traders passing through his territory on their way to Ibadan. Ijebu traders acted as middlemen, buying goods from Ibadan and selling them at higher prices to British traders. Britain and Ibadan were united in wanting to establish direct trade between each other and to remove Ijebu middlemen and Ijebu tolls. Since Ijebu refused to allow free trade or free movement through its territory, Britain decided to solve the matter by war.

The British force that attacked Ijebu consisted of 13 European officers, about 300 African police, 70 West Indian regular soldiers and 100 Ibadan soldiers. The British had breech-loading rifles with smokeless cartridges, three maxim machine guns and three cannon. The Ijebu army which resisted the British consisted of about 7,000 men. The majority were battle-experienced in the Yoruba wars and they nearly all had guns, but they did not know how to use them properly. The Ijebu fired their Snider breech loaders while standing up instead of lying down and so presented an easy target for the British to shoot at. They had plenty of ammunition but no smokeless cartridges, so concealment was difficult. Junwase, the awujale, could not use all his soldiers against the British because he had to keep men in reserve in case of an Ibadan attack. Ijebu tactics were poor: they tried to hold fixed defensive positions against superior British firepower, and were defeated at the Battle of Yemoji River near Imagbon, when about one thousand Ijebu were killed. After the battle, Ijebu surrendered. Soon afterwards, in 1893, Governor Carter of Lagos and a British force toured all Yorubaland (except Ilorin which was an emirate of Sokoto), and the Yoruba states each accepted British protection. Thus the Sixteen Years' War between Ibadan and its neighbours came to an end. Ibadan had hoped to gain from its alliance with Britain but like the other Yoruba states had to submit to British rule.

After the making of the 1893 treaties the British had to use force in order to impose effective authority in Yorubaland. In 1894 they arrested Ogendengbe of Ibadan for pillaging in Ilesha. In 1895 they bombarded Oyo town after Alafin Adeyemi of New Oyo had exercised his traditional rights to punish criminals according to Oyo law. Between 1893 and 1897 Ilorin frequently raided the British-protected Yoruba states. But a Royal Niger Company expedition led by Goldie and equipped with machine guns and artillery conquered Ilorin in 1897. Black missionaries and their converts were almost unanimously in support of the British invasion. Samuel Johnson, the historian-missionary, supported the expedition against the 'refractory and irreconcilable Ijebus'. The extreme lawlessness and disruption of trade in Yorubaland from 1877 onwards enabled even the early nationalist newspaper editor, John Payne Jackson of Lagos, to describe British annexation of the interior as 'an act of the most prodigious and urgent necessity in the cause of humanity and philanthropy'. Only a few Creole leaders opposed the war. The Reverend James Johnson of the Breadfruit Church of Lagos condemned the British invasion of Ijebu as an unrighteous war, which he believed would serve not God by spreading the Gospel but only Mammon, in the form of profits for traders.

The Niger delta—Opobo and Itsekiriland

The British Consul Hewett signed protection treaties between 1883 and 1885 which 'bound' the Niger delta rulers not to enter into agreements with other European powers. Men like Jaja of Opobo and Nana of Ebrohimi in Itsekiriland interpreted the treaties as treaties of alliance with the British—not as the British did, as surrenders of sovereignty to Britain. The 1884 treaty between Hewett and Jaja allowed the Opobo king a monopoly of trade and the exclusion of British traders from his own territory. These terms were unusually good for Opobo, because Hewett normally insisted on free trade clauses in protection treaties. All the same, trade conflicts between Opobo and Britain arose. Britain wanted to fix the price of oil bought from Opobo traders, but Jaja managed to prevent this. Moreover, he stopped British traders moving through his territory to trade in areas of the hinterland north of Opobo, and his neighbours from trading with the British. British traders naturally resented Jaja's actions. Jaja also upset Britain by rejecting missionary work and continuing both slavery and the slave trade.

Jaja was overthrown by blackmail in 1887. The British consul, Harry Johnston, invited him to a meeting on a British warship, HMS Goshawk, promising the king he 'would be free to go' afterwards. At the meeting, however, Johnston told Jaja that he could either surrender himself to Britain or leave, but that if he left he would be treated as an outlaw and the British Navy would attack Opobo. Jaja surrendered, partly to save his country and people, but also because he believed he would get a fair trial and be acquitted of the various charges. However, the trial at Accra was rigged and Jaja was deported to the West Indies, where he died in 1891.

Nana Olomu of Ebrohimi, like Jaja, had insisted in his 1884 treaty with Hewett that clauses providing for free trade and entry of missionaries he excluded from the agreement. In 1893 Itsekiriland became part of the Oil Rivers Protectorate. The next year Britain decided to destroy Nana's trading monopoly, and at the same time end the slave trade and slavery.

Because he was so powerful Nana was blamed for all the troubles in Itsekiriland. In 1894 Major Claude Macdonald, the British Consul-General of the Niger Coast Protectorate declared Nana deposed. Nana did not intend to give up his position without a struggle. In early 1894 the acting British consul, Ralph Moor, made repeated requests to Nana for a meeting—all of which were refused. In August Moor summoned all the Itsekiri traders to a meeting and demanded that they sign a treaty which would allow missionaries to enter their country and establish free trade. All except Nana signed the new treaty. Nana failed to attend because he feared that he would be seized and deported like Jaja had been. Nana's refusal to attend marked him out as the chief opponent of the British and allowed Moor to persuade the Foreign Office that it was necessary to take action against him.

Moor's first action was to destroy a number of villages suspected of being friendly to Nana. Attempts were made by Nana to negotiate a settlement through the Governor of Lagos, but these failed and a direct military clash became inevitable. The British eventually defeated Nana's small army and captured his capital, Ebrohimi, but only after they had been compelled by strong Itsekiri resistance to withdraw three times. Nana had one considerable advantage: the site of Ebrohimi was reclaimed land in the middle of dense mangrove swamp, which was difficult for an enemy to reach. Moreover, the capital was defended by stockades manned with cannon and by infantry with modern rifles and one machine gun. In the end, however, several factors led to defeat. The British forces—three gunboats of soldiers, 350 men in all—had more modern weapons then Nana's men, and could back up cannon, machine gun and rifle fire with gunboat fire, rockets to fire over stockades and dynamite to blow them up with.

Throughout the engagement with the invaders Nana attempted to delay the British forces from reaching Ebrohimi. He realized that he could not win a pitched battle and hoped that a negotiated settlement could be reached during the time the British forces were delayed. Moor was determined not to negotiate. A number of men were killed in the first three attempts to reach Ebrohimi but Moor called up reinforcements and eventually captured the town. However, Nana had fled shortly before the fall of Ebrohimi. Eventually after a period of guerilla resistance he surrendered to the Governor of Lagos believing that he would be treated leniently. He was then handed over to the authorities of the Niger Coast Protectorate, tried for making war on Her British Majesty and sent into exile. His exile lasted from 1894 to 1906 when he was allowed to return home, finally dying in July 1916.

The Royal Niger Company

Sir George Goldie's Royal Niger Company ruled the Niger territories between 1886 and 1899. These consisted of the northern part of the delta, the banks of the Niger in western Igbo country, and the southern emirates of the Sokoto caliphate, like Nupe and Ilorin which were conquered in 1897. The southern and central parts of the delta were under the administration of the British government, which even hoped to be able to hand over the responsibility for, and expense of, its new coastal protectorate to the Company. Yet in 1899 the British government felt itself compelled to take over the Company, largely because of Company misrule. The following two case-studies of the Company's misrule in the western Igbo states and its clash with the delta state of Brass, reveal not merely the lack of wisdom but also the evil of handing over the government of colonial peoples to a chartered company of businessmen concerned almost exclusively with profit, and prepared to resort to violence in order to ensure such profit.

The Niger Igbo suffered less from Company blockades than from Company violence. The people of Onitsha reacted to blockade by producing less for export, reducing the scale of their palm-oil trading, and concentrating more on domestically-based agriculture. But they could not escape the bombardment of their town and burning of their buildings. Asaba suffered the dubious distinction and the misfortune of being chosen as a centre of Company administration. The Company's soldiers lived in a compound surrounded by an iron railing as protection against Igbo attacks. In reality the townspeople needed protection from the soldiers, who regularly stole livestock and other property from them. In 1888 the Company destroyed half of Asaba ostensibly to enforce the abolition of human sacrifice. There was, however, extensive looting.

The Company did almost nothing to develop the areas it ruled. Its officers were mainly traders, adventurers and military men with little concern for African welfare. It built no roads or railways, and no hospitals or schools. Its major contributions to development were to establish botanical gardens to develop new cash crops and to begin tin-mining at Bauchi.

Brass became a British protectorate in 1884 and later part of the British Niger Coast Protectorate. It welcomed British protection against trading threats from the French. In 1895, however, Brass fought a war of resistance not against the protectorate but against the Royal Niger Company which was destroying its trade.

In the early 1890s the Company secured control of trade in areas of

Brass's hinterland in the northern part of the Delta and thus greatly weakened the Brass palm oil trade. The African Association, a group of Liverpool palm oil traders, was also cut off from the palm oil-producing hinterland by the Royal Niger Company and decided to help Brass to break into the Company's Niger Territories and smuggle palm oil from there. Goldie was unable to stop the smuggling so he offered contracts to detach firms from the African Association until it was so weak that it was virtually forced to sell all its assets north of the Coast Protectorate to the Company, and agreed to stay out of the Niger Territories. The Brass people were now abandoned by their European allies.

The results were an abrupt decline in Brass's trade. Smuggling in the Niger Territories was now put down by firm Company police action. Brass traders were unable even to collect debts from Ijo palm oil producers in Company territory. The Company seized food canoes bringing yams and cassava from its territories to Brass, and the people of Brass began to starve. During this crisis the King of Brass, Ebefa, continued to support the British connection, but in 1894 smallpox killed Ebefa and Koko became king. In 1895 the Royal Niger Company's headquarters were attacked by the Brass army. This was, in the words of Goldie's biographer John Flint, 'a desperate nihilistic bid for revenge against the Company'. Koko had no intention of rebelling against the Niger Coast Protectorate or the British government. Koko led a thousand men in thirty war canoes armed with cannons, some rifles, but mainly spears and axes. Akassa was only lightly defended since the Company's forces were elsewhere. The Brassmen easily captured Akassa, destroyed property there, and withdrew with many prisoners, mainly African employees of the company, most of whom were sacrificed and eaten.

The British reaction to the destruction of Akassa was to employ greater violence. Although the British government sympathized with Brass's grievances against the Royal Niger Company, it could not condone the destruction of the Company's troops and the British Navy destroyed Nembe, Brass's capital, and Twon, its port, drove the inhabitants of the towns into the mangrove swamps, where many of them starved, confiscated all Brass war canoes, and fined Koko heavily. The British government ordered an inquiry into the affair. Although the Royal Niger Company was criticized it continued to strangle Brass's trade and was even encouraged by the British government to expand its Niger Territories and conquer the Emirates of Nupe and Ilorin in 1897.

Eventually the Company had its charter taken away by the British government but the oppression of Brass was not the reason for this. The government had become unhappy at the use of the Company's constabulary on punitive expeditions against African communities which challenged the Company's monopolistic practices. It was unhappy, too, about the Company's monopoly, and in particular with the Company's exclusion from its vast territories of rival white British traders and British African traders from Sierra Leone, Lagos, and the delta. However, the Colonial Secretary, Joseph Chamberlain, was primarily worried by the Company's failure to prevent French expansion into northern Nigeria. Chamberlain decided that direct action by the British government was required. He set up the West African Frontier Force under Lugard in 1897 to stop the French advance in Borgu, and then settled the boundaries of Northern Nigeria by making the Anglo-French agreement of 1898. Since the British taxpayer was now doing Goldie's work for him, Britain ended the Charter of the Royal Niger Company on January 1, 1900 and began to administer its territories directly with Lugard as High Commissioner for Northern Nigeria.

Benin

In 1897 the British invaded the ancient Kingdom of Benin and overthrew Oba Ovonramwen, who had reigned since 1888. A variety of reasons can be advanced for the conquest. The British wanted to stop the slave trade, the practice of slavery and human sacrifices in Benin, and to enable Christian missionaries to enter the country. Benin was notorious for human sacrifice although Europeans exaggerated its extent there. Another reason was political. Benin was an independent state surrounded on all sides by British colonial territory. Economic matters also led to disputes.

Itsekiriland is between Benin and the coast. The Itsekiri people were part of the British protectorate in the 1890s. Ovonramwen charged high customs duties on Itsekiri traders who traded in Benin. These duties had to be paid in the form of presents. In 1896 the Oba demanded from Itsekiri traders a thousand corrugated iron sheets to roof his palace as a condition for allowing them to trade again in Benin. This demand annoyed the British Consul Phillips who refused to let the Itsekiri traders send the iron sheets to Ovonramwen. The Oba therefore continued to forbid them from entering Benin.

Another cause for dispute between Britain and Benin was the 1892 Gallwey Treaty. In this treaty Vice-Consul Gallwey had written that the Oba allowed complete freedom of trade in Benin to all foreigners, which would include the Itsekiri and the British. However, since Ovonramwen would not have agreed to this, Gallwey did not honestly explain the terms of the treaty to the illiterate Oba and Bini chiefs. After signing the treaty, Ovonramwen refused to allow foreigners to trade in Benin. The British were able to claim that the Oba was breaking the treaty and to use this as another excuse to conquer Benin.

Why did Ovonramwen keep foreign traders out of Benin? As the Oba, he had a monopoly of Benin's rich palm oil and ivory trades.

He was thus able to keep the price of these exports high. He was also able to impose high customs duties on foreign goods. The British traders and their Itsekiri allies wanted an end to the Oba's monopoly and to high customs duties. British traders also wanted to exploit the rich rubber-producing trees of Benin's forests.

The casus belli, or incident that sparked off the war between Britain and Benin, was the killing of Phillips, the Acting British Commissioner and consul for the Niger Coast. Early in 1897 Phillips invaded Benin with a force of nine Europeans and two hundred Itsekiri carriers. His object was to spy on the Benin army. Ovonramwen, when he heard of the invasion, wanted to negotiate with Phillips because he believed armed resistance to British military power was unrealistic. However, he was opposed by a powerful party among Benin's chiefs who wanted to offer armed resistance to the British, for two reasons. Firstly, Phillips had entered the country without permission and at a time when he would disturb Benin's religious ceremonies. Secondly, the chiefs took action because they feared Phillips would seize the Oba as Johnston had seized Jaja of Opobo and because of what had happened to Nana in neighbouring Itsekiriland. Therefore, part of the Benin army, which had been ordered into action by the 'rebel' chiefs, ambushed Phillips's party. Phillips and most of his men were killed and only a few survivors escaped to the British-controlled coast.

Later in 1897 the British sent a large expedition of 1500 men to conquer Benin and avenge Phillips' death, as Ovonramwen had feared. It was the usual story of modern repeater rifles, machine guns, large cannon and better training and discipline versus old-fashioned rifles, spears, axes, swords and bows and arrows. Ovonramwen abandoned the capital to the enemy and took refuge in the countryside for six months before he was finally forced to surrender. When the British soldiers captured Benin city they looted 2500 bronze art treasures, including sculptures and decorated doors, and took them to Britain where many were sold to museums. A vast quantity of ivory was taken from the palace. Once the looting was over, the city was burnt down. Oba Ovonramwen was deported to Calabar. He died in 1914. No new Oba was appointed by the British. Instead they ruled Benin with European district officers and those Benin chiefs who co-operated with them.

Sokoto

At the time of the European invasion, the Sokoto caliphate— never a centralized political unit—was less politically cohesive than it had ever been. In the second half of the nineteenth century many of the emirs, especially those ruling states far from Sokoto, acquired almost independent authority and the caliph's control over his vast territories was considerably weakened. The political divisions made it easier for Britain to conquer the caliphate but at the same time meant that the process took longer than would have been the case with a single, politically united state.

There were three stages in the British conquest of the caliphate: the Royal Niger Company's 1897 campaign against Nupe and Ilorin, the southernmost emirates, the West African Frontier Force's 1898–9 campaign on the middle Niger, and Lugard's 1901–3 campaigns to occupy the whole caliphate.

The Royal Niger Company's campaign against Nupe and Ilorin was undertaken both to punish the two emirs for allowing slave raids on areas in the Niger Valley under the rule of the Company, and to occupy these emirates before the French did. The latter were advancing south-eastwards down the Niger towards Yorubaland, and also eastwards from Dahomey. The Company force of five hundred Africans led by Goldie and a few European officers, and carrying many modern weapons, captured Bida, the capital of Nupe, and Ilorin city. However, the Company's resources were limited, so effective European occupation of the two emirates did not follow Goldie's campaign but had to wait until Lugard reconquered Bida in 1901.

The West African Frontier Force's 1898–9 campaign against small states on the southwest edge of the caliphate succeeded in stopping a renewed French advance down the Niger. The WAFF was set up on the orders of the British Colonial Secretary, Joseph Chamberlain, who appointed Lugard, the conqueror of Uganda, to take command. The campaign resulted in the 1898 Anglo–French agreement which settled the north and west boundaries of the British sphere of influence in the Niger basin.

Lugard's 1901–3 campaigns resulted in the effective occupation of the whole of the caliphate by Britain. In 1900 Sokoto had been declared a British protectorate, as part of Northern Nigeria, of which Lugard was the first High Commissioner. This had to be confirmed by effective occupation. Britain also wished to end of slave trade which was still carried on by various emirs in spite of British attempts to stop it. It was also necessary for Lugard to forestall the French who were expanding along the southern edge of the Sahara towards Lake Chad, and the Germans who were expanding north from Cameroon to the Benue River. In 1901–3 Lugard fought successive and successful wars of conquest against Nupe, Kontagora, Yola, Bauchi, Kano, Sokoto and Burmi.

In the first war Lugard deposed the powerful Emir of Nupe to show the other emirates the futility of resistance to Britain. But Lugard also promised Britain would not attack Islam. Therefore, the Caliph Attahiru Ahmadu and his advisers and emirs were unsure whether to resist or co-operate with Lugard. They feared British power but could not accept infidel rule in spite of Lugard's promise to respect Islam.

Attahiru hesitated over what policy to adopt and while he did so Lugard's military commander, Colonel Morland, dashed north in 1903 with a small force to attack Sokoto city. The Emir of Gwandu had chosen not to fight, thus making the rear of Morland's column secure in an attack on Sokoto. The Sokoto leaders were divided on battle tactics against Morland. The majority wanted to fight behind the city walls, but the walls had not been maintained, so Attahiru drew up his line of battle outside the walls and relied on cavalry charges. An army of 30,000 Hausa-Fulani charged against the British square of 600 men who were armed with artillery, maxim guns and repeater rifles. The result was a hundred Sokoto men and one British carrier dead. Attahiru who was not keen on armed resistance put up only a token fight at Sokoto and fled to the east with many of his followers. His ultimate destination was Mecca, which he had never visited. He wanted to fulfil the ambition of every Muslim by making a Haj to Mecca, where he intended to settle. However, the caliph never left the caliphate.

Lugard assumed Attahiru was organizing a jihad against Britain and that flight was merely a tactical military retreat. The first Battle of Burmi in 1903 was a British defeat but the caliph offered to surrender if he were allowed to leave the country. However, Lugard would not countenance anything but unconditional surrender, so Attahiru decided to fight on, without hope of victory, but for the sake of honour. At the second Battle of Burmi a stronger British force managed to breach the walls, and although resistance was fierce and prolonged, Attahiru was defeated and killed, together with about nine hundred defenders including many leaders of Sokoto, Kano, Katagum, Bauchi and Burmi.

Islam was a powerful factor in the strength of Attahiru's final resistance. It helps to account for the fanatical defence at Burmi, and explains why Ali Bouri Ndiaye the King of Djolof in Senegal after his earlier defeat by the French trekked eastwards to Sokoto and helped his brother in Islam, Attahiru, to resist the British. Islam, bravery and heroism were, however, no adequate substitute for technical sufficiency. Sokoto was bound to lose a war with Britain, as Attahiru understood only too well, because of the disparity of weapons. However, Sokoto's lack of organization and adoption of unsuitable tactics did not help either. Each emir in the caliphate had his own army. There was no unified military command. This meant that Lugard was able to conquer the emirates one by one and then Sokoto itself. Moreover, the fortress mentality—defence of walled towns—coupled with cavalry charges had proved disastrous to the Tokolor against the French, but somehow the lesson was not learnt by the Fulani and Hausa. Attahiru might have had more success if he had been bold enough to adopt an offensive strategy and attack Morland's small column before it reached Sokoto. Yet it seems unfair to reproach Attahiru for inadequate military leadership when he preferred peace to war, and when Lugard made it impossible for him to surrender honourably.

The Igbo

We have seen already how the Igbo of the Niger River city-states, like Onitsha, reacted to the invasion of the Royal Niger Company. However, the Igbo-speaking areas away from the river were not brought under British control until after the demise of the profit seeking company that had concentrated on the river.

Igboland at the end of the nineteenth century was a collection of many small states. There was no large Igbo state that could fall at a single blow like Benin or Sokoto. Both British conquest and Igbo resistance were piecemeal and lasted from 1898 until 1917.

Some Igbo communities put up armed resistance to the British from the beginning of the period of colonial expansion. The West Niger or Ika Igbo prevented the establishment of effective British administration in Igboland west of the Niger, until 1911. The Igbo resistance was dominated by men of the Ekumeku secret society, an underground movement that relied on guerilla tactics and on co-operation between clans. Ekumeku benefited from the existence of a tradition of resistance to Benin, and from the profound desire of the Ika Igbo to preserve their political, economic and religious independence from foreign rule. It took three major British expeditions, one by the Royal Niger Company in 1898 and two by the British government in 1902 and 1909, before the Ika accepted British rule. Armed resistance to the British was also put up by the Ezza in north-eastern Igboland, but they were defeated in 1905.

Another feature of Igbo resistance was a form of diplomacy, trying to keep the British away by long *palaver*, or negotiations and talks, but when in the end palaver failed, armed resistance was resorted to. The Aro traders tried palaver between 1896 and 1901; but diplomacy could not work when the Aro were not prepared to accept even a measure of British rule and the British in their turn were not prepared to recognize Aro independence.

Aro raids on Igbo communities under British protection led to the 1901–2 Aro expedition, the capture of Arochukwu town, and the destruction of the place of the famous oracle. However the spirit of the oracle was not destroyed, according to many Igbo, whose belief in it led to a revival of resistance in the 1920s and 1930s. The Afikpo of eastern Igboland also attempted palaver until the Aro defeat showed its ineffectiveness. Armed resistance was tried in 1902–3 but Afikpo courage was no match for British artillery.

So the Igbo like almost all other societies in West Africa came under colonial rule. Faced with a determined and technologically superior European power West African societies had little chance of preserving their independence.

3
European Scramble and African response: East Africa

The European Partition

The Scramble in East Africa began with Bismarck's recognition of the treaties signed by Karl Peters with a number of African chiefs in the area of Kilimanjaro. Britain was unable to resist these German moves in March 1885 because of the situation in Egypt.

The Egyptian Sudan had been convulsed by the activities of the Mahdi who had led a popular and successful revolt against Egyptian rule. Britain had sent General Charles Gordon to evacuate British and Egyptian officials from the Sudan, but the general disobeyed his orders. He decided to remain in occupation of Khartoum: it was captured by the Mahdi in January 1885 and Gordon was killed. This provoked a storm of protest in Britain over the government's failure to send troops to rescue Gordon. In March 1885 Britain also faced a crisis with Russia over Afghanistan. Quite clearly she could not afford to antagonize Germany and so the Anglo–German Agreement of 1886 which split East Africa into German and British spheres of influence was signed. Germany was apportioned land south of a line from the Umba River to Lake Victoria. She also retained territory further to the north around Witu. It was also agreed that a commission should be set up by Britain, France and Germany to decide the extent of the territories of the Sultan of Zanzibar. In due course the commission restricted the sultan to a strip of land ten miles wide, along the coast. This brought bitter protests from the sultan but there was nothing he could do to alter decisions taken by the European powers.

The Anglo–German Agreement had not decided the future of Uganda. A race for Uganda now began between the German East Africa Company and the Imperial British East Africa Company. The latter was granted a charter in 1888. Kabaka Mwanga was persuaded that an agreement with the German Company would leave him with more independence. In February 1890 he signed a Treaty with Karl Peters, and when Jackson of the IBEA Company reached Buganda in April 1890 Mwanga refused British protection. However, the future of Uganda was settled not in East Africa but in Europe.

By 1889 Britain was convinced that her occupation of Egypt was likely to be lengthy. She was determined that no European power should gain control of the Nile, the life blood of Egypt. In July 1890 Britain and Germany signed the Heligoland Treaty. This laid down that Germany would surrender her claims to Witu and Uganda and recognize British control of Zanzibar. Britain thus secured control of the headwaters of the Nile. In return Britain would give Germany the small North Sea Island of Heligoland and would persuade the Sultan of Zanzibar to sell his coastal strip south of the Umba to Germany. As in West Africa, European considerations were a major factor in drawing up the boundaries of the new states.

African response: an overview

East Africa shows a pattern of varied initial response to the imposition of colonial rule—involving four different techniques. The first technique—active or armed resistance—was employed not only by organized political communities, such as Uhehe and Bunyoro, but also by segmented communities like the Nandi and the Acholi. The second technique—passive resistance—was applied by communities which, while not approving of the establishment of European rule, either did not need to or could not resort to military solutions. Rwanda and Burundi in the far west of German East Africa did not feel any need to fight because the Germans had few men and limited funds, their influence was comparatively weak and they did not upset significantly the local balance of power in the area. Communities such as the Shambaa, Haya, Maasai and at one time the Kikuyu were unable to resist. They had been hit by natural disasters such as cholera, smallpox, and rinderpest epidemics, locust invasions and famines, which raged over northern Tanzania and southern Kenya in the 1880s and 1890s. Other communities, such as the Pare, could not offer armed resistance because they were very weak politically. The third technique—adaptation or diplomacy—often took the form of alliance with European invaders against powerful local enemies, within the same ethnic group or a neighbouring one. This technique was widespread and amongst its most famous examples are Rindi of Uchagga, Mumia of Wanga and the Ganda Protestants. The fourth or mercenary technique—assisting the European invaders by being recruited into their armies or by fighting as auxiliaries alongside them—for the reward of either loot or money, was used as an additional technique by many of those who also used diplomacy.

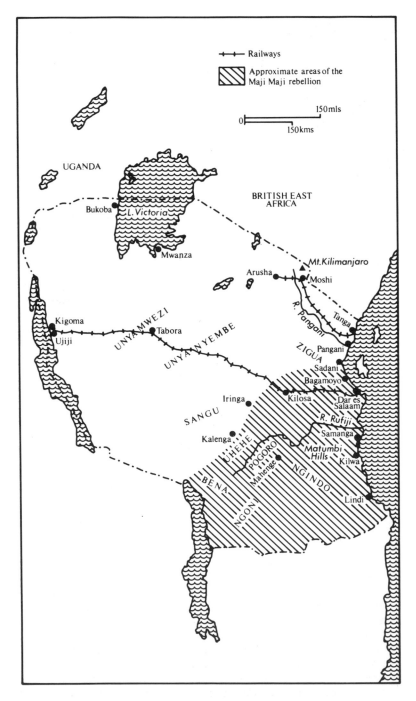

Map 6.   Tanzania

Tanzania

The establishment of German rule

Karl Peters' treaty-making in 1884 with illiterate chiefs in parts of Usagara, Uzigua, Nguru and Ukami, launched the German East African empire. Peters' treaties were meaningless in a number of ways. Firstly, the chiefs who made them regarded them as treaties of alliance and friendship and not as treaties of protection. Secondly, Peters wrote far more into the treaties than the chiefs either agreed to or understood. Thirdly, the chiefs concerned had authority over only their own villages, so the treaties could not properly apply to more than a very few thousand people. Fourthly, the written versions of the treaties referred to the cession of land which the chiefs could not have agreed to. The customary laws of the peoples involved never treated land as property of any one person, not even rulers, and the chiefs could not give away land which belonged to the community. These factors did not stop the German government ratifying the treaties and declaring a protectorate, in 1885, and granting a charter to the Society for German Colonization to rule it. Later in the year the Society was replaced by the German East Africa Company.

Die Deutsche Ost Afrika Gesellschaft (DOAG) (anglicized as the German East Africa Company) was from the beginning short of capital, because Peters had deliberately kept the number of shareholders small in order to ensure his personal control of the Company. Moreover, German capitalists were hardly interested in East Africa, since Germany was rapidly industrializing in the 1880s, and it was far more profitable for them to invest at home than abroad. The Company tried to introduce settlers to grow crops which would provide revenue, but Usagara proved to be unhealthy for Europeans and the German settlement scheme was abandoned. The few Germans who did come tried plantation farming, but the initial cost of establishing plantations severely strained the Company's limited finances, as did the cost of building administrative stations. The heavy initial capital expenditure on the plantations led the Germans to seek quick profits at almost any cost. The Company's attempts to trade were a failure, since the Germans were unable to compete with the long-established Arab, Swahili, Indian, Nyamwezi and Zigua traders in the area. The Company had no interest in any 'civilizing mission'. It was neither obliged by its charter to end slavery nor did it attempt to do so. It did not construct any public works of a developmental nature. The Company's economic failure in the first three years of its rule led to its seeking control over the coastal belt ruled by the Sultan. In 1887 German pressure on the Sultan led to

Barghash leasing control of the customs at Dar es Salaam and Pangani to the Company. In 1888 the new Sultan, Sayyid Khalifa, granted the Company the administration of all his territory between the River Umba and the River Rovuma. The Company hoped that these concessions, by giving it control of the coastal ports and a route to its inland protectorate, would lead to its economic salvation. Instead, they produced, almost immediately, a widespread armed resistance by the coast peoples which destroyed the Company.

The coast resistance of 1888–90

The resistance commonly known as 'Abushiri's Rebellion' in fact comprised three separate attempts to drive out the Germans: one led by Abushiri in the northern coast area in and around the port of Pangani, another in the more southerly ports of Dar es Salaam, Kilwa and Lindi, and a third in Uzigua under Bwana Kheri. Strictly speaking, they were not rebellions, because the Company had not had time to establish its authority at the coast before the fighting began. The Company began to set up administration in the coastal ports in August 1888 and large-scale resistance broke out in September.

Resistance started in earnest in September at Pangani, under the leadership of the most prominent Swahili-Arab trader of the town, Abushiri bin Salim al Harthi. The resistance at first was spontaneous. The Germans were quite unprepared for it and were defeated in its early stages. A few Company officials were killed, and the Germans were expelled from the coast, except from Bagamoyo and Dar es Salaam which were besieged. Abushiri led the resistance at Pangani and directed the siege of Bagamoyo. The leading coast traders at Dar es Salaam led resistance there. At Kilwa the Sultan's ex-governor, Mataro, was responsible for expelling the Germans. In the northern hinterland of Uzigua, a Swahili, Bwana Kheri, the Sultan's ex-governor of the port of Sadani, led many Zigua against the Germans.

It would be incorrect to characterize the resistance as the reaction by a Swahili-Arab plutocracy to the loss of their economic power. Clearly, Abushiri, Mataro, Bwana Kheri and their trader supporters were stunned at the transfer of customs duties from themselves to the Germans. Undoubtedly, too, they feared German competition in the ivory trade and that the Germans would end the slave trade. However, they were equally alarmed by another German threat to their economic position: the threat to their property. Throughout 1887 and 1888 the Company demanded Arab houses as German residences. Then Vohsen, the Company administrator, issued an ordinance that owners of land and property should register the amounts within six months, after which all land not registered would be treated as public, that is Company, property. Most owners, not being able to produce legal proof of ownership, feared loss of their property. All classes of the coastal population detested foreign rule and they were all involved in the resistance.

A significant feature of the resistance was inter-ethnic cooperation. Many men from the coastal Bantu communities, especially Zigua and Bondei, fought alongside Abushiri. Later in the course of the fighting, Abushiri hired Maviti mercenaries in the interior. At Kilwa the Yao supported Mataro, on one occasion mustering a force of several thousands along the beach to prevent a German force from landing from warships. Bwana Kheri's resistance was a combined Swahili-Zigua affair. The Tanzanian coastal resistance of 1888–90 was not, as the Germans claimed at the time, a revolt by Arab slave-traders against civilization, but nationalist resistance by Arabs and Africans alike to the onset of colonial rule.

The German government succeeded, where the Company had failed, in suppressing the resistance. Chancellor Bismarck had originally supported colonization by the Company in order to save the German government expense, but at the end of 1888 he was concerned with restoring German prestige whatever the cost. Major von Wissman was sent to Tanganyika in 1889 with a large mercenary force of Turkish police, Nubian Sudanese, Somalis and Zulus. Wissmann had an immediate advantage because the resistance forces were unco-ordinated. Abushiri had very loose contact with the leaders at Dar es Salaam and none with either Mataro or Bwana Kheri. The German forces also had the advantage of superior arms and discipline. Moreover, Abushiri was a poor general, employing the wrong tactics in the face of superior German weapons. He first tried open warfare and then defence from stockades. The Germans also had African allies, such as Kingo Mkubwa, a Zigua chief, who preferred diplomatic activity to resistance. He stayed neutral until it was clear the Germans would win, then he made an agreement with them, supplied troops and, most useful, guides in Zigua country against Bwana Kheri. Kingo Mkubwa was duly rewarded with the colonial chiefship of Usagara. Many Nyamwezi porters, too, served the German forces; they seem to have been motivated by traditional trade rivalry with Swahili-Arabs who were prominent in the resistance.

Wissmann conquered the northern coastal towns first. Abushiri retreated to the interior where he hired five thousand Maviti. They did not help him at all, because once they had pillaged the countryside, they deserted in large numbers with their loot. As a result of their activities Abushiri lost support among interior communities. In December 1889 Abushiri, by now deserted by most of his followers, was betrayed to the Germans by Magaya, a *jumbe*, or village headman, in Usagara. He was arrested and hanged at Bagamoyo. In 1890 Wissmann captured the southern towns, and then turned north to deal with Bwana Kheri, who had been driven out of Sadani in 1889. When the German forces pursued him into the interior he organized a skilful guerilla resistance, building a series of forts which the Germans had to destroy one after another. He was reinforced by six hundred men sent by Mohamed bin Kassim, an Arab trader in Tabora. The famine of 1888–92 in north-east Tanzania which reduced his troops to starvation, forced Bwana Kheri to come to terms with the Germans in 1890.

Active resistance: the Hehe

Mkwawa of the Hehe, who had considerably expanded Hehe power before 1880, continued to extend the area of Hehe domination in the late 1880s by increasing the tribute-paying region rather than by outright territorial conquest. At the same time as he was expanding to the coast the Germans were moving inland, and a clash between the most powerful military nation in Europe and one of the most powerful military states in Africa became virtually inevitable. Mkwawa had no intention of submitting to German rule and the Germans could not allow him to raid Africans under German rule or remain an independent ruler without peril to their own position. Mkwawa's control of the trade routes from the coast to Unyamwezi was a major cause of conflict.

Mkwawa first found armed resistance necessary, when in 1891 his proffer of gifts did not meet with a positive response from the Germans. They misunderstood this gesture as a sign of weakness and willingness to submit to German authority, whereas it was customary for leaders in East Africa to exchange presents as a preliminary to negotiations. The Germans, instead of sending presents to Mkwawa in return, sent a military expedition, commanded by Zelewski, to punish the Hehe for taking prisoner Africans in Usagara which was under German rule. Mkwawa's army, using spears at close range in an ambush that rendered German firepower less effective, destroyed Zelewski's force at the Battle of Lugalo. Ten Europeans including Zelewski, two hundred African soldiers and a hundred porters were killed; only a few survivors managed to retreat to the safety of German-occupied territory. Hehe losses in the battle were heavy, with seven hundred men killed, but they had successfully preserved their independence, at least for a time. The Germans were unable to send a larger expedition against Mkwawa immediately. They were demoralized and they had to deal with resistance by other African leaders, like Isike of Unyanyembe.

In 1894 the Germans sent a stronger expedition against Mkwawa. It stormed Mkwawa's stone fort at his capital, Kalenga, killed many of the Hehe soldiers and destroyed Mkwawa's supplies of gunpowder. The Hehe were heavily defeated, but Mkwawa managed to escape capture. There can be little doubt that Mkwawa made a tactical error in deciding to defend his fort. He believed it was unconquerable, and it probably was by other East Africans. However, German artillery was able to destroy it easily. Moreover, the Hehe had very little experience in fighting defensive battles.

After capturing Mkwawa's fort, the Germans withdrew from Uhehe, believing Mkwawa would now submit. Instead he hit back, raiding German-occupied territory. In 1896 the Germans invaded Uhehe once again and built a garrison town at Iringa in order to bring Uhehe under effective control and as a base for expeditions to attack and destroy Mkwawa's forces. Mkwawa continued to resist, employing guerilla warfare in which the Hehe soldiers were expert. However, the German scorched earth policy, which resulted in widespread hunger and disease, gradually wore down Hehe resistance, and many of Mkwawa's soldiers were reluctantly forced into surrender. Resistance ended in 1898 when Mkwawa, whose surviving forces were too weak to continue the struggle, committed suicide to avoid capture. The Germans found only his corpse.

Mkwawa, like all great men, had his faults. He was very ruthless, having many of his enemies and even some of his relatives put to death. He appears to have been emotionally unstable. One of his praise names means 'The madness of the Year'. This instability made him ruthless at one moment, and indecisive the next. When the Germans stormed Kalenga he wanted to commit suicide there, even though it was possible to escape; but his soldiers dragged him away into the bush, where he broke down and wept.

The reasons for Mkwawa's defeat were the disparity of weapons, which proved to be decisive from 1894 to 1898, and the assistance some African groups gave to the Germans. The Sangu under Chief Merere helped the Germans against the Hehe in retaliation for earlier Hehe raids on Sangu trading caravans and on Usangu. The Kimbu, traditional enemies of the Hehe, following the defeat of Mwambambe during Mkwawa's rise to power, also allied themselves with the Germans in order to pay off old scores against the Hehe. In the early 1890s Mkwawa proposed an alliance against the Germans to Chabruma, *Nkosi* (Chief) of the Ngoni, and to Isike of Unyanyembe, the most powerful Nyamwezi state at the time. However, Chabruma rejected the proposal because at the time the Germans were not a direct threat to the Ngoni and because he could not rise above the traditional enmity between the Hehe and the Ngoni. Chabruma learnt a lesson from the separate defeat of the Hehe and the Ngoni by the Germans and he was foremost in the inter-ethnic resistance of the Maji Maji Rebellion. Isike realized the value of the proposal too late and accepted it only on the eve of his defeat. Mkwawa ranks with Samori in his appreciation of the urgency of uniting African communities in order to meet the colonial threat, and in his efforts to do something positive about it.

Mkwawa was able to resist the Germans so forcibly and for so long for a number of reasons. He adopted the correct tactics most of the time, of avoiding pitched battles and so reducing the effectiveness of German firepower. Secondly, in the years before the German incursion the Hehe had built up a powerful army by imitating the tactics and weapons—such as short stabbing spears—of their enemies the Ngoni. These were more effective in the hands of soldiers trained to use them than were guns which they had been inadequately trained to use.

In the Hehe army all booty was handed over to the ruler, who then distributed it to officials and soldiers as a reward for loyalty and bravery in battle. Therefore, Mkwawa's men tried to serve him well. Hehe culture was as dominated by military values as was that of the Prussian officers the Hehe resisted. Hehe men who disliked war or who were afraid of battle were compelled to do women's work or act as porters. Mkwawa ruled a well-organized state, improving the structure created by his father. His policy of royal centralism strengthened the state. Only a disciplined policy could have kept the Hehe people and armies so well supplied with food during a long period of resistance. Hehe supplies ran out in 1898, but what is remarkable is that they did not run out sooner.

Varieties of response within Unyamwezi

The Nyamwezi are here considered as an example of a Tanzanian community in which active resistance and diplomacy were both used as techniques of response to the Germans, but by different groups in Nyamwezi society. In 1890 Emin Pasha, with over a thousand soldiers passed through Tabora on his way to Uganda and declared Unyanyembe a German possession. In 1891 the Germans tried to make this a reality by setting up a military post at Tabora, but the result was a war of resistance in 1892 and 1893, led by Ntemi (Chief) Isike. In 1892 Isike nearly destroyed a German column, but he was soon on the defensive and in 1893, the Germans laid siege to his fort. The German force, led by Von Prince, was small, but it was heavily reinforced by the forces of Isike's local enemies. These local allies included Nyaso, a distant relative of Isike, who claimed the throne of Unyanyembe, and the rulers of Urambo and Ukimbu, traditional rivals of Unyanyembe from the days of Mirambo and Nyungu-ya-Mawe. Urambo had welcomed Emin in 1890, and in 1892–3 defeated reinforcements sent to Isike by Rumaliza, the powerful Swahili-Arab trader at Ujiji. Urambo's diplomacy had been so successful that the Germans provided forces in 1890 to help Urambo defeat the Tuta Ngoni who were marauding through Urambo.

Isike defended his fort with a force of over a thousand men, many of whom had guns—but only twenty of which were breech-loaders. He put up a long and heroic struggle. When the Germans finally broke into the inner enclosure, Isike blew up himself and his family in his powder magazine to avoid the shame of capture by foreigners. He was still breathing when Von Prince found him, and in his dying state he was at once hanged—surely the most unchivalrous and most brutal act of the German occupation. Nyaso was duly rewarded with the ntemiship of Unyanyembe.

The defeat and death of Isike did not mark the end of all Nyamwezi armed resistance to the Germans. In 1893 the Germans found it necessary to storm the stone-walled fort of Nkandi, Ntemi of Kahama, who resisted with a cannon and a variety of guns. In 1895 the Germans expelled the Ntemi of Urambo, Katuga—Mirambo's grandson—for his anti-German attitude; he then took to the countryside and organized armed resistance until his capture in 1898, when he was deported to the coast.

Passive resistance

The Shambaa were in political decline at the time of the German occupation. Many provinces had broken away from central control in the succession disputes and civil wars that racked the kingdom after the death of Kimweri the Great. In the early 1890s Semboja was still the real leader of the state, and when his son, King Kimweri Maguvu, wanted to fight the Germans, he persuaded him not to. Instead, Semboja pursued diplomatic contacts with the Germans. Semboja's policy was workable only because the Germans were initially prepared to leave the Shambaa alone. When the powerful Semboja died in 1895, the Germans carried out a coup during the funeral, sending a small force which seized all of Semboja's arms and ammunition. They arrested King Mputa, who had succeeded Kimweri Maguvu, and accused him of murder. Mputa had ordered the killing of a man who had entered the royal village and slept with one of his wives. Mputa was hanged in public in front of all the leading Shambaa chiefs, who had been rounded up and forced to witness the execution. Without either arms or a leader the Shambaa could offer no more than passive resistance. The Germans replaced Mputa with a puppet, Kinyashi, who served them as a labour recruiter. The early colonial period in Usambara was marked by a series of natural disasters which further weakened Shambaa ability and will to resist. In 1898 there was a jiggers plague; in 1898 half of the royal capital, Vuga, burnt down; in 1899 there was famine; and in 1902 the other half of Vuga burnt down, and the town was not rebuilt afterwards.

The powerful, warlike Ngoni of the south-east, organized in the Njelu and Mshope chiefdoms, naturally enough prepared for armed resistance against any German attempt to impose colonial rule over them. However, the German occupation was carried out in such a way that the Ngoni were unable to fight. The Boma Massacre nipped in the bud active resistance by the Njelu Ngoni, and the Chilembo Incident deterred the Mshope Ngoni from taking up arms. The Boma Massacre occurred in 1897 when a German party sent to the Ngoni built a strong wooden *boma,* or fort, near the camp of the powerful Njelu *induna* Songea, and invited the Njelu leaders to inspect it. The *nkosi* (king) Mlamira Gama, four indunas (ministers) including Songea, and several generals, accepted the invitation. As soon as they were inside the boma, the Germans started to arrest them. Some of the war generals tried to escape by jumping over the fence and five of them were shot dead. The surviving leaders, including Mlamira Gama and Songea, were detained for a time, and released after surrendering unconditionally to German authority. Nkosi Chabruma of the Mshope kingdom was forced to submit after he had sent his most important induna and war general Chilembo, to raid a border district of neighbouring Njelu. The Germans shot Chilembo dead and Chabruma then reluctantly accepted the German flag.

The Ngoni, with their military tradition and culture, were very conscious of their failure to fight in 1897. A significant factor in their decision to participate in the Maji Maji Rebellion eight years later was their keen desire not only to avenge the Boma Massacre and the killing of Chilembo, but to recover their military honour.

The failure of the Imperial British East Africa Company

The period of Imperial British East Africa Company rule lasted from 1888 to only 1894, when its territories and responsibilities were taken over by the British government. The bankruptcy of the IBEA Company in 1891, only three years after being granted its charter, is explicable largely in terms of conflicting objectives. It tried to serve both the British government's political ends and its own need to make profits. The Company was severly restricted by the 1887 agreement with the Sultan of Zanzibar and the terms of the charter of 1888. Duties on imports collected at the Kenya coast were restricted to five per cent; subjects of foreign states were exempted from any taxation other than customs duties; the Company had to accept freedom of trade within its area of operations, and had to pay an annual subsidy to the Sultan that was so high that it would eliminate virtually all profit unless there were dramatic mineral discoveries at an early date.

The Company was undercapitalized as much as Peters' was. It started with only £250,000 much of which was consumed in capital expenditure on infrastructure, like piers, roads and telegraphs at Mombasa, which brought no direct or immediate profit. Much time and money had to be devoted to developing communications since existing caravan trails in the Company's sphere ran southwards to German-controlled ports. Expensive reconnoitring expeditions had to be sent through mostly unknown country to find new routes. At the same time there was a lack of mineral wealth and other exportable commodities, apart from ivory, which made it impossible to derive quick profits to offset the capital expenditure.

The potentialities of Uganda and Kenya lay largely in agricultural development, which is a slow process with long-term profits, and which could only have occurred after the building of a railway which was beyond the Company's resources. Ivory was profitable, but because of the dependence on human porterage, which was both costly and slow, profits were low. It took three months for a caravan to march from Buganda to the coast. Resistance to Company rule by the Sultan and people of Witu, the port at the mouth of the Tana River, during 1890–3, prevented the Company from utilizing this navigable river which led to a rich ivory area. Similar efforts by the Company to use the Juba River as a quick route to ivory country were frustrated by Somali resistance. The resistance by the Tanzanian coast peoples to the Germans during 1888–90 added immeasurably to the Company's difficulties, because not only did hostilities in the German zone disrupt trade over a wider area including the British zone, but also a British blockade embraced the Kenya coast to prevent the Swahili-Arabs to the north supplying Tanzanian coastal peoples. However, what really destroyed the Company's economic position was Mackinnon's policy of aggressive expansion far inland. He believed that the Company would never make sufficient profits to pay its way if it concentrated on developing the coast and the areas near the coast. He hoped that the occupation and development of Buganda and the surrounding states would bring in large profits. The occupation of Buganda was a financial gamble which did not come off; not only did it not bring in profits, but it brought additional non-profit-making governmental responsibilities.

Uganda made the Company an annual loss of £50,000. Additional symptoms of the Company's failure were its lack of experienced officers, its shortage of officers whether experienced or not, and the two-year delay in recruiting a police force. It took two years before de Winton was appointed as permanent administrator in 1890; he was hardly suitable because of his age and lack of vigour. However, none of these symptoms were root causes.

Uganda

The coming of the Company

The coups and religious wars in Buganda from 1887 to 1890 led to the transfer of effective power from the Kabaka to an oligarchy of young Christians, and to the defeat of the Ganda Muslims. They also

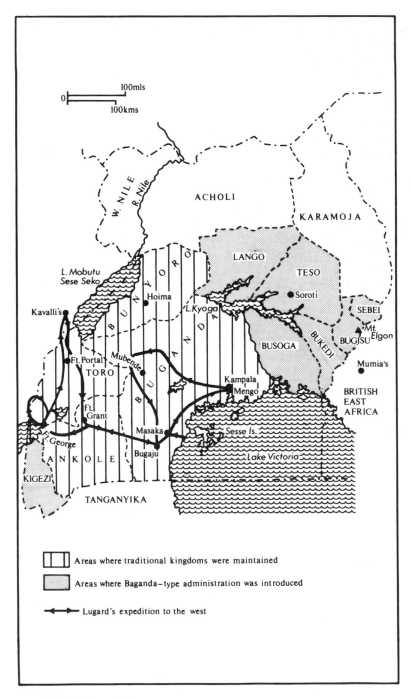

Map 7. The Uganda Protectorate.

led to the emergence of intense rivalry between the Protestant and Catholic leaders within the new ruling group, and to the emergence of rival parties. The *Ingleza* party was composed of the Protestants led by the katikiro, Apolo Kagwa. The *Fransa* party consisted of the Catholics and the Kabaka Mwanga and his supporters. Mwanga believed neither in the old religion nor any of the new ones in Buganda. He was a Catholic from 1890 to 1892, but only a nominal one. He adhered to the Fransa party because, like the Catholics, he feared the expanding imperialism of the British in East Africa in the shape of the IBEA Company. The Catholics feared the British who they identified with the Protestants, since the Protestant missionaries in Buganda were British.

A German expedition arrived in Buganda in early 1890 and offered Mwanga a protection treaty, which the Kabaka accepted on the advice of the French Catholic White Fathers. Mwanga rejected a treaty offered by Frederick Jackson who had led an IBEA Company expedition to Buganda. The Fransa appeared to have won a great diplomatic victory. However, the Anglo-German Agreement of July 1890 declared Uganda to be a British sphere of influence. The IBEA Company then sent a second expedition to Buganda, this time fifty Swahili and Somali soldiers under Captain Frederick Lugard, who arrived at Mengo, the Kabaka's capital, in December 1890.

The weaker Protestant Ingleza welcomed Lugard as an ally in the Ganda internal power struggle against the numerically stronger, better armed and anti-British Catholic Fransa. From 1890 to 1892 the Ingleza used diplomacy as their response to Lugard, whereas the Fransa showed passive resistance until in 1892 they resorted to active armed resistance. In December 1890 Mwanga reluctantly signed a protection treaty with the Company. There were a number of reasons for his signing. Very strong pressure was put on him by Apolo Kagwa and even the White Fathers influenced him to sign. The continuing threat from the Muslim Ganda forces on the Bunyoro border made it imperative for the Fransa to make common cause with both the Ingleza and Lugard. The Catholics within the Fransa party knew that Lugard's presence helped to keep under control the basic anti-Christian feelings of the kabaka, and the White Fathers seem to have believed Lugard's promise to be impartial between Protestants and Catholics. However, Mwanga showed no enthusiasm at the signing ceremony and for two years he refused to fly the Company flag.

In 1891 Lugard led a predominantly Christian army to defeat the Ganda Muslims on the Bunyoro border. Next he marched into Toro and drove out the Bunyoro army which had conquered the area in 1876. He then restored as *Mukama* (King) of Toro a Mutoro prince named Kasagama, an outstanding opportunist who had been in exile in Buganda and had thrown in his lot with Lugard. Afterwards

Lugard marched to Kavalli's on Lake Mobutu to meet the Sudanese of the former Egyptian garrison who had refused to accompany Emin to the coast in 1889. He persuaded them, under their leader Selim Bey, to enlist in the Company forces. Lugard used some of them to man the new forts he set up along the Toro-Bunyoro border, while he took the rest with him to Kampala to augment his limited power there.

The Ganda War of Resistance 1892

Lugard's wars with the Ganda Muslims and Bunyoro in 1891 proved to be only a temporary rallying point for the rival Christian factions in Buganda. The wars removed the persistent threats of attack from those quarters which had hitherto kept the Christians from fighting each other. Moreover, Lugard had received a letter from the Company instructing him to evacuate Buganda. This he was not prepared to do even though he shared the pessimism of the heads of the Company about its economic future. Lugard now decided to force the Fransa to accept more completely the authority of the Company so that he could show, as part of a compaign to retain Buganda, that the country was under close Company control. Lugard began to side increasingly with the Protestants.

Lugard's mishandling of the Mugoloba Case finally led to war. Mugoloba, a Catholic leader, killed a Protestant, allegedly in self-defence. Mwanga tried the case according to Ganda law and acquitted Mugoloba. The Protestants believed that the Catholics were using the kabaka against them, so they appealed to their new patron, Lugard, against the kabaka. Lugard openly sided with the Protestants in the case by demanding that Mwanga order Mugoloba's execution. When Mwanga refused to do so and conflict seemed inevitable Lugard issued about 500 guns to the Ingleza.

The Battle of Mengo was fought on January 24, 1892. The Protestants opened fire first, but since this was to counter a Catholic invasion of Kagwa's compound, it seems pointless to blame either side for the beginning of hostilities. Lugard stayed out of the battle at first. In the early stages the Protestants were successful and they succeeded in destroying the Catholic Church and Mission. It seemed they would do Lugard's work for him. However, Gabriel Kintu, the *Mujasi*, or army commander, and a Catholic, kept the Catholic forces back for a counter-attack, and when he began his advance the Protestants began to fall back. The battle was by no means decided at this stage, but Lugard was not prepared to risk a Protestant defeat which would have put his own position in peril, so he intervened. His maxim gun scattered the Catholic forces and his Sudanese captured the kabaka's palace and pursued their enemy to the lakeshore. Lugard's intervention in the battle was decisive in ensuring a Protestant victory. Mwanga and the Fransa chiefs fled to Bulin-gugwe Island in Lake Victoria.

The Battle of Mengo revolutionized the political situation in Buganda. The Protestants were now the ruling class, and they had the largest share in the new land settlement. The system of dividing offices and lands equally between Catholics and Protestants agreed in 1890 was replaced by a geographical partition. However, the partition was most unequal: the Catholics, who were far more numerous than the Protestants, were allocated the large but single province of Buddu; the Muslims were given three small counties; the Protestants were rewarded with the rest, which was most of Buganda. Mwanga was able to return to the capital and keep his position as kabaka. Both the Company and the Protestants needed to make the victorious Ingleza regime, which held a disproportionate number of senior posts, appear legitimate to the Ganda people, who held the kabakaship in immense respect. They believed that the return of Mwanga would achieve this. However, a new treaty between Mwanga and the Company reduced his independence still further, and he became nothing more than a constitutional monarch, a position he would not willingly hold for long. Many of the defeated Catholics were given sufficient land and offices to reconcile them to the new regime—their leader Stanislaus Mugwanya was made an extra katikiro in 1893. There were, however, still many dissatisfied Catholics.

The year 1892 marked a revolution in Buganda in more ways than one. The new land settlement led to the migration of thousands of families, and the solidity of the old social order was profoundly shaken. Christianity now began to spread much more rapidly into the provinces. In 1893 the first Anglican deacons were ordained, including Henry Wright Duta and Sebwato, and in 1893 and the following year nearly one hundred Anglican converts were sent out all over the country to set up reading houses. The Catholics displayed similar evangelical zeal, with similar successful results. However, it is time to turn to a group which, because it was politically defeated, has been largely neglected by historians, but which played a significant role in early resistance to colonialism: the Ganda Muslims.

The Ganda Muslim revolt, 1893

The Ganda Muslims, who had resisted British colonialism in 1891, were given a very small share in the land settlements of 1892 and 1893. Moderates like Prince Mbogo, the late Kabaka Mutesa's brother, lost control of the Muslim party to extremists like the young Juma Nyenje, a fanatical jihadist. Nyenje planned a revolt against the infidel regime, and entered the discussions for an alliance with his co-religionists, the Sudanese soldiers of the Company. Selim Bey, who had been used by Lugard in 1892 to persuade the Ganda Muslims to return from the Bunyoro border and settle in the heart of Buganda, felt keenly in 1893 that they were being mistreated and disregarded and he openly sympathized with their grievances. Macdonald, the British officer left in charge of the country, decided to take no chances and acted swiftly and decisively to pre-empt possible concerted action between the Ganda Muslims and the Sudanese. He arrested and deported Selim and disarmed the Sudanese at Kampala. In spite of this the Ganda Muslims rose but they were defeated by a combined Protestant-Catholic army in a battle at Rubaga near the capital. They retreated to Toro, whence they were pursued by a Protestant army under the brilliant general Semei Kakungulu and defeated again. The Muslims had already suffered a blow when Mbogo had refused to join the revolt at its outset; they suffered another in Toro when Taibu Magato led a large body of them into surrender. Magato had come to believe what Mbogo had always believed: that the British would safeguard Islam in Buganda. After Magato's capitulation, the other rebels abandoned the unequal struggle. The Muslims now had two of their three counties taken away from them so they suffered severely economically. Selim Bey, who was dying of dropsy at the time of his arrest, died on the way to the coast.

Bunyoro's resistance to the British invasion

Mukama Kabalega of Bunyoro was able to offer determined and prolonged armed resistance to Britain largely because of his achievements in reorganizing his country in the pre-colonial period. Such resistance was made possible largely by his administrative reforms that brought greater centralization and efficiency into his government, his social reforms that brought greater unity and cohesion among the various social classes in Bunyoro, and his creation of the *abarusura*, a regular army of professional soldiers equipped with guns.

The spread of British authority in Uganda in the 1890s made a conflict between Britain and Bunyoro almost inevitable. In the 1870s and 1880s Kabalega had reasserted Bunyoro's authority in many parts of Uganda in a bid to revive the glory and the extent of the ancient empire. In the early 1890s he was continuing this policy. So expanding Bunyoro imperialism collided with expanding British imperialism.

In 1891 Kabalega committed only a small part of his army to resist Lugard's advance to Kavalli's because he was taken by suprise, and because he was not yet ready to fight the British who had the latest type of rifle. Lugard expelled Kabalega's garrisons from Toro without much difficulty. From 1892, however, Kabalega organized skilful resistance to Britain. He attacked the British forts along the Toro-Bunyoro border, frequently interrupting their communications and cutting off their supplies.

In 1893 the British withdrew from most of their Toro forts. A special commissioner, Gerald Portal, had been sent to investigate the situation in Uganda by the British government. He began a policy of reducing the bankrupt IBEA Company's expenses and concentrating on Buganda. This gave Kabalega the opportunity, which he promptly took, to reinvade Toro, reoccupy the country which Lugard had taken from him in 1891 and expel the British puppet king Kasagama. This induced Portal's successors, Macdonald and Colvile, to endeavour to restore British prestige in Uganda generally. They also wished to forestall a rumoured Congo Free State advance from the west towards the Nile. So in late 1893 Colvile invaded Bunyoro proper and established a line of forts across the country to secure a route to Lake Mobutu. Naturally, Kabalega attacked these forts, so Colvile decided to attempt to destroy Kabalega and his army and remove the threat from Bunyoro for ever.

In 1894 Colvile invaded Bunyoro with a combined British-Buganda force of eight European officers, 400 Sudanese and 15,000 Baganda. In the Buganda army—as in the campaign of 1891—the Catholics allied with the Protestants. Kabalega was fully determined to resist the threat to Bunyoro of combined British-Buganda imperialism. However, at the beginning of the struggle the Mukama made a serious strategic mistake by dividing his army into four scattered divisions. One division was assigned to guard the border with Toro; another to garrison Bunyara on the southern shore of Lake Kioga; a third to cover the main frontier with Buganda; and the other to form a general reserve. Colvile was then able to advance without meeting serious resistance. Faced with the consequence of dividing his army—the overrunning of his country by the enemy—Kabalega recovered his strategic skill and refused a general engagement. He abandoned his capital, Mparo, and prevented Colvile from achieving the primary objective in warfare, the destruction of the main body of the enemy. Instead, he retreated to Budongo forest to gain time to reorganize his forces. He could always retire faster than the British could advance, so he sensibly avoided a serious engagement and committed his forces only to a series of rearguard actions. He retreated across the Nile into Lang'o, the country of the Lang'i. As Kabalega retreated, Colvile occupied Bunyoro, but failed to subdue Kabalega.

Bunyoro suffered severely from Colvile's invasion of 1894. Five and a half counties of Bunyoro, including Mubende, the former centre of the old kingdom and the burial place of many Bunyoro kings, were awarded to Buganda. Toro, too, was enlarged at Bunyoro's expense. Economically, Bunyoro was ruined as farms and homes were destroyed by the invaders. The prolonged guerilla warfare waged by Kabalega from 1894 onwards completed the ruin of the country.

Many of Kabalega's *abarusura* officers surrendered after the defeats of 1894. A few even collaborated with the British and later became colonial chiefs. However, many others regrouped their forces in their various hideouts and continued to resist, some under Kabalega's distant leadership from Lang'o, and some independently. The mass of the people, the peasants, did not resist, because they were neither trained nor armed to do so.

Kabalega's resistance of 1895 was much stronger than the resistance of 1894. Not only did he return to Bunyoro from Lang'o, but he even invaded Toro in the south, in an attempt to obtain arms and ammunition from Swahili-Arabs operating from German East Africa. At Kijumbira island near Masindi in Bunyoro he defeated a British-Buganda force of several thousand, compelling the occupying force to withdraw to Hoima to reorganize. Later in the year a large British force with 20,000 Baganda attacked Kabalega's stockade on the Lang'o bank of the Nile, and captured it, but Kabalega escaped, though with the loss of most of his property and followers.

In 1896 Bunyoro was declared part of the Uganda Protectorate, but the British still did not control the country effectively. Kabalega prevented a British-Baganda advance across the Nile by employing a scorched earth policy of destroying crops so that the enemy forces were deprived of food. A revolt in the Lost Counties—those districts of Bunyoro given by the British to Buganda in 1894— succeeded in destroying a British fort and a mission. Ganda chiefs who had been introduced into the area as colonial agents were chased out. The British and the Baganda restored their authority in the Lost Counties only with great difficulty.

Kabalega continued his guerilla resistance throughout 1897. In 1898 he was offically deposed by the British who set up a council of regency to act for the new mukama, Kabalega's son Kitahimbwa. This did not dampen Kabalega's determination to fight on. At this time Mwanga escaped from German custody and began fighting in southern Bunyoro. This encouraged Kabalega to take the field against the British in northern Bunyoro, and British Indian troops only managed to reconquer the area after encountering some of the fiercest resistance of all, directed by Kabalega's brilliant guerilla generals, Ireta and Kikulule. The climax of the Banyoro resistance of 1898 was the destruction of the British post at Hoima.

In 1899 Kabalega and his new ally Mwanga, were eventually betrayed by some Lang'i chiefs, and were deported to the Seychelles Islands. In 1923 Kabalega was allowed to return to Uganda, but he died at Jinja on the way home. The crucial factor in his ultimate defeat was his inability to obtain modern weapons.

The capture of Kabalega and his banishment marked the end of

Banyoro armed resistance to the imposition of British rule, but the courage with which he had resisted to the last possible moment meant that, until his death nearly a quarter of a century later, many Banyoro still regarded him as their legitimate king, rather than his son who was imposed by the British.

A notable feature of Kabalega's resistance was inter-ethnic co-operation. Many Lang'i had fought for Kabalega in the war of succession that brought him to power in the wars of expansion in the 1870s and 1880s. The Lang'i fought on his side against Colvile in 1894 and in the long guerilla war that followed, and allowed him to use their country as a base to fight the British. Kabalega also received considerable help from the Acholi, some of whom had fought for him before the British arrival. Mwanga, too, linked up with Kabalega in flight. One wonders what might have happened if the two kings had made common cause against Lugard in 1890.

Mwanga's Rebellion

Apolo Kagwa diagnosed the causes of the 1897 Rebellion in Buganda in this way: 'The king hates the Europeans because they stopped his gross immoralities. The chiefs hate us because a Christian is expected to have only one wife and because no slaves are allowed; and the people hate us because they say they are obligated to carry loads, and to make roads . . . and because the old heathen customs are dying away!' This diagnosis tends to indicate that many of the rebel supporters of Mwanga were looking backwards rather than forwards, which was generally true. However, Kagwa under-estimated the role in the Rebellion of Catholics and Muslims, and clearly misrepresents Mwanga's motives.

The kabaka led the revolt because he had a fierce distrust of European colonial rule. There were a number of matters to which he particularly objected: the stopping of tribute from the Soga to Buganda, which had been one of his major sources of income; the enactment of a law ending the kabaka's prerogative as the sole giver of land and allowing anyone to buy land; the purge of his pages in 1896. In that year, alarmed at the revival of homosexuality and drunkenness at Mwanga's court and the steady increase in his personal entourage, the Christian government leaders had hundreds of young men and boys removed from the kabaka's service. It is not surprising that the kabaka should wish to act against men who were more powerful than he was and against the British administration that sustained them. He wanted both the restoration of his old political power and recognition of what he regarded as his personal right to appoint his own servants.

By 1897 many of the Kabaka's subjects, too, were disenchanted with Protestant-British domination. Many of the Catholic leaders had not become reconciled to the regime since their defeat in 1892.

Many Muslims, too, could not accept Protestant domination. There were even dissident Protestants with anti-British sympathies, like Yona Wasswa, the *mukwenda* (a very senior minister), who was arrested just before the rebellion. Above all, there was the great body of traditional leaders who lamented the suppression of customary practices such as bhang-smoking, and who suffered economically from the banning of slave-trading.

When in 1897 Mwanga left the capital and raised the standard of revolt in the mainly Catholic province of Buddu, thousands of Ganda from all religious parties and sections of the population joined him. Loyalty to the kabaka was so deeply ingrained that many chiefs who had suffered from his tyranny in the past now threw in their lot with him. However, equally as strong as attachment to the kabaka was the attachment of the ruling oligarchy to their new regime. The rebellion was resolutely opposed by the senior Protestants such as Kagwa, and the senior Catholics such as Mugwanya, who held senior government posts, and whose very positions and power depended on their diplomatic alliance with the British. The senior Muslim leaders like Prince Mbogo and Taibu Magato also threw their power and influence on the side of the colonial regime.

A combined army of the British forces and the followers of the senior Ganda leaders defeated Mwanga and his fourteen thousand supporters at Kabuwoko Hill, maxim guns once again carrying the day. Mwanga now made a serious error of political and military judgement. In spite of the defeat at Kabuwoko, he managed to escape capture and, since he had considerable popular support, he could have stayed in Buganda and been the focus for guerilla resistance. Instead, he fled to German East Africa where he was interned by the Germans. Later he escaped from Mwanza and returned to his country to keep the dying embers of rebellion alive, but by then it was too late. His flight had led to the collapse of his support. He had already been deposed and replaced as kabaka by a one-year old baby, Daudi Cwa, who could be no threat either to British rule or to the senior Christian politicians. Three regents ruled for the kabaka; they were the three most senior Christians: Kagwa and Kisingiri (Protestants) and Mugwanya.

Gabriel Kintu organized Mwanga's surviving followers in brilliantly conducted guerilla warfare for two years until the final defeat of 1899. Mwanga's return from Mwanza certainly inspired this lengthy resistance, but his earlier flight had meant the loss of the initial momentum of the rebellion. Still, he gained new supporters: some Bahima leaders in Nkore, and some Soga traditionalists and Muslims. Kintu was eventually defeated by the Ganda Protestant forces and escaped to German territory. In 1898 Mwanga linked up with Kabalega in Lang'o and was captured with him there by an army of Ganda Protestants and British troops. He shared Kabalega's exile in the Seychelles but died there.

In 1899 the British Government sent Sir Harry Johnston to Buganda as Special Commissioner to investigate and make recommendations on the future administration of the country. Johnston duly made the Buganda Agreement of 1900 which both rewarded the senior Christian leaders for their loyalty to the British during Mwanga's Rebellion and a mutiny of Sudanese troops in 1898, and defined the basis of the British colonial system in Buganda. British rule had been firmly established in the lake kingdom; from 1900 Buganda could be formally administered. However, at this time there were still large areas in northern Uganda independent of Britain.

Semei Kakungulu and Ganda sub-imperialism

The career of Semei Kakungulu illustrates the crucial part played by the Ganda Protestants in spreading British imperialism throughout Uganda. Kakungulu emerged during the Christian-Muslim civil wars of 1888–90 as the most able Protestant general, and captured Mengo from the Muslims. In 1892 he subdued Busoga for the IBEA Company and in 1893 played a significant part in the Ganda–British campaign against Bunyoro. In 1895 he helped the British conquer the Bukusu in western Kenya; and in 1899 he helped to capture Kabalega. Kagwa's dominance deprived Kakungulu of the chance of political leadership he aspired to in Buganda, so he sought outlets for his ambition in the conquest of regions outside British control. From 1899 to 1902 he subdued an area of about ten thousand square miles to the north-east of Buganda and Busoga, between Mount Elgon and Lake Kioga: these were the lands of the Padhola, Gisu, Kumam and Teso. The communities west of Elgon had no centralized political authorities to organize effective armed resistance. Kakungulu divided the conquered peoples into five administrative counties ruled by his own appointees as chiefs, along the lines of the provincial administration in Buganda. He was simply paving the way for British rule. When the British took over the area from 1903 they made very few changes in his administrative system, and for some time retained the Ganda administrators he had appointed.

The Sudanese Mutiny

After the campaign against Mwanga in 1897, the Sudanese troops in the British army in Uganda were sent to Eldama Ravine in present-day western Kenya, and put under the command of Major Macdonald, a tactless move after his mistreatment of their former officer and leader, Selim Bey, in 1893. To make things worse, he was to lead them on an expedition to the southern Sudan in order to stop a rumoured French advance from the northern Congo basin towards the upper Nile. The Sudanese needed a rest. For years they had been fighting battles for the British, and had marched thousands of miles to do so. Now they were ordered to make a longer march than any they had made before; moreover, they were told they could not take with them the women who usually accompanied them on long marches. Equally important, their pay was in arrears, and they were paid less than a coastal porter. However, perhaps the most important factor was their belief that they would be made to fight the Mahdists, their Muslim co-religionists. They mutinied at Eldama Ravine and at Lubwa's where they were besieged by forces loyal to the British. The Christian Ganda sent a large force to Lubwa's, but the British also called in Indian troops. In 1898 the mutineers broke the siege of Lubwa's by breaking through the British-Ganda lines. The mutineers retreated to Mruli in Lang'o on the Nile, and were heavily defeated there. The survivors scattered, some making their way northwards into the Sudan, and some continuing to resist the British expedition from hideouts in independent Lango and Acholiland. A British expedition in 1901 dispersed the remaining resisting mutineers in northern Uganda. Thus the most serious threat to the British position in Uganda was removed.

Kenya

Kenya showed the same pattern of varied response to European invasion as Tanzania and Uganda. Some parts of the coast put up armed resistance during Mbaruk's Rebellion in 1895. Mbaruk led one group of the powerful Mazrui family against Britain while another branch of the family supported the British. The Kamba were divided between those sections led by individual *athani*, or war leaders, who were prepared to play diplomacy with the British and those who were prepared to fight the invaders. The Maasai, in spite of their warlike reputation, did not offer armed resistance to the British. Lenana used diplomacy to win British aid against his rival for the laibonship, his brother Sendeo, and to loot Kikuyu cattle in joint military operations with the British. The following case studies illustrate the nature of Kenyan resistance in greater detail.

Initial Kikuyu response to British invasion

Cege wa Kibiru, the most famous Kikuyu seer of the late nineteenth century, apparently prophesied that peculiar strangers would come to Kikuyuland from out of the big water to the east. They would look like small white frogs, their dress would resemble the wings of butterflies, they would carry sticks that would spit fire, and they would bring an iron snake which would belch out fire as it travelled between the big waters to the east and west. He warned the Kikuyu against attacking these strangers; advice that was taken by

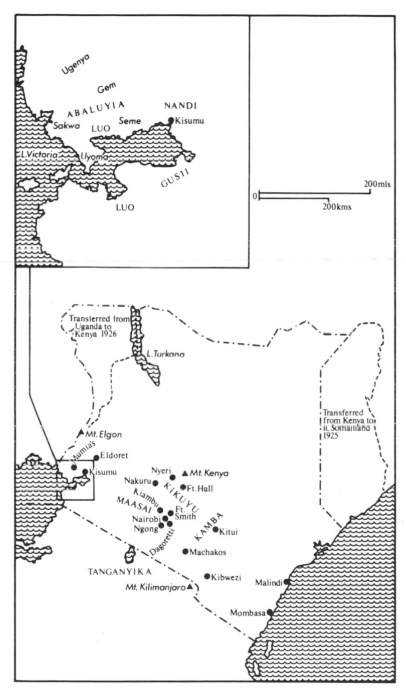

Map 8.   Kenya.

some but not by others. The Kikuyu offered a varied response to British invasion. A uniform reaction was virtually impossible from a society that lacked central political organization and in which local loyalties tended to be very local indeed.

The first stage in Kikuyu response runs to 1894, when the IBEA Company was supplanted by the British government. This stage was marked by armed attacks on Company forts in the Nairobi area, Company punitive expeditions, and the arrest and death of Waiyaki. In 1890 the Company built a fort at Dagoretti, on the southern edge of Kikuyuland in present-day Nairobi, to provision caravans bound for Uganda. The presence of weak administrators, unable to discipline the largely Swahili soldiers, encouraged the Swahili, who were underfed by the Company, to steal food and livestock from the Kikuyu. This theft led to armed resistance which forced the Company to abandon the fort in 1891 and withdraw its forces to Machakos in Kambaland. The Kikuyu then burnt the abandoned Dagoretti fort. However, later in 1891 the Company returned to the Nairobi area and built Fort Smith which, despite the occasional breakdown of its relationships with the local Kikuyu, generally managed to obtain food supplies with little trouble.

Waiyaki was a prominent leader of the Kikuyu of the Nairobi area. He lived in a large fortified village, and both fought and traded with the neighbouring Maasai, to whom he was related. He welcomed the British as potential trading partners who would augment his wealth. He could not resist posing to the British as a ruling chief and even paramount chief of all the Kikuyu, especially as the British, who did not understand the Kikuyu system of government, were looking for rulers to make protection treaties with. The Kikuyu chiefs, including Waiyaki, were not titled office-holders but outstanding individuals called upon to lead their people by the choice of the people. There was certainly no paramount chief. Yet in order to please the British, and to secure their friendship as a preliminary to profitable trade, Waiyaki made treaties with the Company on behalf of all the Kikuyu, which neither he nor any other Kikuyu had the right to do. His pretence to paramountcy redounded to his disadvantage in 1892. Some Kikuyu killed a number of Company soldiers who were trying to loot their village, and the Company planned a punitive expedition. Waiyaki was afraid that his own livestock, which were being herded by the people who lived in the area that was to be attacked by the expedition, would be killed or captured. He secretly warned the people of the impending expedition, which was a failure. Unfortunately for Waiyaki the British found out he had warned the people and came to the erroneous conclusion that not only was he a 'traitor' but that, as 'Paramount Chief', he probably instigated the killing of the soldiers. This misunderstanding led to Waiyaki's arrest at Fort Smith, during which he was wounded. A few days later he was marched off to Mombasa for trial, but died en route and was buried at Kibwezi. The anger of the people of his area at his mistreatment resulted in intermittent armed resistance against Fort Smith for the rest of the period of Company rule. Generally however, reactions remained friendly as the Company made no real attempt to rule the area effectively.

After 1894 the resistance of the southern Kikuyu was greatly weakened by a series of natural disasters. Locust invasions, smallpox and famine, resulting from drought and cattle plague, led to the deaths of over half the southern Kikuyu and the migration of many survivors to live with relatives to the north. During the period of natural disasters from 1894 to 1899 many Kikuyu men were reluctantly forced to accept service with the British as porters and soldiers in exchange for food. The opportunity for armed resistance was extremely small.

The most prominent of the Kikuyu of Kiambu to ally with the British was Kinyanjui. Initially he was a very poor man, an *ahoi* or tenant, who lived by hunting wild animals. He became Waiyaki's servant, then an interpreter with the IBEA Company and later a trader selling agricultural produce to the British caravans and expeditions. When he was given a gun as a reward for his services he raided his fellow Kikuyu with it. In the late 1890s he 'sold' land to the first European settlers in Kikuyuland. It was not his land: it belonged to the community, and other families were living on it. Later, he became a colonial chief and the leader of the Kikuyu colonial chiefs. He was less a diplomatist than a self-seeking opportunist, who became very rich through his contact with the colonial system.

The final stage in Kikuyu resistance to the British invasion was the reaction of the central and northern Kikuyu. In 1900 the British set up Mbirri station (Fort Hall) in Murang'a in central Kikuyuland, where a prominent individual, Karuri wa Gakure, excelled in the diplomatic technique as a response to the British. From 1898 to 1900, Karuri played a major role in encouraging Kikuyu in Murang'a and Nyeri, to the north, to cooperate with the new British administration in the area. He even provided the British with men to help conquer those Kikuyu who did resist. He became very wealthy, receiving presents from other Kikuyu leaders who knew he had the ear of the colonial government. Another successful diplomatist was Wang'ombe, a prominent chief in Nyeri. He also allied with Boyes, a prominent British trader, and gave building sites to the British.

Gakere, on the other hand was a Nyeri leader who decided on armed resistance, and after his defeat in 1902 he was captured and deported to the coast. The attempt by the British to enforce their rule in northern Kikuyuland provoked strong resistance in some areas, especially Tetu and Mathira. An attack in Tetu in 1902 led by Meinertzhagen almost met disaster. His troops were only saved by the use of machine guns and a fearless counter-attack by Maasai mercenaries. By 1903 a full company of troops was stationed at Fort

Hall and new weapons were issued to them. During 1904 and 1905 a number of expeditions were mounted against the Mathira Kikuyu and it is estimated that at least 1500 were killed. Whereas the southern Kikuyu had initially faced the rather weak IBEA Company which basically wished to safeguard food supplies on the route to Uganda, the northern Kikuyu faced a British administration determined to enforce its rule and to begin an efficient system of revenue collection.

Nandi resistance

The Nandi numbered probably about forty thousand at the time of their armed resistance to the British. Of these, about six thousand at any one time were soldiers. Yet in East Africa only the Banyoro equalled them in the vigour and constancy of their resistance. The Banyoro lived in a large, well-organized and comparatively well-armed state; the Nandi were not a single political unit and fought only with spears. How were a few spearmen able to resist the British empire for eleven years?

Firstly, the Nandi possessed a number of advantages from their environment. Their country was mountainous, with steep, heavily wooded valleys and little open country. It was ideal for guerilla warfare and unsuitable for the Maxim gun. It greatly reduced the effectiveness of rifle power. The wet and cold climate had a dispiriting effect and caused a high incidence of exposure and respiratory infections among the invading forces. Secondly, the mixed economy practised by the Nandi reduced the effects of crop burning and confiscation because they could live off their livestock. Moreover, as Nandi agriculture was on a subsistence scale only, British expeditions could not live off the land. The mobility of expeditions was reduced by the large number of porters who had to carry food. Thirdly, the Nandi had an ardent martial spirit and a disciplined and efficient army, which had considerable experience of warfare against the Maasai and other neighbouring peoples. Traditional Nandi military tactics, involving night fighting and ambushes, required little adjustment against the British. The Nandi had no defensive strongpoints that would have been ideal targets for superior British firepower. The Nandi fought in separate companies according to their clan and residence. There was no unified military command. Even this helped the resistance for the Nandi could continue the struggle with other companies if one were located and destroyed. Their democratic system of electing officers meant that if a commander were killed or captured resistance did not collapse but continued under a freshly-elected successor.

In the pre-colonial period the Nandi had developed the office of the *orkoiyot*, a ritual expert who acted as a religious leader and a political and military prophet. He could not initiate raids; he could only interpret whether the omens were favourable for a war the army was planning. By the last quarter of nineteenth century a degree of centralization had been reached whereby the orkoiyot had a *maotik*, or agent, in each district, so that there was considerable co-operation between districts in war. In 1890 the orkoiyot Kimnyole had been put to death because he was blamed for an outbreak of epidemics, such as smallpox and cattle diseases, and for defeats of raiding parties by the Luo. For nine years there was an interregnum until a new orkoiyot, Koitalel arap Samoei, was appointed in 1899. The revival of the orkoiyotship was a response to the impending menace of the white man, and Koitalel was a strong nationalist completely opposed to any accommodation with any foreigners. Though the orkoiyot had no defined political authority, there is little doubt that the revival of the office was a major unifying factor and a significant aid to resistance. A further factor in the determination of their resistance that Europeans failed to understand, was the Nandi feeling of cultural superiority over all other people, especially Europeans, whose colour and dress resembled those of devils in Nandi mythology.

Nandi reaction to the coast traders who entered their country between 1850 and 1890 foreshadows their later reception of the British. Arab and Swahili traders were either expelled or killed. In 1895 a British trader, Andrew Dick, quarrelled with the Nandi on the edge of their country. In retaliation the Nandi killed another British trader, Peter West and most of his party, and made a series of attacks on the Uganda Road which skirted their country and was the British lifeline between Buganda and Mombasa.

In 1895 a punitive expedition was sent by the British against the Nandi. It consisted of six Europeans, and several hundred Sudanese and Swahili. The British force lost thirty killed and the Nandi, according to British official records, two hundred. However, the Nandi were so elusive that no fine or treaty could be imposed. In 1897 the Nandi attacked and destroyed a British mail party. This time the British added four hundred Maasai auxiliaries to their punitive forces, and Chief Odera of the Luo provided many porters. This expedition made little impression on the Nandi as it was suddenly disbanded and the troops were sent to deal with Mwanga's rebellion. In 1899 the Uganda Railway reached Nandi country, and the Nandi carried out a whole series of raids in 1899 and 1900, killing Indian railway workers and looting telegraph wire for making ornaments and weapons. They also continued to raid the caravans using the road to Uganda and to raid British-protected communities such as the Luo and the Luyia. There were as many as three punitive expeditions in 1900, the British using Maasai and Ganda auxiliaries to reinforce Swahili and Indian troops, but the Nandi were not conquered. The British needed peace so that the railway construction could proceed, and the Nandi were tired of fighting and living in the forests, so both sides agreed to negotiation and a period of peace. The British still did not rule the Nandi. Their forts in Nandi at Kipture, Kaptumo and Kapkolei were not administrative centres; their prime function was to safeguard the Uganda Road and the Railway.

The negotiation of 1900 produced only a short-lived peace. Soon the Nandi resumed their resistance, attacking the railway, killing maintenance workers, looting wire and rails, and raiding the new European farms to the north and east of Nandi country, thus forcing the settlers to leave. The British replied by preparing and equipping an expedition to crush the Nandi once and for all. The 1905 expedition consisted of 1,500 soldiers and police, largely Indian, Swahili and Somali, 1,300 auxiliaries, mainly Maasai, 900 armed porters, 10 machine guns, and two armoured trains.

Before the actual war began the British killed the Nandi orkoiyot in a shameful incident. The British officer in Nandi, Captain Meinertzhagen, had planned, according to his diary, 'to kill or capture the Laibon on the first day of operations'. He believed that if Koitalel could be removed from the scene Nandi resistance would collapse. He arranged a meeting with Koitalel at the orkoiyot's home, and turned up there with a small British force. According to Meinertzhagen he was fired on first and hit by Nandi arrows, the British fired back, and Koitalel was killed. According to Nandi accounts Meinertzhagen offered his hand to Koitalel and pulled the orkoiyot towards him. This was a signal to the British soldiers to start shooting. Koitalel, most of his maotik and many other Nandi present were killed. As the British party retreated to Kaptumo fort they killed more people. The death of Koitalel demoralized the Nandi, but not to the extent that they did not offer strong resistance to the invasion that followed, in October and November 1905. Several hundred Nandi were killed while they managed to inflict only ninety casualties on the invaders. The Nandi were defeated because for once the enemy was not only exceptionally well-armed but also had considerable manpower.

The Nandi leaders accepted peace terms in December 1905, including the removal of the south-east Nandi clans, the Kamelilo and the Kapchepkendi, to a northern reserve away from the railway. The reasons for imposing this forced resettlement were a desire to protect the railway from Nandi attacks, to prevent them uniting in armed resistance with the Kipsigis to the south and to protect the European farms and make available more land for European settlement. When these sections refused to move, the British expedition, which was now occupying Nandiland, moved them by force in a 'drive' in January 1906. Many Nandi resisted the 'drive'. Many British forts were built in Nandiland in 1906 and effective administration began.

The Nandi now resorted to passive resistance for the rest of the colonial period.

Diplomacy versus military resistance among the Luyia

Shiundu served as *Nabongo* (ruler) Wanga from 1841 to 1882, and allowed Swahili traders to establish a camp at his capital Elureko (later Mumia's), largely because he welcomed their military support against his hostile neighbours—the Bukusu and other Luyia sub-tribes, and the Luo of Ugenya. Shiundu's son, Mumia, who was nabongo from 1882, continued his father's policy of diplomatic friendship with well-armed strangers and welcomed Joseph Thomson the explorer in 1883 and Jackson's 1889 expedition to spread IBEA Company rule. In 1895 the British were allowed by Mumia to set up an administrative post at his capital, Mumia's. They needed a base from which they could establish their authority over surrounding communities who made their caravan route unsafe. There were a variety of reasons for Mumia's cooperation with the British. He realized the power of guns, which the British had in abundance, whereas he had very few, and the British were prepared to ally with Mumia against his African enemies. The British carefully cultivated his friendship because Wanga was on the caravan route to Buganda in a fertile area where food was plentiful and cheap. Mumia's itself was only a mile from the River Nzoia ford. Mumia's effective authority was limited to a small area around his capital and did not extend beyond Wanga itself, yet he claimed to rule a much wider area, a claim that was patently false.

One group of Luyia who resisted the British were the Bukusu who had suffered badly from Swahili-Arab and Wanga raids. They saw no reason to welcome Mumia's friends, the British, especially as the British employed Swahili in their forces. The notorious British Ketosh expedition (the British thought the Bukusu were called 'Ketosh') arose from an incident when the Bukusu of Majanja's village killed a number of British Sudanese and Swahili soldiers who were trying to recover rifles sold to the Bukusu by deserting porters. The expedition was sent to avenge the dead soldiers and to force the Bukusu to recognize Wanga-British hegemony. The British forces consisted of a hundred and fifty Sudanese, nine hundred Ganda volunteers under Kakungulu, two hundred Maasai and allies in the Wanga army. These forces were heavily armed with guns. The Bukusu had very few guns and almost no ammunition, yet they offered very strong resistance in their walled villages, originally built as defence against the Nandi, and killed or wounded about half the invaders. However, four hundred and twenty Bukusu were killed and their armed resistance was crushed.

Mumia provided the British with soldiers to fight not only other

Luyia but other ethnic groups. In 1897 he sent thousands of his men to assist the British expedition against the Luo of Ugenya and successfully defended Mumia's against the Sudanese mutineers on their way from Eldama Ravine to Lubwa's. In 1899 he provided men to help the British conquer the Luo of Seme, Sakwa and Uyoma.

Luo response

Many Luo leaders, aware of the political divisions of their society, approached the British through diplomacy, but others offered armed resistance.

Gunda Mera, a prominent elder of the Kisumu area, accepted a Company flag from Jackson in 1889. Chief Odera Ulalo of Gem, west of present Kisumu, provided porters for British expeditions against the Nandi, and soldiers to help the British crush armed resistance by the neighbouring Luo sections of Seme, Sakwa and Uyoma. His motive appears to have been desire for loot, especially livestock. Kitoto, a Luo leader at Miwani east of Kisumu, provided men to guard the railway against Nandi attacks.

The Kager clan of the Luo of Ugenya, north-west of Kisumu, had been conquering large parts of southern Buluyia, especially Wanga, for settlement purposes, in the 1880s and 1890s. In 1896 Mumia sent a large army reinforced with armed Swahili traders against the Luo of Ugenya. Nevertheless, the Luo won a decisive victory, smashed Mumia's army, and advanced deep into Wanga. Mumia had to depend on British help to preserve his domain. The 1897 British punitive expedition against Ugenya had another object apart from bolstering up Mumia: the Luo of Ugenya had prevented government parties passing through Ugenya from Mumia's to Port Victoria, an important link in the chain of communications with Uganda. Several hundred Ugenya soldiers were killed.

The British expedition of 1899 against Seme, west of Kisumu, was caused by the raids of its people on caravans, on government servants and on Luo friendly to the British administration. To a large extent such hostility had been provoked by the British themselves, whose forces had frequently raided the Seme to get grain and livestock to feed the Kisumu garrison. Maasai, Wanga and even Luo followers of Odera Ulalo, assisted the British. Hundreds of resisters were killed, and 2,500 cattle and 10,000 sheep and goats were seized. In south Nyanza the British also faced armed resistance when they set up an administrative post at Karungu in 1903.

Amongst the Luo, however, passive resistance was much more widespread then either active resistance or diplomacy, yet it was largely unrecorded and is less memorable. It became more noticeable as the colonial system became more established and interfered with the cultural practices of the people. It was expressed in traditional religions like Mumboism (see Chapter 8).

Gusii response

The British did not attempt to bring the Gusii under their authority until 1905, and did not succeed in establishing effective authority in Gusiiland until 1908. The Gusii are a Bantu community of the most south-western section of the Kenya Highlands. They were a decentralized society, made up of seven sub-groups, each having its own territory. Despite having a common language and culture, the sub-groups rarely acted in unison even in matters of defence, and were often at war with each other. Significantly, the weaker sub-groups sought British support against their enemies, whereas larger ones, loath to lose their supremacy, resisted the British.

Sakawa of Nyakoe, the greatest Gusii diviner of the late nineteenth century had foretold the advent of white strangers and advised against fighting them, thus preparing the Gusii for a peaceful introduction to British rule. Unfortunately, however, the British made a violent entry to Gusiiland and provoked resistance. The Jenkins expedition of 1905 was ostensibly a punitive exercise to avenge British-protected Luo killed in a Gusii cattle raid. Its real purpose was to survey Gusiiland to find a site for an administrative station. It hoped to divide the Gusii by supporting the pro-British Ombati, the leader of the weak Muksero sub-group, against his enemies in the Kitutu and Wanjara sub-groups. The expedition was not immediately followed up by the establishment of an administrative station because the British had to concentrate in 1905 and 1906 on subduing the Nandi, but in 1907 a British administrative officer, Northcote, did set up a station. His attempts to collect hut tax led to the armed resistance of the Kitutu in 1908.

The elderly Moraa, a famous Kitutu prophetess, incited her foster-son, a young man named Otenyo, to attempt to assassinate Northcote, and Otenyo managed to wound him with a spear. Many of the Kitutu, falsely believing Northcote was dead, were inspired to rise up in a spontaneous armed resistance. Northcote managed to defend his station until relief forces arrived. Mackay's expedition of 1908 not only relieved Northcote but killed considerable numbers of Gusii and seized thousands of their cattle in ruthless reprisals. Angwenyi, a prominent Kitutu elder, made peace with the British, handed over Otenyo to them, and was made a colonial chief. He was motivated mainly by a desire to protect the Kitutu youth from being massacred further by British guns. Moraa surrendered herself, was severely reprimanded and was set free. Otenyo, however, was not so lucky. He was taken to Nairobi, where it is believed he was executed.

A variety of responses to the incoming Europeans was evident in East Africa but whatever the response by 1914 the colonialists were in dominant control of the region.

4

The Scramble in Central and Southern Africa

Overview

In 1885 the two oldest colonial powers in Central and Southern Africa were Britain and Portugal. The latter in particular made grandiose claims to territory stretching across the continent from the Atlantic to the Indian Ocean. In the aftermath of the Berlin West Africa Conference Portugal was forced to face reality: many areas claimed by Portugal had never been effectively occupied and her claims were ignored.

Even before the Berlin Conference was over Portugal was forced to concede some of her claims. Finding herself unsupported she surrendered her claims to all areas north of the Congo River except for the small enclave of Cabinda. In the interior a number of incidents occurred between Portugal and the Congo Free State but Leopold was much more effective in his occupation of the interior than Portugal. In treaties dated 1891 and 1894 the boundaries between Angola and the Congo were fixed.

Attempts to retain territory in the interior of Central Africa also failed. Portugal negotiated her colonial boundaries with France and Germany between May 1886 and July 1887 in the hope that these two countries would support her against Britain. However, the British government, partly pushed by Cecil Rhodes and partly by public opinion, was determined to extend her influence. In 1885 Bechuanaland was declared a protectorate to prevent German expansion. By 1887 Britain was expressing disquiet that Portugal was laying claim to Manicaland, Matabeleland and the regions around Lake Malawi where British missionaries were working. Portugal, however, continued to push her claims until a crisis was precipitated by an expedition, led by Serpa Pinto, into the Shire region. In 1890 Lord Salisbury, the British prime minister, issued an ultimatum to Portugal to remove her troops from Mashonaland and the Shire. Portugal was forced to accept the ultimatum as neither Germany nor France were prepared to offer anything more than moral support. Boundary settlements were worked out but were not finally agreed until 1891 when the boundaries between the former British and Portuguese colonies were fixed at roughly their present positions.

Whereas the boundaries of the colonies of Germany, Britain and

Portugal were fixed with little danger of war, the Scramble in South Africa itself brought war between the British and the Boer states of the Transvaal and Orange Free State. Britain was determined to safeguard her interests at the Cape and believed that to do so it was essential to create a united country out of the separate British- and Boer-ruled areas. The Boers were equally determined to maintain their independence and the inevitable war broke out in 1899.

The discovery of diamonds in Griqualand West in the 1860s and gold on the Witwatersrand in the 1880s had set the stage for the ruthless, violent and bitter struggle between Boers and British, who competed with each other to exploit the vast mineral resources of South Africa. The discovery of gold on the Rand helped to formulate a myth that Central Africa was a similar Eldorado of vast mining wealth. The greed of Europeans—German, Belgian, British and Portuguese—and their desire to become rich overnight led not only to war between two groups of Europeans in the south, but also to the loss of land and independence by Africans in Central Africa.

Namibian response to initial German invasion

At the Berlin Conference of 1884–5 the coastline and its hinterland between the Orange and Kunene Rivers was recognized as a German sphere of influence. German attempts to impose their rule in South West Africa met with only limited success in the 1880s and 1890s. The Nama and Herero peoples of the interior resisted German invasion from 1884 to 1894, when a truce was signed. However, it was not until after the failure of the 1904 Nama and Herero wars of independence that the Germans could be said to have brought these peoples under effective control.

The Nama, part of whom were ruled by Hendrik Witbooi, made an armistice with their traditional enemies the Herero, and resisted the Germans strongly before 1894. In 1894 Witbooi successfully negotiated a peace treaty with the Germans who were anxious to end a war that severely overstrained a limited colonial budget. The Nama were allowed to keep their firearms. Witbooi stated as a reason for negotiation: 'You are powerful in weapons and the comforts of civilization.' In fact, this was false modesty. Nama expertness in the use of modern repeater rifles had helped bring the Germans to the discussion table. Between 1894 and 1904 Witbooi's Nama served as allies of the Germans, using their firearms against other African societies who were resisting the Germans.

The Herero under their ruler Maherero defended themselves against German invasion until his death in 1890, after which a

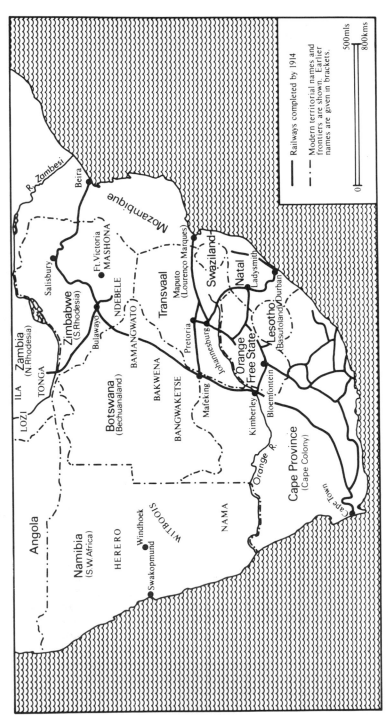

Map 9. Southern Africa.

succession dispute enabled the Germans to exploit Herero divisions and impose some control over them. Their new ruler, Samuel Maherero, was recognized by the Germans as paramount in 1894, and like Witbooi he assisted the Germans against resisting groups.

The Nama and Herero resumed armed resistance in 1904 partly because the German government did not honour the terms of its protection treaties with these communities, and allowed German settler-farmers to alienate African land (see Chapter 9).

Tswana response to British invasion

Khama was ruler of the Bamangwato from 1875. During the Scramble he acted in consultation and concert with two other Tswana rulers, Gaseitsiwe of the Bangwaketse and Sechele of the Bakwena. Faced with a double threat from the Boers and Ndebele, these three wise men used Britain as a pawn to protect the Tswana and played off Britain against the Boers and the Ndebele. The land later known as Botswana was declared a British sphere of influence in 1885, and became an official British protectorate in 1891. The British occupied the area as a response to Boer pressure from the Transvaal and German activity in South-West Africa. But Khama and the other Tswana leaders were as much interested as the British in forestalling the establishment of a Boer or German protectorate by a British one.

In 1885 the three main Tswana leaders negotiated with Britain: they demanded a prohibition on the sale of land but at the same time they offered some for European settlement. Khama granted land that belonged to the Ndebele, and Gaseitsiwe and Sechele offered stretches of desert. The British were more concerned with keeping their European rivals out of Tswana country than with ruling and exploiting it and so accepted the bargain. As a result, for many years the new Bechuanaland Protectorate served no purpose apart from protecting the Tswana from the Boers. Bechuanaland was a rare example of a protectorate that actually lived up to its name.

Khama's relations with Cecil Rhodes were friendly at first. He provided guides to take the Pioneer column into Mashonaland in 1890 and Tswana soldiers to fight alongside the British South Africa Company against the Ndebele in 1893. But in 1894 Rhodes made a formal request to the British government for the right to administer Bechuanaland. He had built the telegraph line through the Protectorate in 1890, and was building the railway from Cape Colony to Bulawayo. The British government at first gave favourable attention to Rhodes' request. Rhodes had reckoned, however, without the determination of the Tswana leaders to remain under British government control, which was light, and avoid the heavy hand of the Company. In 1895 Khama, Sechele and Bathoen (Gaseitsiwe's son and successor) travelled to London to rouse support for their cause. Missionary influence in governing circles and the direct protests of the Tswana rulers persuaded the new Colonial Secretary, Joseph Chamberlain, to compromise with them. The protectorate was partitioned: virtually all Tswana-settled areas became reserves for each sub-tribe; the largely unoccupied lands along the borderland with the Boer Republics and Southern Rhodesia came under Company administration. Khama's attitude to the compromise was that 'British protection is worth more than our unoccupied lands.'

Thus most of the Tswana communities came to terms with the Scramble for Africa. The change from time-honoured independence to colonial rule was requested as simply the lesser of two evils.

Swazi response to the Scramble for Africa

The Swazi state managed to survive the Scramble for Africa by diplomatic tactics, although the Swazi had far less room for manoeuvre than did the Tswana. Before 1880 the foundation of Swazi foreign policy was an alliance with the Boers of the Transvaal against the Zulu. In 1879 a Swazi regiment had fought on the Boer and British side against the Bapedi. From the Boer point of view, Swaziland was a buffer state between the Transvaal and the Zulu. However, the destruction of the military power of the Zulu and Bapedi by the British in 1879 destroyed the basis of Swazi dealings with Europeans. The Boers no longer needed Swazi allies. The result was that the Swazi King Mbandzeni, who ruled from 1875 to 1889, was forced into granting extensive concessions, mainly to Boers, covering land, mining and grazing rights and even the collection of revenue.

The economic partition of Swaziland by the granting of concessions to Europeans continued in the 1890s during the nominal reign of young Bunu and the real rule of his mother, the Queen Regent. The 1890 Anglo-Transvaal Treaty, followed up by the 1894 Convention, established a Transvaal Protectorate over Swaziland. The Boers were particularly interested in building railways from the Transvaal through Swaziland to Kosi Bay on the Indian Ocean in order to facilitate the export of Rand gold and to escape the tariffs of the British colonies of Natal and Cape Colony. German activity in Kosi Bay in cooperation with the Transvaal President Paul Kruger alarmed Britain sufficiently for her to annex Tongaland, including Kosi Bay, in 1895. Thus the Boers failed to get their own port on the

Indian Ocean, but their influence in Swaziland was paramount until their defeat in the Second Anglo-Boer War, when Britain took over the protectorate.

The Second Anglo-Boer War (1899–1902)

The Scramble for South Africa long preceded the Scramble for Africa as a whole. The European scramble for South Africa's agricultural land began in the 1820s and continued up to the end of the century. From the 1870s South Africa witnessed a feverish scramble by Boers and British for mineral resources and African migrant labour. The dominant figure in the Scramble for South Africa's mineral wealth was Cecil Rhodes.

Rhodes, a migrant from England, arrived in South Africa in 1870 at the age of seventeen. He made an early and massive fortune as a mining businessman on the Kimberley diamond fields. He began by buying up cheaply the claims of bankrupt owners, and soon acquired the wealth to buy up more profitable concerns. After an epic struggle with his business rival Barney Barnato, Rhodes managed to bring together nearly all diamond production in South Africa in his company, De Beers Consolidated. However, Rhodes' ambition encompassed a wider vision than the accumulation of wealth. Like many millionaires he planned to gain money and use it as a means to an end: in his case, political power. Rhodes was determined to build a vast British empire in Africa. He intended 'to paint the map red' from the Cape to Cairo. His vision was to win for Britain a continuous belt of territory from South Africa to Egypt, linked by a railway and telegraph. He became Prime Minister of Cape Colony in 1890, with Afrikaner (Boer) support, but his political career in South Africa was destroyed by his attempt to overthrow the Transvaal government, which lost him his Afrikaner backing.

In 1886 a gold-bearing reef was discovered on the Witwatersrand in the Transvaal. The discovery rapidly led to the development of Rand gold-mining which in turn led to a transformation of African society and a revolution in economic and political power in South Africa. Rand gold-mining, even more than Kimberley diamond-mining, transformed many African communities from economic self-sufficiency into rural reservoirs of unskilled mining labour. African migrant labour in the mines was shamefully exploited by recruiting agencies and mining companies. The agencies hired men for contracts of six months or a year. Hiring was little different from slave-trading, especially in Portuguese territory. There was no real freedom of contract. The Portuguese colonial administration rounded up so-called 'recruits' for a fee which was paid to the government, not the recruits. Many chiefs were bribed to provide 'voluntary' labour. And when the labourers got to the mines they were subjected to very low wages for highly dangerous work, and to appalling living conditions in the mining compounds. Men were not allowed to have their families in the compounds; the result was moral and social degradation and the break-up of thousands of families.

The development of Rand gold-mining turned the Transvaal, hitherto the poorest of the white-ruled states in the sub-continent, into one which was economically viable. Civil servants' salaries could be paid, arms could be bought, and the presence of a large mining population provided a vast new market for Afrikaner agricultural products. The British now feared a new wave of Afrikaner expansion, especially as the success of the Transvaal in its war of independence in 1881 had given a tremendous boost to the developing national feeling of the Afrikaners, as the Boers now called themselves. This feeling was epitomized by Paul Kruger, the Transvaal president. Kruger had gone on the Great Trek as a child. He was elected president three times, in 1888, 1893 and 1898. He aimed to consolidate the Transvaal's new economic independence by establishing an outlet to the sea that was independent of the British ports of Durban and Capetown. The building of lines from the Cape and Natal was delayed until Kruger was certain that the Pretoria-Lourenco Marques line would be built. However, Kruger proved to be no match in the end for British imperialism.

Rhodes' British South Africa Company which sent the Pioneer Column of settlers to Rhodesia failed to find gold in desirably large quantities in Mashonaland and Matabeleland in the early 1890s. It was available on the Rand. Although Rhodes and his business associates made enormous profits by investing in Transvaal gold-mining, they planned to seize power there and thus prevent the Afrikaners turning their revenue from gold-mining into political power. Following his political successes in Rhodesia and in Cape Colony, where he became prime minister with the support of Hofmeyr, the leader of the Afrikaner Bond, Rhodes thought Kruger could be swept aside quickly. This proved to be a serious error of judgement. Rhodes planned an armed raid by his BSA Company police, led by Jameson, on the Transvaal, believing it would inspire the *uitlanders*, the non-Afrikaner, predominantly British, white mining population on the Rand, to rise up in revolution against Kruger who had denied them the vote and other civil rights. The British Colonial Secretary, Joseph Chamberlain, gave his consent to the coup, since the removal of the Afrikaner government in the Transvaal would strengthen Britain's strategic position on its southern flank to India. But the Jameson Raid failed ignominiously. The uitlanders failed to rise: they were divided by separate national origins and social classes, and their interest was in economic and financial concessions rather than political power. Jameson's British volunteers, left in the lurch by the uitlanders, were surrounded and forced to surrender before they reached Johannesburg. Rhodes' political career in the Cape was shattered.

The Second Anglo-Boer War was a natural aftermath of the Jameson Raid because the British were determined to avenge Jameson's failure. Britain was also motivated by world imperial strategy. The German Kaiser William II sent a telegram to Kruger congratulating him on defeating the Raid, and the Transvaal now turned to Germany for arms and diplomatic support. The Kaiser's interference in South African politics alarmed Britain sufficiently for her to revive the old scheme of a confederation of British and Afrikaner states, which would safeguard British supremacy in the Cape hinterland. Milner, the British High Commissioner to the Cape from 1897, was a fanatical imperialist and a strong proponent of confederation. His hopes of a peaceful setting up of a confederation were ruined by the re-election of the conservative Kruger and the defeat of the Transvaal 'liberals' in the elections of 1898. In 1899 Milner, like Frere with the Zulus twenty years earlier, provoked a war with a community which was an obstacle to a British-dominated Confederation of South Africa.

The war, which broke out in October 1899, did not lead to the quick and easy British victory that Milner expected. The Orange Free State and many Cape Dutch, like Smuts, joined the Transvaal. The initial phase of the war, until early in 1900, was marked by severe British defeats. The Afrikaners took full advantage of their superior mobility and markmanship and their home ground. Then the Afrikaners made the mistake of laying siege to the British garrisons at Kimberley, Ladysmith and Mafeking. By besieging the British garrisons in the early stages of the war, instead of sweeping on into the heart of the British colonies while they were undefended, the Afrikaner commander, Joubert, lost the opportunity to capture Durban and to inspire a full-scale Afrikaner rising in the Cape. He also allowed the British time to pour in troops from Britain and other parts of their empire, first to relieve their beleaguered garrisons, and secondly to overrun the Afrikaner republics. The second stage of the war from early 1900 to June of that year, was one of British victories, as the generals Lord Roberts of Kandahar and Lord Kitchener of Khartoum relieved the besieged British towns and captured the main Afrikaner ones. Roberts and Kitchener won their victories at appalling cost because of their reliance on frontal attacks on Afrikaner positions, but they pushed relentlessly on to Pretoria because of their massive superiority in manpower. They had 450,000 troops and outnumbered the Afrikaner forces by five to one.

The third and final stage of the war, from June 1900 to May 1902, was marked by guerilla resistance from Afrikaner commandos.

Kitchener forced them into submission by destroying their farms and herding their women and children into concentration camps, where 25,000 died from disease and malnutrition. Finally, at the compromise Peace of Vereeniging, the Afrikaners surrendered their independence, in return for a British promise that no non-white franchise would be granted in the former republics of the Transvaal and Orange Free State until they had been restored to responsible government. Naturally once the Afrikaners had regained responsible government they would block the grant of a non-white franchise. The British victory proved to be irrelevant to Africans.

In many ways, the war was a triumph of one type of white imperialism over another. In Britain there was much opposition to the war. It was considered to be unjust by many British people, notably the rising Liberal politician David Lloyd George, and by people in Europe generally, because the victims of imperial aggression were European: great concern was felt in Britain for the Afrikaner women and children who died in the camps.

There was little interest in the fate of those Africans who died in separate camps, and whose death rate of 32% was roughly similar to that of the Afrikaners. The Africans were herded into camps for the same reasons the Afrikaners were—so that their homes might be destroyed, to deny succour and shelter to the Afrikaner commandos. Conditions were even more appalling in the African camps. After the war Afrikaners received fairly generous compensation, whereas the Africans had relatively little (£114,000). African levies which fought for the British were shot out of hand whenever they were captured by the Afrikaners, on the grounds that it was equivalent to an act of murder for any black man to take up arms against a white man—although the British used African troops only in a non-combatant capacity: as scouts, bearers and wagon drivers. They refused to arm the Swazi, Zulu, Xhosa and Sotho who offered their services. Africans did sometimes join in the fighting independently. The Bapedi of the northern Transvaal settled some old scores with neighbouring Afrikaner farmers. The Zulu wiped out one Afrikaner commando, killing fifty-six. This African military intervention, though uncoordinated with the British, hastened the guerilla leaders' decision to seek a truce, on the principle that British rule was better than an African uprising.

Generally, Africans were pro-British in the war. They believed that the British were more humane and just as rulers than the Afrikaners. The Africans of the Transvaal were soon disabused of this notion. When the British army captured Johannesburg from the Afrikaners the African miners of the town celebrated by burning their Pass books. The British severely punished them for breaking the Afrikaner law on passes, and made them carry out forced labour on road and railway building. Colonel Robert Baden-Powell, famous as the defender of besieged Mafeking and the founder of the

Boy Scouts, was appointed commander of the new para-military South African Constabulary, a white settler force whose first achievement was to disarm the Transvaal Africans, something the Boers had never been able to do.

The response of the Zimbabwean peoples to the British South Africa Company, 1890–3

According to Shona oral traditions, their spirit medium, Chaminuka, forecast that both the Ndebele and the Shona would be conquered by white men without knees and Lobengula, the Ndebele king, had him executed for this. The historical record also shows that Lobengula did everything he reasonably could to avoid war with Cecil Rhodes, and that it was Rhodes' settlers who provoked the British-Ndebele War.

Lobengula had followed a policy of diplomatic contact with the Europeans long before Rhodes' appearance on the Central African scene. During the succession crisis which brought him to power in 1870 Lobengula had forestalled the threat that Europeans seeking mining concessions would combine with the Zwangendaba regiment, which supported a rival candidate, by granting a concession to Thomas Baines of the Durban Gold Mining Company. However, the concession affected a part of Mashonaland not directly ruled by the Ndebele, so there was little Ndebele resentment.

The European threat became much more serious and more difficult for Lobengula to handle in the 1880s. The Portuguese to the east were trying to extend their rule up the Zambesi. From the south the Afrikaners in the Transvaal were intending to expand. In 1885 the British appeared to threaten Lobengula's territory by establishing the Bechuanaland Protectorate on the south-western border of his kingdom. Then the discovery of gold in the Transvaal in 1886 fostered a widespread illusion among Europeans that land to the north must be equally rich in gold. This led to a trickle of European mining prospectors seeking concessions from Lobengula becoming a flood. In his efforts to cope with the heightened interest in his kingdom Lobengula received no help from missionaries, in contrast to his neighbouring rulers Khama and Lewanika. The missions had had no real success among the Ndebele. Nor was Lobengula helped by the attitude of his own people. The young Ndebele soldiers wanted to drive out all the Europeans by force. However, Lobengula was aware of the military strength of the Europeans and feared that any war with them would lead to his own defeat and the conquest of his kingdom. So he hoped to make enough concessions to the

Europeans to satisfy them and so avoid the loss of independence, but not so many concessions that his soldiers would rebel and overthrow him. In fact Lobengula failed to find a middle way that would satisfy all and this failure led to his dowfall. It is extremely doubtful, however, if such a middle way could ever have been found. A number of factors made it almost inevitable that the Ndebele nation would be destroyed. The first factor was the determination of South African-based capital to exploit the region between the Limpopo and the Zambesi. Rhodes and his associates in the Cape cast greedy eyes on an area considered to be rich in gold and certainly favoured with a good soil and a climate suitable for white settlement. Secondly, Matabeleland's geographical position made it an obvious target for the Cape's expansion. It lay on the direct route from the south to the further interior. Thirdly, the Ndebele were a military nation and, like the Zulu from whom they sprang, were unlikely to surrender their independence without fighting.

In 1887 the Transvaal attempted to extend its influence over Lobengula. An ambassador, Piet Grobler, was sent to Bulawayo, Lobengula's capital, and signed a treaty with the king. Britain was alarmed by the Grobler Treaty, so in 1888 John Moffat, a British envoy, visited Lobengula and signed a treaty with him, aiming to check Afrikaner expansion. Lobengula promised in the new treaty not to hand over any part of his country to anyone else without the agreement of the British government. Lobengula's independence, far from being ensured, was now threatened more seriously than ever. In 1888 Rhodes sent his partner Rudd to negotiate a mining concession from Lobengula. The Ndebele king hoped that by making a fairly large concession to one group he would succeed in excluding all the other concession seekers. Under the Rudd Concession, Rhodes and Rudd were to give Lobengula £100 a month and a thousand rifles in exchange for exclusive mining rights in Lobengula's country and in areas of Mashonaland that were in fact independent of Ndebele control. Thus Lobengula diverted Rhodes' imperial designs to Mashonaland.

Lobengula, too late, regretted having signed the Rudd Concession and soon repudiated it. However, having got his concession Rhodes was determined to exploit it. He formed the British South Africa Company for which he hoped to get a charter from the British government. A charter would give the Company political powers as well as economic rights in the area claimed by Lobengula as his kingdom. In 1889 the British government granted the Company a charter in spite of opposition by some rival businessmen, and missionaries who feared Rhodes would ignore African interests. The government looked on their arrangement with the Company as an inexpensive means of establishing a British protectorate north of the Limpopo, keeping the Portuguese and the Afrikaners out of the area, ensuring the fabled mineral wealth of Central Africa for Britain and isolating the Transvaal in the hope of forcing it into a political federation within the British empire. In return for the charter Rhodes had to promise to build a railway through Bechuanaland, thus bringing trade to the government protectorate and helping to bring about the unification of British possessions in southern Africa. The Charter of the British South Africa Company was granted for 25 years, although it could be revoked at any time. It gave the Company the right to make treaties, to pass laws and to have a police force. The Company could make grants of minerals and land. The Charter stated that these rights could only be exercised with the agreement of the African communities. The Ndebele and the Shona had not agreed to any of this, and Lobengula's concession to Rudd had granted only mineral rights and given Rudd and Rhodes no right to own or rule land.

Rhodes organized a 'Pioneer Column' to march north from Bechuanaland and occupy Mashonaland. At this stage Rhodes wished to avoid direct confrontation with the Ndebele because he did not yet feel strong enough to fight them. The column consisted of two hundred white settlers and five hundred company police, nearly all recruited from Europeans living in South Africa. Each settler was given a contract for fifteen gold-mining claims and a 3,000 acre farm. This was contrary to the Rudd Concession which had granted no land. The column entered Mashonaland in 1890. The Ndebele army demanded that Lobengula allow it to attack the column but Lobengula refused to let them as he feared that any attack on the British South Africa Company would provoke an attack by the British government seeking to avenge it.

The Shona offered hardly any armed resistance to the Pioneer Column, nor did they accommodate themselves to its arrival by co-operating with it. They believed it had come to trade and then go away, like earlier Portuguese expeditions. They had no idea the column intended to settle and take land by force. In any case, Shona political fragmentation would have prevented them putting up any co-ordinated initial resistance. It was not for a year or so that the Shona realized what trouble had come into their midst, and only then did they begin to work out ways of expelling the invaders.

In 1891 the British government recognized the Company's occupation and issued the Mashonaland Order in Council. A British administrator and judge were sent but all other administration was left to the Company. A clash between the Ndebele and the Company now became almost inevitable. The Ndebele considered that the Shona were their subjects, and that they were entitled to raid them for cattle and women. The Company believed that the Shona were ruled by them alone, and that they could use them for labour on European farms. (Naturally the Shona shared neither of these views.) Moreover, Rhodes and Dr Jameson, the leader of the Pioneer Column, had expected to find gold in Mashonaland. There was none and as a result the shares of the company were losing value. Now they hoped to find gold in Ndebele territory, which would restore the prosperity of the Company. The Company promised prospective white settlers in Matabeleland 6,000 acre farms and shares of Ndebele cattle. Only the defeat of Lobengula in war could bring this about. However, Lobengula still hoped for peace.

In 1893 an incident at Fort Victoria, one of the European settlements, provided Jameson with his opportunity to invade Matabeleland. In an Ndebele raid some Shona servants of Europeans were killed. Jameson, now reinforced by many more settlers and by Imperial troops, used this as an excuse for an invasion of Ndebele territory. To make sure that war would take place, Jameson had Lobengula's peace envoys murdered, an act that incited Lobengula to armed resistance.

Part of the Ndebele army was out of action before the war started. The best regiment, just recalled from Bulozi, had contracted smallpox there, and was isolated in quarantine in special kraals, and thus took no part in the Ndebele War of Resistance of 1893. However, it is doubtful if its participation would have made any difference to the result of the war. The Ndebele were heavily defeated because they failed to adapt their Zulu military system and tactics to the new conditions of warfare laid down by superior European weapons. At the Battles of Shangani River and Mbembezi, Ndebele frontal assaults were destroyed by Maxim guns fired from the tight defensive laagers of the invaders. Moreover, in 1893 the Ndebele fought with their old military system. The subject peoples and lower castes took no part in the fighting. In contrast the British had on their side many of the Shona, eager for loot, contingents of Tswana men sent by Khama, and even some Ndebele. Their chief guide was Nyenyezi, of the house of the king's brother, Umhlaba, whose family had been wiped out by Lobengula.

Lobengula was neither killed nor captured by the Europeans. He fled north to escape their advancing forces, but before he could cross the Zambesi he died, probably of smallpox, in January 1894. After his death the indunas, the leaders of the Ndebele regiments, surrendered. The British government issued the Matabele Order in Council in 1894, which recognized Company rule in Matabeleland. The immediate aftermath of the British victory was mass starvation among the Ndebele whose cattle were seized by the British and who were prevented from ploughing and sowing until they had fully surrendered. Much of their land was taken, too. But the Ndebele were not cowed. It was only three years later that they rose up, with the Shona, in a great war of independence.

Zambian response to the coming of British rule

Lewanika of Bulozi (Barotseland) is best known as the central African king who did not resist European occupation but instead co-operated with the colonialists. By negotiations and treaties with the British he preserved both his kingdom and his position as king into the colonial period, whereas all other central African kingdoms were destroyed at the beginning of the period of colonial rule.

The Lozi had established friendly relations with the British in the pre-colonial period. In the 1870s George Westbeech sold guns to the Lozi; in 1878 Coillard, a French Protestant missionary who was friendly to the British, came to Bulozi and in 1886 Lewanika allowed him to found a permanent mission station. Coillard and Lewanika were on good terms and, although Lewanika never became a Christian, he sent his sons to Coillard's mission school. Coillard was his unofficial adviser on foreign affairs and had great influence over him. Another influence on the king were the Lozi men who had gone south to work in the Kimberley diamond mines. When they returned they described the power of the white man. The chief of the Ngwato, Khama, was a friend and ally of Lewanika because both the Lozi and the Ngwato suffered from attacks by the powerful Ndebele. Khama's acceptance of British protection in 1885 in order to safeguard his people from threats of invasion from the Ndebele and the Transvaal Boers greatly influenced Lewanika's decision to seek British protection also.

The Lochner Treaty of 1890 put Lewanika's kingdom under the protection of the British South Africa Company. Lewanika gave the Company mining rights throughout his kingdom, while the Company promised in return to protect the kingdom from outside attacks, to pay the king £2,000 a year, to develop trade, and to build schools and telegraphs. Lochner only secured the treaty because he deceived Lewanika that he was a representative of Queen Victoria not of Rhodes. Lewanika wanted to come under British government, not Company, protection. When, after the treaty had been made and Lochner had gone, Lewanika learnt he had put his kingdom under the Company's protection he repudiated the treaty.

In the 1890s Lewanika became alarmed at the extension of the Portuguese colony of Angola inland towards his kingdom, and a new treaty in 1900 finalized the establishment of British rule. Lewanika was recognized as Paramount Chief of the Barotse (Balozi) and allowed considerable authority within the central part of the kingdom where the Lozi lived. However, the Company had most authority in the large outlying parts of the kingdom, such as Ila and Tonga country. Bulozi became part of the British colony of Northern Rhodesia, later Zambia. The Lozi system of government continued to operate, as Lozi chiefs collected taxes for the Company. The Lozi sub-imperialism was similar to Ganda sub-imperialism over non-Ganda people in British Uganda. However, in the colonial period after 1900 Lewanika's authority was reduced and the Company failed to keep its promises of development.

Elsewhere in Zambia the response to Company invasion varied

from diplomacy to war. The Bemba of the north-east were politically divided into numerous states. Mwamba, the most powerful of the Bemba rulers, had welcomed both the White Fathers led by Bishop Dupont and the Company representative, Robert Young, as allies against his Bemba and non-Bemba local rivals. When Mwamba died in 1898 his state and the neighbouring Bemba polities were taken over by the Company and little or no armed resistance was shown.

Among the Ngoni in Mpezeni's kingdom, a division of opinion emerged between Mpezeni himself who favoured a treaty and his son Nsingu who supported war against the Company. Nsingu got his way, but in the resulting war a large British force from Nyasaland (Malawi) was sent to reinforce the Company troops, Nsingu's forces were defeated, and Mpezeni was forced to surrender.

Malawian response to the coming of British rule

British claims to Nyasaland (Malawi), based on missionary and trading activity since 1860, clashed with historic Portuguese claims, based on penetration from Mozambique in the seventeenth and eighteenth centuries. The Portuguese hoped to link Mozambique with Angola but they came up against a Britain whose imperial activity in Malawi was spearheaded by Cecil Rhodes, who wished to preserve the road to the north for his Cape to Cairo dream. Portuguese imperial initiative in the 1880s hastened British activity to forestall it. In 1882 the Governor of Quelimane sent an armed force along the lower Shire valley. In 1884 Lieutenant Cardosa led a Portuguese force up the Rovuma valley as far as Mponda's, making many treaties with the Yao. Then in 1889 Major Serpa Pinto with seven hundred men marched into the Shire highlands. Serpa Pinto's expedition galvanized Britain into action.

Harry Johnston, of Niger delta notoriety, and now Consul at Mozambique made a string of protection treaties over a wide field north of the Zambesi including the Shire valley. Johnston played a dual role: he was employed by the British government and also by Rhodes who offered to pay for the administration of the protectorate in the hope that it would eventually be given to his Company. Johnston's treaty-making with Swahili, Tonga and Yao rulers was strongly supported by British Protestant missionaries. The latter feared extension of Catholic Portuguese rule to the Lake Malawi region and hoped a British protectorate would bring an end to the slave raiding that was endemic to the area. However, it was the Kololo, left behind by Livingstone in 1864, rather than Britain who prevented Pinto's advance. The partly successful armed resistance of the Kololo to Pinto made it easier for Britain to put pressure on Portugal to withdraw Pinto in 1890, and impose on the weaker power the Anglo-Portuguese Treaty of 1891, which placed the Shire Highlands in the new British protectorate.

Johnston as Commissioner and Consul-General now had to impose effective occupation, and suppress the slave trade, against some fairly determined resistance. From 1891 to 1895 Johnston with two gun boats and two hundred Sikhs from British India, largely financed by Rhodes, steadily overcame resistance by the Yao slaving rulers Chikumba, Mponda, Makanjira, Matapwiri and Zerafi, destroying their towns and freeing many slaves. Yao resistance was not simply slave-trader resistance to progress, but also resistance by Islam to Christianity. As such, Yao response to British invasion was in the same pattern as that of the Swahili traders round the Lake. Jumbe Kisutu, the most prominent Swahili halfway up the Lake, had developed an alternative to slave-trading. His base of Kota Kota was already a centre of agricultural economy. Kisutu found it, therefore, easy to adapt himself to the British invasion; he did not resist but cooperated with Johnston. Not so Mlozi, the powerful slave-trader at Karonga at the northern end of the Lake. The British captured Mlozi's stockaded village only after a heavy bombardment. Mlozi was tried and executed by the local Nkonde people, who allied with Britain against a longstanding local oppressor.

The Maseko Ngoni put up armed resistance, but the Ngoni of Mbelwa accepted British rule. Mbelwa was guided by his existing contact with the Livingstonia Mission, and the entry of his people into a cash economy. He was probably influenced also by his military decline and the rise of neighbouring leaders such as Mwase Kasungu with ample supplies of guns and ammunition.

Angola and Mozambique: African response to the extension of Portuguese rule to the interior

During the Scramble for Africa the weakest of the colonial powers—Portugal— made grandiose claims for territory. But if the Portuguese claims were historic, being based on the penetration of their traders in the interior in early centuries, such claims were also unrealistic. Portugal lost its claim to control of the Congo River to Leopold II of Belgium, and the attempt to link up Angola with Mozambique was prevented by Rhodes' drive to the north from South Africa. Portugal had neither the power nor the authority to impose its claims against the British. The 1891 Anglo-Portuguese

Treaty which recognized British claims to the 'Rhodesias' and Malawi was in reality a British ultimatum imposed on Portugal. British gunboats patrolled Mozambique waters to put pressure on Portugal to sign. Yet in spite of these developments the Portuguese gained far more than they had previously occupied, and were faced with the problem of effective occupation of vast interior regions in the hinterland of their coastal settlements. Conversely, African communities of the interior which had previously experienced Portuguese commercial penetration now had to fight in an attempt to preserve their political independence.

The peoples of the interior of Angola continued to resist the Portuguese after 1885 just as they had done for over three hundred years. The two regions where opposition was most persistent were the Dembos, the country north-east of Luanda at the headwaters of the Dande River, and the area of southern Angola west and south of Moçâmedes. The Portuguese attempt to occupy Humbe in this southern area provoked major opposition from the Cuanhama peoples. One of the worst setbacks for Portugal in this area occurred in 1904 when an encampment about halfway between Humbe and the frontier to the south was attacked and over 300 men killed. A force of 2,000 was sent in 1906 to restore Portuguese authority. Only in 1915 was the area finally brought firmly under Portuguese control when General Pereira D' Eça routed the Cuanhama. A revolt in the Bié Plateau area in 1902 was put down with great brutality and thousands of Africans were killed.

The struggle with the Dembos was the most difficult of the campaigns of the Portuguese against the Angolan people. The Dembos were chiefs of the area about 100 miles north-east of Luanda. By the last third of the nineteenth century the chiefs had become so exasperated by the Portuguese in their area that they drove them out. Only a two-year military campaign restored some semblance of Portuguese authority. As late as 1907, however, only a few Europeans lived in the area—and even they had to pay taxes to the chiefs. In 1907 a determined campaign was started to bring the area under effective Portuguese occupation. Captain João de Almeida, with about a thousand men moved through the area and fought a series of engagements from village to village. There was no real attempt to cooperate to resist the Portuguese and within three years the area had been effectively occupied. Of course not all Africans resisted the Portuguese. Some seized the opportunity of increased trade to produce coffee, rubber, groundnuts and palm oil. Many cooperated with the Portuguese because they believed it was to their economic advantage to do so.

In Mozambique, the supra-prazo polities either allied with the Portuguese or resisted them by fighting defensive wars. In Makanga in 1885 the new prazero, Chicucuru II, at first cooperated with Lisbon to the extent of allowing Portugal to establish a military post

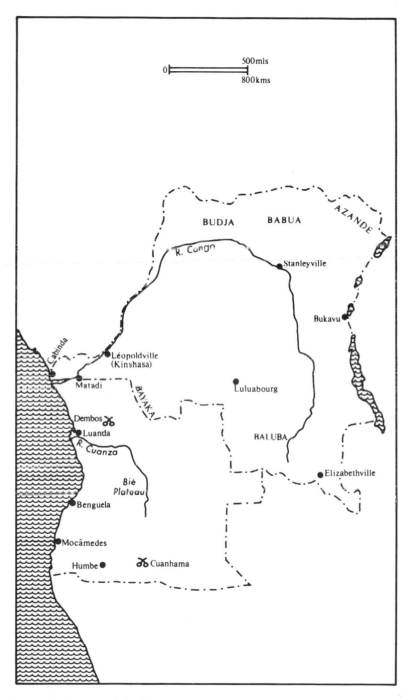

Map 10.   Angola and the Congo.

on his prazo. However, when the Portuguese began to attempt to collect taxes and institute laws, and invite Tete merchants to trade in the area, opposition grew rapidly. Attacks on foreign traders and hunters, the refusal to pay taxes and the harassing of the Portuguese military post resulted in the withdrawal of the Portuguese. Chicucuru attempted to form an alliance of prazeros and others against the Portuguese but failed to do so. He was defeated by the Portuguese in 1889. Makanga was then ruled by Chigaga and from 1890 by Chinsinga who was forced to sign an agreement with the Companhia da Zambézia.

Opposition to the Portuguese continued and burst into the open in 1901 when Chinsinga was ordered to send 2,000 men to work in Angonia. An attack by Chinsinga against Europeans was foiled by a pre-emptive Portuguese attack. Heavily defeated Chinsinga killed himself by drinking poison and the Portuguese at last gained control of Makanga.

The supra-prazo of Massingire surrendered its independence in 1882 to the most powerful prazero Gouveia, who was acting as a Portuguese imperial agent. Gouveia, acting for Lisbon, crushed the Massingire Revolt of 1884, which had been caused by the attempt of the Portuguese to interfere in the selection of a successor to Matequenha II. As in Makanga, however, the spirit of independence was not completely crushed. A number of Manganja chiefs who had been associated with Massingire led uprisings against the Portuguese in 1887 and 1896. Only after 1896 were the Portuguese able to establish effective control over the whole of Massingire.

The kings of the supra-prazo Massangano put up prolonged but ultimately unsuccessful resistance from 1887 to 1897. The refusal of King Chatara to renounce the independence of Massangano provoked a major Portuguese attack in 1887. Seven thousand troops with rapid-firing rifles converged on Chatara's capital but the king was able to escape before the Portuguese arrived. Chatara was forced to abdicate and was replaced by Mtontora. To the astonishment of the Portuguese Mtontora not only recaptured Massangano but also heavily defeated an expedition sent against him. A second Portuguese expedition of 5,000 men was too strong for Mtontora. The Portuguese were held off for six months but only at the cost of 6,000 dead for Mtontora's forces. Mtontora was forced to flee. He continued to fight until his death in 1892 but some of his followers continued their resistance, at least on a limited scale, until 1897.

Even after the death of Gouveia in 1891 opposition continued in the area formerly ruled by him. Cambuemba, one of his lieutenants, allied with the Sena and Tonga in a rebellion in 1897 which was only put down by a Portuguese force of some 3,000 men.

Resistance to the Portuguese in Mozambique spread far beyond the supra-prazo polities. Unfortunately much of it was characterized by a parochial outlook. The frequent peasant rebellions lacked any

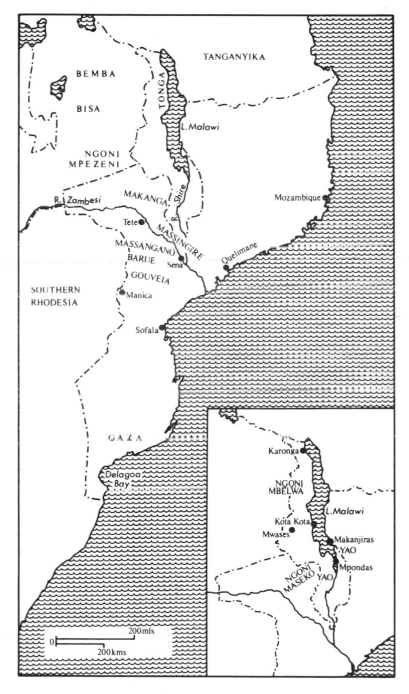

Map 11. Mozambique and Nyasaland.

long-term goals. After a period of unrest which included attacks on labour recruiters, driving away tax collectors and burning stores and warehouses the peasants usually returned to their homes. The peasants were reacting to immediate abuses rather than being driven by a general opposition to foreign rule. However, during the period 1878 to 1904 there were 23 well-documented peasant revolts in Mozambique. Opposition to the Portuguese was also shown by flight across the frontiers into British territory and by the setting up of settlements beyond the reach of the Portuguese in the more inaccessible parts of the colony.

One centre of opposition to the Portuguese was the Barue people. Their defeat of Gouveia and their ability to remain independent of the Portuguese gave them considerable prestige in the colony where they became a symbol of resistance. The Barue gave assistance to Cambuemba in his fight against the Portuguese and sent troops to fight with the Shona peoples on the Mozambican-Rhodesian border in 1900. Gradually Hanga, the Barue ruler, built up a series of alliances which challenged Portuguese control of the Zambesi. The Portuguese determined to crush this resistance and in 1902 sent a expedition against the Barue. This met stiff resistance but the superior Portuguese armament eventually triumphed and Hanga and a number of his supporters fled to Rhodesia. A key factor in the triumph of the Portuguese had been their ability to recruit large numbers of Africans into their forces. However, the Barue will to resist had not been killed by their defeat. In 1917 they were again to rise against the Portuguese.

The Shangane of the Gaza kingdom were unsuccessful in their armed resistance to Portugal. Gungunyane succeeded his father Mzila as king in 1884 and continued his father's ineffectual policy of trying to preserve his people's independence from Portugal by pursuing the chimera of an alliance with the British in Natal. Gungunyane's ambassadors to Natal were ignored as Mzila's had been. The 1891 Anglo-Portuguese Treaty placed Gaza firmly in the Portuguese sphere. In 1895 the Portuguese invaded Gaza in force and easily defeated the Shangane army, which had once been organized on a powerful basis along Zulu lines, but had been in serious decline for a generation because of labour migration to South African mines and increasing alcoholism. Gungunyane was captured, paraded through the streets of Lisbon, and exiled to the Azores Islands, where he died.

The Congo: contrasting responses to De Brazza and Stanley

Makoko of the Bateke had welcomed De Brazza in his territory in 1880 in the hope that this particular white man would mediate in the political and economic disputes that were preventing the peace and development of the Bateke. On his march from Gabon to the Congo River De Brazza had been very careful to establish peaceful relations with the communities he passed through. Makoko heard of De Brazza's pacific reputation before he reached Bateke country, and he heard about Stanley's violent methods too. De Brazza was infinitely preferable to Stanley. Moreover, Makoko traded with the coast on a small scale and was anxious to develop this trade with the French.

De Brazza's 1880 Treaty with Makoko placed only some of the Bateke under French protection. The Berlin Conference acknowledged a huge French sphere on the north Congo bank. De Brazza's expedition of 1883–5 brought vast regions under French rule largely by peaceful talk, as the politically fragmented communities of the region followed Makoko's lead in using the white man as an arbiter in litigation and a partner in trade.

Stanley's occupation of the south bank for Leopold quite naturally provoked a hostile response from the people. Between 1879 and 1884 Stanley imposed treaties by force on four hundred Congolese rulers over an area a thousand miles inland, as far as Stanley Falls. The political fragmentation of the people and their reluctance to unite made physical resistance ineffective. For example, the powerful trader-ruler Ngalyema, who controlled the down-river approaches to Stanley Pool was prepared to resist at first. Ngalyema was a remarkable man who had risen from slavery by trading in ivory, grown rich, bought his freedom, and built a powerful political position based on an army of a thousand slaves armed with muskets. A show of force by Stanley intimidated Ngalyema's would-be local allies and because of his lack of support from local communities he changed his response from armed resistance to economic cooperation and an acceptance of the International Association's control of his territory.

Stanley left the Congo in 1885, but Leopold employed equally ruthless and militaristic men to occupy the 900,000 square miles given to him by the Berlin Conference. The Zairean peoples put up strong resistance to European invasion for over thirty years. The most notable wars of defence were those of the Azande of the north-east (1892–1912), the Bayaka of the south-west (in 1895) and the Bashi-lele of the east (1900–16). Tippu Tip accommodated himself to the European Scramble for Africa. In 1887 he accepted the position of Governor of Stanley Falls under Leopold, but when the

Belgian monarch made clear his intention of breaking Swahili-Arab control of the east Tippu Tip retired to Zanzibar in 1892. However, his lieutenants like Rumaliza put up strong armed resistance in 1894. Rumaliza was defeated and retreated to German East Africa, eventually reaching Zanzibar where he, too, retired. The Yeke king, Msiri, one of the great Nyamwezi state-builders, was murdered by Belgian agents of Leopold in 1891, when he refused to accept a treaty, and his army was destroyed by machine guns.

Even after Leopold had established effective occupation of the Congo, there were repeated rebellions against him and the Belgian regime that took over the rule of the colony in 1908. The Bayaka rebelled in 1902 and 1906, the Baluba of the south-east from 1907 to 1917, the Babua of the north in 1903–4 and again in 1910, and the Budja from 1903 to 1905. These rebellions were fundamentally responses to the consolidation of European political control.

5
North and North-eastern Africa during the Scramble

Tunisia

The French occupation of Tunis in 1881 reflected two aspects of European imperialism in Africa in the late nineteenth century: how European economic penetration in the form of bondholders prepared the way for political occupation in North Africa, and how Africa was frequently seen by European political leaders as a pawn in their games of Great Power diplomacy in Europe. The Tunisian response demonstrated the divisions in North African society both between social classes and between rival Muslim groups.

Tunis was nominally part of the Ottoman empire but in practice was independent. In 1877 the reforming Tunisian prime minister, Khair al-Din resigned and was replaced by Muhammad Khaznadar and later by Mustafa b. Ismail. Corruption and embezzlement then became the order of the day and by 1878 the government was unable to meet its obligations to the International Financial Commission which had been set up by Italy, France and Britain in the 1860s when Tunisia had been unable to repay its debts. France in particular became concerned about this and in 1879 attempted to negotiate a treaty of protection with Mustafa b. Ismail. This failed largely because of opposition by the French public to colonial adventures. However, the campaign mounted against French interests by the Italian consul in Tunis after 1878 quickly roused passions in France which allowed the government to take action in 1881.

One of the French motives for the occupation of Tunis in 1881 was to safeguard the eastern flank of French Algeria against occupation by another European Power, especially Italy who already had many settlers in Tunis. The excuse for the French invasion was Tunisian raids on Muslim villages in Algeria. In fact, the French moved into Tunis in 1881 because of the meddling in North African affairs of Bismarck, the German Chancellor. The key to Bismarck's foreign policy was to divert France's interest from European affairs and from its desire to revenge its defeat by Germany in 1870–1. Therefore, in 1881 Bismarck secretly tipped off France about Italy's plans to occupy Tunis and France swallowed the German bait. Britain had no objections to this extension of French activity in the Mediterranean because it was part of a bargain by which France recognized the British acquisition of Cyprus from Turkey.

At first the French occupation changed little in Tunisia. A protectorate was set up and the bey remained titular head of state. A French Resident was imposed on the existing Ottoman administration. But between 1882 and 1890 the government of Tunisia was gradually but surely gallicized. In 1883 the Financial Commission of Control was brought to an end. The French government paid off the debts of the bondholders, and proceeded to reimburse itself by exploiting the country. French settlers began to arrive, but were compelled to buy any land which they wished to farm. On the one hand, this kept down the numbers of settlers. On the other, the settlers tended to be men with capital who were able to develop Tunisian agriculture. As late as 1901 only 24,000 Frenchmen were living in Tunisia.

The Tunisian response to French occupation was mild. The urban aristocracy accepted French rule out of self-interest and kept many posts in the administration, as well as their lands. Moreover, the French were seen as allies against the Tunisian masses. Even the Muslim reformers (disciples of Khair al-Din) accommodated themselves to French rule in the interests of modernization, and accepted the French as allies against the traditional Sufi orders. The docile Tunisian response was understandable since the French did not create another Algeria in Tunisia and ruled through a Grand Tunisian Council and municipal institutions on which Tunisians as well as French settlers were represented. In legal matters Muslim justice continued to be administered to most Tunisians. In any case, Tunisians were long used to alien rule and accepted French paternalism as they had tolerated Ottoman domination. There was armed resistance in 1881–2 in southern Tunisia which had been less effectively controlled by the Ottomans, and was therefore less ready than the north to accept French hegemony. But the southerners' resistance was defeated and many of them migrated, paradoxically, to Ottoman-ruled Tripoli.

Egypt

The Egyptian economy was eroded by unrestrained European economic penetration during the reigns of Muhammad Ali, Sa'id and Ismail. In turn this erosion of the economy led to the setting up in 1876 of Dual Control, the arrangement whereby the Ottoman sultan remained nominally Suzerain of Egypt with the khedive nominally representing him in Cairo, but the real rulers were the European members of the Commission of the Debt. The Commission, in its attempts to raise money to repay European bondholders, succeeded in stirring up the first Egyptian nationalist revolution of 1881–2.

The man who inspired the revolution was a great scholar, Al-Afghani, who taught at Cairo's Al-Azhar university and the man who led it was one of his former students, Colonel Ahmed Arabi. Al-Afghani preached reform within the framework of Islam and pan-Islamism. He believed all Muslim peoples should develop partly by adopting western technology, in order to withstand western economic and political power, and that Muslims must unite to oppose Western political and religious encroachment. The actions of the European financial commissioners turned Al-Afghani's intellectual movement into a mass-supported revolution. Egyptians were opposed to European control of their finances even though the system of taxation introduced by the Commission was more equitable than that of the khedive. The many civil servants and soldiers who were dismissed for reasons of economy naturally opposed the new regime. Some of the Commission's moves were extremely unwise. For instance, of the 2500 army officers who were dismissed, almost all of them were junior officers and Egyptians. The Turkish senior officers kept their posts. A nationalist movement soon arose around Colonel Arabi, an Egyptian of *fellaheen* (peasant) origin.

Arabi's nationalism was both anti-Turkish and anti-European, and he was supported by both the Egyptian liberal intelligentsia and the fellaheen. Their first success was the removal, in January 1881, of the hated Turkish War Minister, Osman Rifky, following military demonstrations. Then on September 9, Arabi carried out a successful coup. The army surrounded Khedive Tewfik's palace and forced him to yield to its demands to dismiss his ministers, restore the army to its former strength, and summon the parliament, the Chamber of Notables. A new liberal and nationalist Prime Minister was appointed. The European response to these developments was the Anglo-French Joint Note of January 6, 1882, in which Britain and France made it clear they were determined to uphold the khedive and European financial control. Far from backing down, the Egyptians prepared to resist any Anglo-French invasion, and in February Arabi was made Minister of War. Britain and France stepped up the pressure by a demonstration of their naval strength in Alexandria harbour, and by ordering Tewfik to retire Arabi. Tewfik obeyed, but Egyptian public opinion, expressed in mass demonstrations, forced the khedive to reappoint Arabi only five days later.

Thus Anglo-French pressure simply reinforced the ranks of the Egyptian nationalists, and provoked anti-European violence. In June there were riots in Alexandria in which fifty Christians—European and Egyptian—were killed. The riots and the massacre were spontaneous, but European governments and public opinion blamed Arabi for them. The massacre also created a casus belli for the Great Powers, who now increasingly feared an Egyptian threat to the Suez Canal. Britain and France planned a joint military expedition but the French withdrew from it because of a domestic crisis, and Britain invaded on its own. A naval bombardment of Alexandria in July was followed up by the landing of British troops in August. On September 13, 1882, General Wolseley defeated Arabi at the Battle of Tel el-Kebir, where superior European firepower was decisive. Arabi was captured and banished for life to Ceylon.

The aims of Gladstone's British government were to set up a pro-British Egyptian government which would ensure repayment of European debts and to withdraw Britain from Egypt as soon as possible. However, because of its position on the route to India, Egypt had immense strategic importance. In the end Britain stayed there for forty years. But Egyptian nationalism was not destroyed. It took new forms under British occupation (see Chapter 9).

Sudanese response to Anglo-Egyptian imperialism

The Mahdist jihad against Egypt began in 1881 when Muhammad Ahmad ibn Abdullah declared himself the Mahdi and quickly liberated the Sudan from Egyptian rule. The jihad continued under the Mahdi's successor, Khalifa Abdallahi. To some extent the Scramble for Africa as it affected the Sudan was a response to the Mahdiyya. Yet the Anglo-Egyptian occupation of the Sudan between 1896 and 1899 fitted into the Scramble for Africa in general, because Britain's motive was to keep rival Great Powers out of the upper Nile Valley.

Anglo-Egyptian forces crushingly defeated the Mahdist invasion of Egypt at the Battle of Tushki in August 1889. Britain did not immediately follow up her victory because the Mahdists no longer seemed to be a threat to Egypt. The fear of Mahdism evaporated with a series of Mahdist defeats in the early 1890s. In 1891 an Anglo-Egyptian expedition from Suakin routed the local Mahdist governor, Uthman Diqna, and captured his headquarters. In 1893 a Mahdist expedition into Eritrea was defeated by the Italians at the Battle of Agordat. Then in 1894 the Italians captured Kassala. Then in the late 1890s the whole diplomatic and military situation in the upper Nile valley dramatically changed. In 1896 Ethiopians under Menelik II annihilated the Italians at Adowa. Anglo-Egyptian forces under Kitchener now advanced up the Nile into the north Sudan province of Dongola, not to reconquer the Sudan for Egypt, but to assist defeated Italy by distracting the Mahdists from winning back Kassala from the Italians. The Mahdist forces were defeated in a series of actions and by September 1896 the whole of the province was occupied. However, from March 1897 the British embarked on the full reconquest of the Sudan in order to forestall the French, because in that month a French army officer, Marchand, set out from

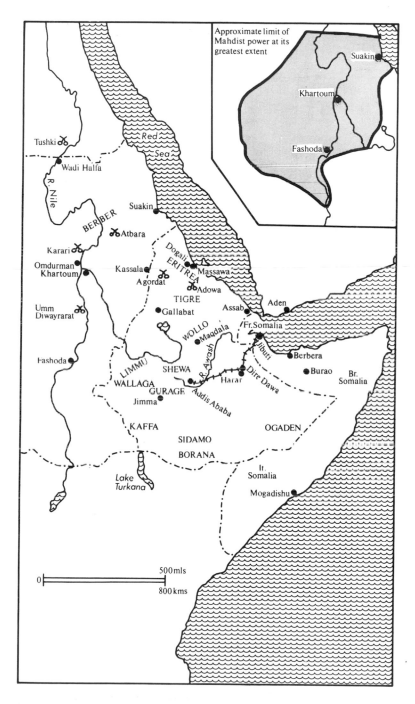

Map 12. Sudan, Ethiopia and Somalia.

Brazzaville for the southern Sudan. Moreover France was not the only imperial power expanding into the southern Sudan. The Ethiopians were closing in on the beleaguered Mahdist state of Khalifa Abdallahi. France and Ethiopia even made an agreement partitioning the southern Sudan between them, the left bank going to France and the right bank to Ethiopia.

The Mahdist army of the north under Mahmud Ahmad found itself steadily driven back by Kitchener's unrelenting advance. The railway which had been built up the Nile from Wadi Halfa in support of Kitchener was now continued to Abu Hamad. Mahmud fell back and gave up Berber without resistance because he could not feed his army. But he made a stand at Atbara in April 1898. The Ansar, although starving, showed all their old fanatical courage, but this availed them little against Kitchener's machine guns. The Battle of Atbara left 3,000 Ansar dead and 4,000 wounded. Anglo–Egyptian casualties were only 81 killed and 500 wounded. Kitchener then pushed on to the Mahdist capital.

At the Battle of Omdurman fought in September 1898 at Karari, six miles north of the capital, 11,000 Sudanese were killed and 16,000 wounded, as against Anglo–Egyptian losses of 49 dead and 382 wounded. The overwhelming British firepower consisted of eight gunboats providing heavy artillery, howitzers on an island in the Nile, cannon in the British square, maxim guns and the latest repeater rifles. Most of the ansar were armed with antiquated muskets or spears.

Khalifa Abdallahi did not surrender after Karari but led his surviving soldiers into Kordofan, where he continued to resist. In November 1899 Abdallahi made a final stand at Umm Diwaykarat, where he was killed with many of his ministers. After Karari, Kitchener raced south to Fashoda, the settlement on a Nile sandbank where Marchand, seven other Frenchmen and 120 Senegalese had already arrived. The French got there first in July 1898, but they did not effectively occupy the southern Sudan any more than had the Ethiopians in their expedition to the White Nile in 1897. Britain and Egypt had a large army in the Sudan and claimed right of conquest. After a brief threat of war between Britain and France over Fashoda, France backed down, mindful of British naval power in Europe.

Ethiopian resistance to the Italians

The British victory over Tewodros at Maqdala in 1868 was remembered in Europe long after the conditions in Ethiopia that made it possible had been forgotten. As a result, the Italians who invaded Ethiopia at the end of the nineteenth century acted on a false assumption of Ethiopian weakness. Ethiopia united was a vastly different proposition from Ethiopia divided

The origins of the Italian penetration of Ethiopia go back to 1869, when Italian missionaries bought the Red Sea fishing village of Assab from a local sultan. In 1882 the Italian government took over Assab and in 1885 Italy occupied the larger port of Massawa. An Italian advance inland was halted by Ras Alula, Yohannis IV's general, who in January 1887 wiped out a small Italian force at Dogali.

After Dogali the Italians attempted to weaken Emperor Yohannis of Ethiopia by inciting King Menelik of Shewa against him. In October 1887 an Italo-Shewan convention of friendship and mutual support was signed. Menelik had no intention of rebelling against Yohannis or of allowing Italy to occupy Ethiopian territory; he was using the Italians to obtain firearms while deceiving them into believing that he intended to break with his emperor. In 1889 after becoming emperor, Menelik signed the Treaty of Wichale with Italy. The Italian version of the treaty made Ethiopia an Italian protectorate but this interpretation was rejected by Menelik who rightly argued that the Amharic version made no mention of an Italian protectorate. In reality Menelik's concessions to Italy at Wichale were limited and insignificant. He recognized Italian occupation of Massawa, the Eritrean lowlands and a few places on the edge of the highlands that had been occupied by Italy in Yohannis's reign. Menelik granted the Italians Eritrea in order to buy time.

After Wichale the Italians attempted to detach from the new emperor the provincial King of Tigre, Ras Mengesha (Yohannis IV's son) and Mengesha's general Ras Alula. But the plan failed. The Italians advanced southwards into Tigre, beyond the boundary line established at the Treaty of Wichale. But far from detaching Mengesha and Alula from Menelik this drove them into his arms.

Mengesha was quite willing to set himself up as a rival to Menelik in Ethiopia, but he was not the kind of man to give up any of his territory to a foreign power, or to accept the status of a puppet ruler in an Italian-occupied state. Indeed Italian dealings with the provincial kings could not match Menelik's diplomatic skill with the rases. All the great provincial chiefs, who had for years been accepting gifts and arms from Italian negotiators, lined up at the Battle of Adowa on the side of their emperor.

The Ethiopian victory over Italy at Adowa was a devastating and decisive defeat for the invading Italians, who had thrown 17,000 men into the battle. More than 6,000 of these were killed, including over 4,000 Italians. A further 1,500 were wounded and about 4,000 were taken prisoner. A prime factor in the Ethiopian victory was her superiority in manpower. Menelik's vast conquests of lands to the south of Shewa in the late 1880s and early 1890s not only made it necessary for him to maintain large armies but also made it possible for him to provide food for them. The Italians estimated Menelik had as many as 196,000 soldiers even before he became Emperor. At Adowa he was able to summon about 100,000 men. A second advantage for Menelik was his superiority to the Italians in firepower. According to one Italian source Menelik was supplied freely with 189,000 modern rifles by his Italian treaty allies between 1885 and 1895. Moreover, the Italians had also given Menelik a loan of four million lire which he used to buy arms all over Europe. At Adowa three out of four Ethiopian soldiers had modern firearms.

The incompetence of the Italian commander, Baratieri, and his officers played a major part in the Ethiopian victory. On the eve of the battle two important Tigrean allies of the Italians defected to Menelik with 600 men and information of the Italian battle positions. In spite of this Baratieri persisted with his original dispositions. He was encouraged to underestimate the Ethiopians because he had been duped by Ethiopian double-agents, who fed him with the false information that Menelik's army had split up and was retreating, and that the Emperor had only 15,000 men left. To make things worse for the Italians their communications broke down. Because of poor reconnaissance and faulty maps the Italian units became separated from each other and got lost. The Ethiopians, led by Ras Alula who was chief of staff at Adowa, were able to prevent the Italian units from reforming and were thus able to defeat them separately. The attitude of the Ethiopians was also an important factor in their defeat of the Italians. They were intensely patriotic, and this was reflected in their loyalty to their emperor and their high courage under Italian fire

The victory of Adowa was not only the symbol of the Ethiopian love of freedom from foreign control, but also the practical proof of a strong and united Ethiopia. Tewodros had revived the vision of a powerful and recovered Ethiopian kingdom: Yohannis and Menelik and their soldiers had made it a reality. Adowa was the result of the movements towards Ethiopian unity and the modernization begun by Tewodros.

Ethiopian expansion during the Scramble for Africa

Besides his conflict with Italians Menelik embarked on a number of wars to expand his kingdom. The wars of expansion in southern and eastern Ethiopia between 1872 and 1898 began as part of the African Partition of Africa and continued as part of the European Partition. Menelik's motives for expansion were varied. Generally he wanted manpower for his army, tribute, and control of trade routes and of agricultural regions. Menelik was equally determined that Europeans would not occupy regions that former Ethiopian emperors had ruled. He brought several million people under first Shewan and then Ethiopian rule, more than doubling the size of the empire. Part of Gurage was overrun in 1875, Jimma and Limmu in the early 1880s, Wallaga in 1886, Harar in 1887, the rest of Gurage in 1889, Ogaden and Sidamo in 1891, many of the Borana Galla in 1896, Kaffa in 1897, and in 1898 the Ethiopian army reached the northern shores of Lake Turkana (Rudolf).

Menelik incorporated conquered states by peaceful methods wherever possible. For example in 1881–3 many of the western Gallas around Jimma submitted peacefully, having been won over by Menelik's Galla general Ras Gobana. Menelik confirmed their former rulers in their positions. However, more frequently the local rulers and peoples resisted and their lands were absorbed by Menelik only after heavy fighting, ruthless punishment and widespread devastation. For example, when Gobana defeated Hassan Injamo, the Muslim Gurage leader, in 1889 he had all enemy captives massacred. Kaffa resisted and was almost completely devastated before it surrendered in 1897. Resistance was common because outside the 'Habash' (Amhara–Tigre) region Menelik was creating not a nation but an empire. There was considerable local opposition to the establishment of military garrisons in the newly-conquered areas and to the new kind of serfdom that was introduced to maintain these garrisons. Muslims, traditionalists and non-Amhara resented the spread of the Amharic language and Orthodox Christianity. However, this cultural imperialism did have the advantage of helping Ethiopian unity. Moreover, Menelik appointed officials on the basis of loyalty rather than ethnic background. Amhara, Tigre, Galla and Somali all ruled as governors of provinces or districts. Menelik ruled his empire through a combination of direct rule by generals or indirect rule by hereditary rulers.

It would be wrong to characterize Menelik's expansion as entirely opposed to peace and stability. Many local wars were ended, such as the Gurage-Galla wars, and law and order was established over vast areas where little peace had existed before. On the other hand, that the nature of Menelik's expansion was colonialist cannot be effectively gainsaid. The effects of Menelik's expansion on the Amaro-Burji and their Konso neighbours provide a case in point. The Amaro-Burji are a Galla-speaking community who lived around the Burji mountain in southern Ethiopia. In 1895–6 they were invaded by Menelik's general Ras Gadi. The Burji ruler, Guyo Aba Gada, advised cooperation because the Burji had no guns, and a treaty of friendship was made. The Burji did not, therefore, experience the destruction inflicted on their neighbours, the Konso, who fought heroically but uselessly, and suffered thousands killed and extensive looting and burning. However, after Adowa and the removal of the

Italian threat Menelik intensified his control of the south. The Amaro-Burji soon lost their freedom as they were rounded up, counted and divided among the occupying soldiers as slave labour. Unoccupied land was declared 'crown land' and the Amaro-Burji were made to work it. The neighbouring nomadic Borana Galla suffered relatively lightly from the Ethiopian central government and army because they could move away from Menelik's garrisons, unlike the settled and agricultural Amaro-Burji. One result of central government and military exploitation of the Amaro-Burji was social dislocation. Many of the Amaro-Burji migrated out of their homeland to other parts of southern Ethiopia where the local representatives of Menelik were less exacting. Another result was an increase in crime as men stole in order to get the means to pay the tribute demanded by the government or to pay bribes to officials. The Amaro-Burji, like most of the people in the outlying provinces of Ethiopia, benefited little from Menelik's occupation of their lands or from his modernization programme.

Ethiopian modernization under Menelik II

Menelik was a man of great ability and foresight who worked extremely hard to attempt to modernize his country. There was considerable progress in a number of fields, but some serious weaknesses remained uncorrected by the time Menelik, who lived until 1913, became paralyzed and unable to govern in 1910.

The achievements were most marked in communications. A Swiss engineer, Alfred Ilg, worked for Menelik from 1878. In 1886 he built the first modern bridge over the Awash River. A French company began to build a railway from Addis Ababa to the French Somali port of Jibuti, but the line was not completed until 1917. It was held up by Menelik when he heard that the Company was planning to hand the railway over to the French government. Modern roads for wheeled transport were built between Addis Ababa and Harar and Addis Ababa and Jimma. The Addis Ababa-Jibuti telegraph was completed in 1903. Postal services had been set up much earlier. Ethiopian postage stamps began to be printed (in France) in 1893. In 1894 post offices were set up with French advisers. In 1911 a state printing press was opened.

Other reforms were in education, health, administration, banking and currency. New modern European-type schools, like the Menelik II school which opened in 1908, were opened to supplement the traditional church schools. Ethiopian students were sent to Europe, especially Switzerland and Russia. The Menelik II Hospital was opened in 1910. In 1907 administrative reforms created the beginnings of a modern cabinet system. In 1905 a Bank of Abyssinia, affiliated to the National Bank of Egypt, was constituted. Already in 1894 a new national currency of coins made in France began to replace the long-established Austrian Maria Theresa dollars and to help considerably the growth of retail trade. In 1903 a mint was set up in the capital.

The weaknesses in Menelik's reforms were largely the result of limited capital resources and limited skilled manpower. In the field of revenue, the changeover from a tribute system to taxation was by no means complete by the end of his reign. Accounting and auditing procedures were so undeveloped that embezzlement was rife. Yet even assuming Menelik had had more time to devote to reform and had had more money and trained men to carry out his modernization schemes, it is doubtful whether he would have gone much further than he did. There was no social and economic revolution in Menelik's Ethiopia as there was in contemporary Japan. Menelik and his nobles intended to preserve their traditional and privileged way of life by grafting on to it those aspects of westernization that would preserve and strengthen rather than destroy it.

Somali response to the European Scramble for Africa

The Somali were not a nation in the nineteenth century but a collection of scattered nomadic clans and urban groups occupying the area from Jibuti in the north at the entrance to the Red Sea to Brava on the Zanzibari-controlled coast in the south. Somali response to Italian, British and French colonialism differed from one area to another, and very often colonial rule seemed very remote. Italian rule seemed no more arduous than the Zanzibari rule it had replaced. However, in 1899 serious resistance to colonial rule began under the leadership of Sayyid Muhammad.

Sayyid Muhammad Abdullah Hassan, who was born in 1864 in northern Somalia opposite Aden became a wandering Muslim preacher and travelled to Mogadishu, Mombasa and the Sudan. In 1894 he visited Mecca and joined the Salihiya order. In 1895 he returned to Somalia and settled in Berbera. There he began to speak out against Christian missions and to demand a return to a pure form of Islam. In 1897 he returned to his birthplace and quickly built up a following amongst the Dolbahanta of the Darod clan. Initially the British welcomed his establishment of authority in the area but in 1898 and 1899 his letters to the British authorities began to cause concern to them. In August 1899 Muhammad and his followers occupied Burao where he declared himself the Mahdi and proclaimed a jihad against the infidels—Ethiopian, British, French and Italian. Shortly afterwards he raided a settlement of the Qadiriyah order at Sheikh and killed its inhabitants. The British authorities in Berbera decided that action must be taken against Muhammad.

Initially little help was given by Britain to the local authorities because the British were pre-occupied with the Anglo-Boer War. Two expeditions in 1901 and 1902 were made up of locally recruited troops but in 1903 and 1904 two further expeditions were made up largely of regular troops from the Indian Army and the King's African Rifles. The campaigns were inconclusive but Muhammad lost so many men that for a while he ceased to be a threat. In 1905 he reached an agreement with the Italians which recognized a specific area as his own territory. Britain also gave her assent to this agreement and four years of relative peace followed.

In 1909, however, Muhammad again resorted to military activities against various Somali communities whom he believed were not following Islam closely enough. Faced with major unrest in the interior the British withdrew to the coast. The result of this was raid and counter-raid by one Somali clan against another and it has been estimated that one third of the adult male population of the British protectorate died in these troubles.

Under the threat of attacks on their coastal settlements Britain created a Somali Camel Constabulary under the command of Richard Corfield. However, in August 1913 his force was ambushed. Corfield himself was killed and the Constabulary almost annihilated. During the First World War there were clashes between British forces and Muhammad. During this period Muhammad began to build fortresses, the largest of which was Taleh. It had towers 60 feet high and walls 14 feet thick. His resistance continued after the war but Britain mounted a major attack upon him. He was defeated and fled into Ethiopia where he died of influenza in 1920. His followers then scattered and the resistance which Britain, often aided by Ethiopia and Italy, had been unable to suppress in twenty-one years now collapsed.

Although initially Muhammad had been concerned only with religious matters he ultimately transformed his movement into a much broader one. He decided that foreign rule was the reason for the superficiality of Islam in much of Somalia and so added to his aims the political objective of attaining independence from foreign rule. As a result, although many Somalis of the Qadiriya order hated him during his lifetime, he is today regarded by many Somalis as a national hero.

Libyan response to Italian invasion

The French occupation of Tunisia in 1881 initially tempted the Ottoman government to use Tripolitania as a base for a propaganda campaign against the French. Although this campaign never really developed a considerable number of Tunisians moved into Ottoman-controlled Libya believing it better to be ruled by foreigners who were Muslim than foreigners who were Christian. Increasing Italian economic penetration of Libya forced the Ottoman government to reconsider its attitude towards the French. Although the border between French Tunisia and Libyan Tripolitania was not finally agreed until 1910 a Turko-French delegation began looking into frontier clashes as early as 1889.

Gradually the European Great Powers came to recognize the predominance of Italian interests in Libya. In 1888 Germany recognized these interests, in 1902 Britain France and Austria followed suit. Italy was only held back from occupying the area by the wish of Germany and Austria to maintain the decrepit Ottoman empire. As she waited she embarked on a programme aimed at consolidating her economic position in Libya. In 1902 Italian medical services and a post office were established in Tripolitania. In 1907 branches of the Bank of Rome was opened in Banghazi and twelve other· towns. These banks financed Italian domination of Libya's export trade in wool, cereals, esparto grass and ostrich feathers. But the Italians were unable to settle as farmers and traders in significant numbers because the Turks made it difficult for them to buy land.

The Young Turk Revolution in Turkey in 1908 led to a complete ban on the purchase of Libyan lands by Italians. Moreover, the Young Turks began to reorganize the Turkish army. The Italians felt they had to attack Libya before Turkey's revival went too far, making an invasion difficult or even dangerous. The renewed attempt in 1910 by the new governor, Ibrahim Pasha, to enforce the law against foreign land ownership and Italy's increasing suspicion of Germany's friendship with Turkey were the immediate causes of the Italian invasion. In October 1911 an Italian force of 34,000 men, 62 artillery guns and 145 warships moved into Libya. The opposing Turkish force was only 7,000 strong.

In the early stages of the invasion the Italians were successful. Within a month they had captured the coastal towns of Tubruq, Banghazi, Tripoli, Darna and Khums. The Italians heavily outnumbered the Turks and applied an effective naval blockade to prevent Turkish reinforcements reaching Libya. The Libyans were divided in their response to the Italian invasion. Some were neutral; others joined the Turks out of pan-Islamic feeling. The Italian invasion caused the Sanusiyya Brotherhood to cooperate with the Turks far more than they had ever done in the past. Resistance was ruthlessly suppressed. The worst incident was at the oasis of Mechiya on the outskirts of Tripoli city. Reuter's correspondent reported that 'Parties of soldiers penetrated every portion of the Oasis, shooting indiscriminately all whom they met without trial, without appeal'. Over four thousand men, women and children died at Mechiya, including several hundred men who took shelter in a mosque. It soon became clear to the Italians that local Libyan resistance to their invasion was going to prolong the war. Threats of a new attack on the Ottoman empire in the Aegean Sea forced the Sultan to negotiate and in 1912 he gave Libya to Italy in the Treaty of Ouchy.

The Sanusi of the desert, under their leader Sayyid Ahmad Al-Sharif, took over the mantle of resistance from the Turks in 1912. When the Turks left Libya the Sanusi sensibly abandoned the failed Turkish tactics of pitched battles against superior Italian firepower, and turned to guerilla war in the desert, at which they were pastmasters. By 1915 Italy had withdrawn from the interior of the country in order to concentrate her military attention on the First World War. Sanusi resistance continued until 1917 when the Italians, defeated by Austria in Europe, made a truce with the head of the Order. The Sanusi were not effectively brought under Italian control until the offensive begun by Mussolini's Fascist government in 1923.

Moroccan response to French and Spanish occupation

France's main motives for occupying Morocco in the early twentieth century were to safeguard the western flank of French Algeria against occupation by another European power, and to remove the danger to French colonialism in Algeria posed by the existence on its western border of an independent Arab-Berber state. France was assisted in taking over most of Morocco by the weakening of the country by an incompetent and foolish sultan, Mawlay Abdul Aziz (1894–1907) and by favourable factors in European Great Power diplomacy.

Abdul Aziz was only sixteen years of age on his accession, and showed a passionate interest in games, ornaments, toys, and luxuries. Unfortunately he never outgrew these youthful passions and he soon exhausted the treasury by massive spending on frivolities. Attempts to reform the system of taxation were opposed by religious leaders and large landowners and in 1903 Abdul was forced to obtain a loan of about £800,000 from French, British and Spanish financiers in order to pay his debts. Then in 1904 he negotiated a loan from French banks of 62.5 million francs. In order

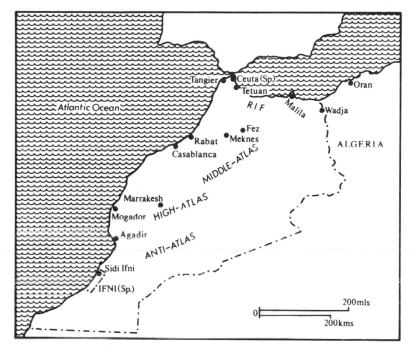

Map 13. Morocco.

to pay off the loan the Sultan imposed new taxes on his subjects
which removed the exemptions on the religious sharifs and shaikhs,
who nevertheless refused to pay. Abdul had other serious weaknesses for a Moroccan sultan: he was not a devout Muslim and he
surrounded himself with non-Muslim European advisers. This was
particularly opposed by the religious leaders in Fez who wanted him
to have only Muslim advisers. Opposition also emerged in the form
of rival claimants to the throne, like the pretender Bu Himara, a
sultan in the Rif Mountains and Ahmed al-Raisuni, a sharif, and
effective ruler of the Jbala district south of Tangier. Ahmed's soldiers
began to kidnap wealthy Americans and Europeans who were
released only after the payment of large ransoms. From 1905 the
Glawis of the High Atlas also turned against the sultan who had
failed to reward them for their help against Bu Himara.

The events known to Europeans as the First Moroccan Crisis
(1905–6) was the first stage in destroying the political independence
of the Moroccan state. In 1904 Britain, alarmed at German naval
expansion, signed a colonial agreement with France known as the
Anglo-French Entente. As part of the agreement Britain gave France
a free hand to dominate Morocco in return for France's recognition
of British control of Egypt. France now prepared to assert her claim

to Morocco but Kaiser Wilhelm II of Germany intervened at the request of Abdul Aziz who hoped to use Germany to protect Morocco from France. The kaiser wished to break the Anglo-French Entente and believed that Britain, when put to the test, would not back up French claims to Morocco. In 1905 Wilhelm visited Tangier and made a speech in which he called the sultan 'an absolutely independent sovereign'. But the kaiser had miscalculated. The crisis which he had begun ended in the 1906 Algeçiras Conference in Spain, at which Britain backed up France and Morocco's sovereignty was reduced, and French and Spanish officers were put in charge of the Moroccan police force in the ports. A Moroccan state bank was to be set up, financed by the European Powers and controlled by France.

The result of the Algeçiras Conference and its decisions was a wave of anti-European feeling and actions in Morocco, and nationalist revolts against the sultan. Europeans were assassinated in both Marrakesh and Casablanca. The attacks on Europeans, however, gave France an excuse in 1907 to occupy Casablanca and the Shawiyya region on the west coast and Wadja on the Algerian border. The French naval attack on Casablanca was a massacre: thousands of Moroccan civilians were killed by the shelling. The Algeçiras terms and the French invasion encouraged further resistance to the sultan's authority by Bu Himara and Raisuni. When Abdul Aziz proposed to call in the French to aid him against provincial revolts a political revolution and civil war broke out in Morocco, in 1907–8. Religious leaders deposed Abdul Aziz, and named a new sultan, Moulay Abdul Hafiz (1907–13). After a civil war Abdul Aziz fled to Tangier and Abdul Hafiz was confirmed in power in Fez. Initially Abdul Hafiz tried to oppose the Algeçiras decisions but the reality of French occupation forced him to accept them.

As the French advanced, the Shrarda and Bann Mtir peoples to the north and south of Meknes rose in rebellion early in 1910. At the same time the sultan was faced with a rival claimant to the throne. Mawlay al-Zain was proclaimed sultan at Meknes. As the threat from these groups to Fez increased the French intervened. Mawlay al-Zain was captured and the rebel attack on the capital repulsed. Then in 1911 the German kaiser made another unsuccessful attempt to break the Anglo-French Entente by sending a German warship to Agadir on the west Moroccan coast, precipitating the Second Moroccan Crisis. Once more Britain supported France, and Germany tried to compensate for a major diplomatic defeat by doing a deal with France. Germany recognized France's claim to Morocco in return for 107,000 square miles of the French Congo which was transferred to German Cameroons. In 1912 the French marched into Fez in force and Abdul Hafiz surrendered without fighting, in return for a French promise not to depose him and the ancient Alawite dynasty, and for French aid against his new Moroccan rivals.

In 1912 Abdul Hafiz began to repent of his deal with the French. The sultan joined Maghrib Unity, the secret Pan-Islamic group formed in Cairo. In 1912 the Maghrib Unity organization tried to foment a nationalist revolt in Morocco against the French. Money was sent to Morocco, arms were smuggled in and Turkish military advisers like Arif Tahif arrived. There seemed a fair chance of a nationwide revolt when Sultan Abdul Hafiz joined the movement. However, the French became alarmed at Abdul Hafiz's reassertion of nationalism, although they knew nothing of his involvement with Maghrib Unity and his plan to revolt. In 1913 the French forced Abdul Hafiz to abdicate, and he joined the previous Sultan Abdul Aziz in retirement in Tangier on a state pension.

Abdul Hafiz had cooperated with the French occupation of the heart of the country in 1912 but there was determination to resist in the south. In 1912 a Mauritanian leader, al-Hiba, declared a jihad, and invaded and occupied Marrakesh, the great city of southern Morocco. Al-Hiba posed a serious threat to the French position in the country. He thrived on the Islamic nationalist feeling of the masses and the fierce desire of the Berber communities of the Atlas to direct their own affairs independent of either central Moroccan or French control. Moreover, Al-Hiba had Turkish military advisers. The French met the crisis by promising the Berber leaders a degree of autonomy, and the Berber leaders changed sides just in time to prevent the rural masses swinging over to al-Hiba. With Berber support, the French were able to defeat al-Hiba. French recognition of the power of the Berber chiefs allowed them to hold the interior of Morocco even when most French troops were withdrawn at the beginning of the First World War.

In 1909 the Spanish had begun the conquest of northern Morocco and the extreme south known as Rio de Oro or Western Sahara. In the north Spain occupied Nador and Salwan and began building roads linking Malila with Salwin and Ceuta with Tetuan. However, Spain's rule was very indirect at first; the resistance movement led by Krim in the Rif Mountains after the First World War was a response to Spanish attempts to make their paper rule effective on the ground.

Thus on the eve of the First World War only Ethiopia remained independent in the whole of north and north eastern Africa. Elsewhere, European economic penetration had paved the way for European political control and European military superiority made that control a reality.

6
Colonial administration

Theories of colonial rule

From about 1900 four main theories of colonial administration emerged. These were assimilation, association, direct rule and indirect rule.

Assimilation was absorption of the African to European culture and European acceptance of the African as a partner in government, business and missionary enterprise. Assimilation had been applied by the French on the Senegal coast since the early nineteenth century. However, the French restricted assimilation to the four communes and did not apply it to the Senegalese hinterland or indeed to any other part of their African territories. The policy of assimilation flourished before the growth and spread of the European racist theory of Social Darwinism (which claimed that Europeans were racially superior to Africans) and the onset of full-scale colonialism at the end of the nineteenth century. After 1900 the French showed markedly less enthusiasm for assimilation of Senegalese even in the four communes.

The Portuguese had officially applied assimilation for centuries, since the beginning of their ventures in Africa. However, slave-trading and other forms of ruthless exploitation had destroyed the basis of the *assimilado* policy. By 1900 only a tiny handful of Africans in the four Portuguese colonies in Africa had been officially granted assimilado status—a situation that remained unchanged throughout the period of Portuguese rule.

Some of the most assimilated Africans in the late nineteenth century were the members of the English-speaking elite in the British West African colonies, especially Sierra Leone. However, Britain did not consciously follow an assimilationist policy or attempt to assimilate western-educated West Africans into English society in the way the French assimilated Africans in the four communes. In any case, the 1890s saw an increase in existing discrimination against westernized Africans in both Church and State, with the de-Africanization of West African missions and the removal of many Creoles from Sierra Leone's civil service.

The policy that the French called *association* but which Michael Crowder has redefined as *paternalism* was adopted when the French colonial authorities outside Senegal found they could not accept assimilation, but did not wish to administer colonies by indirect rule through traditional institutions. These traditional institutions were replaced by new ones imposed by the colonial rulers. They would in principle be best administered by Europeans, but considerations of expense meant that only comparatively small numbers of Europeans were sent as administrators to the tropical colonies. Therefore Africans had to be used in the administration and 'associated' with colonial rule. Since there were very few western-educated Africans, traditional rulers had to be employed as agents of the administration. In practice, association often resembled indirect rule because under both systems the Europeans used traditional African rulers in administration. However, the differences were important. The British tried to apply indirect rule almost everywhere as part of a deliberate attempt to rule their African colonies through both local political leaders and local institutions. Association, on the other hand, was a reluctant recourse to the use of traditional rulers in the absence of enough Europeans and a Europeanized African elite, and it involved the use of African personnel rather than institutions.

Direct Rule would have required a vast population of European administrators to implement the details of colonial policies. Not even in white-settler colonies like South Africa and Southern Rhodesia (Zimbabwe) was direct rule by Europeans over Africans applied generally. Large areas of the white south were governed by policies that resembled either paternalism (as in the Transkei and Natal) or indirect rule (as in Zululand, Lesotho and Botswana). Only the Africans who lived and worked on white-owned farms and in the mines could be said to be under direct rule by Europeans.

Indirect Rule was attempted almost everywhere in British-ruled Africa, though it was applied with far more success in some areas than in others. Lugard, the ruler of Northern Nigeria (1900–6) and of all Nigeria (1912–20), is generally regarded as the apostle of indirect rule, though he was certainly not its founder. Lugard applied and made use of the system of ruling vast territories and different communities that the British had developed in India and the Gold Coast. Already in 1891 Sir Claude Macdonald had introduced indirect rule in the Niger Delta. In Northern Nigeria Lugard took over the existing Fulani system of indirect rule through emirates, which had been successful for a century.

Indirect rule had practical advantages. Indigenous rulers did not have to be paid high salaries nor would they take time to know the area and people, like European administrators. It was also peculiarly well-suited to the British worldwide imperial system, which gave autonomy to British colonial administrations (whereas the French, German and Portuguese colonies were under far closer metropolitan control). The system of administration in each colony could be varied to make use of the differing systems of government already developed by African communities. Another advantage of indirect rule, according to Lugard and his disciples, was that it was the best way of preparing the way for eventual African self-government, because it tied development to the exercise of responsibilities by African leaders. Lugard believed Britain had a 'dual mandate' in tropical Africa: to develop the colonies politically and economically and to exploit them for the benefit of the metropolitan economy. He did not believe that the British empire would last for ever and was sincere in his hopes for African development. However, was indirect rule the best instrument for African progress?

On the surface, Lugard's arrangements for administration in Northern Nigeria seem moderately enlightened. He wrote, 'The attitude of the Resident is that of a watchful adviser rather than of an interfering ruler'. He supported a system of courts under local judges to apply customary law. British district officers would attempt to 'improve' local law by influencing rather than tampering with it. Lugard did not favour passive indirect rule, where there would be stagnation in traditional ways of life and politics, but wished for a positive reformation of traditionalism by well-timed and well-judged European intervention to remove abuses and speed up development. Unfortunately, Lugard had little faith in African ability to reform and develop without European help. Like many Europeans of his age, he detested western-educated Africans whom he could not fit easily within his narrow mental horizons, in which the Europeans were seen as the masters and the Africans as subordinates. As Governor-General of Nigeria, Lugard had bad relations with the educated African elite of Lagos, especially with John Payne Jackson, the editor of the *Weekly Record*. Jackson called Lugard's policy 'maintenance of so-called "white prestige" at all costs.'

Indirect rule was unsuitable as a foundation for future self-government. It usually buttressed conservative elements in traditional government, and in areas like Northern Nigeria was a positive barrier to modernization. Moreover, indirect rule was not an African system of government. It was an alien system imposed on the Africans. Under it the traditional rulers might rule their people, but above them was a pyramid of European district officers, provincial commissioners (or residents) and governors and governors-general. Traditional rulers suffered many limitations on their political and judicial powers. Bishop Tugwell of Nigeria shrewdly summed up indirect rule as 'direct rule by indirect means'.

Another weakness of indirect rule was that it could be applied only to centralized communities with an established governmental hierarchy, such as the Fulani-Hausa, Baganda, Lozi and Ngwato. Indirect rule was inapplicable to those many communities which lacked centralized administration, notably the Igbo and Tiv in eastern Nigeria and most Kenyan communities. In some areas without chiefs the imperialists made use of sub-imperialists. The British were able to use the Baganda and Lozi to rule their neighbours on behalf of the colonial government. But such successes were few. There were disastrous failures in the attempt to apply indirect rule in areas without traditional centralized government. Chiefs had to be created for these areas and they were invariably unacceptable to the people they were appointed to rule.

To sum up, Lugard and his followers in the British colonial service wrongly assumed that African societies were static with a fixed and unchanging system of government. They supported indirect rule partly because they believed the African could progress only very slowly. They did not know or understand recent African history, and did not realize that considerable adaptation and innovation had taken place in African government in many states in the immediate pre-colonial period.

Colonial finance

Whatever system of rule was adopted by the colonial powers, one thing was common to all of them. None of them wished their colonies to become a drain on their finances. At the very least the colonies must be financially self-sufficient. This essentially was the view of French, German and British colonial officials. The Portuguese hoped that their colonies would produce a financial surplus while Leopold of the Belgians unashamedly demanded maximum profit from the Congo. In the early days of colonial rule, it was acceptable that grants from the colonial power might have to be made, but these were to be limited, both in terms of amount and the length of time for which they would be given. Uganda's grant in aid from Britain which was never very large, came to an end before the First World War.

In order to make the colonies financially self-sufficient, taxes had to be revised. Customs duties were charged, but these were rarely sufficiently large to pay for a colony. Various taxes therefore had to be levied. Taxation on Africans generally took two forms: labour and cash. All Africans in French colonies had to perform twelve days' labour free of charge. On top of this, there was often compulsory labour in return for payment. Labour was used most commonly on roads and on *les champs administratifs* to increase agricultural production. Labour was also sometimes provided for commercial companies. The Ivory Coast provides a particular example of this. In some cases, compulsory labour was requisitioned for the building of railways or other public works.

The British also used forced labour as a form of taxation. In the British colonies there was never the compulsory recruitment of labour for commercial companies or the compulsory culture of crops. However, forced labour was still important. In The Gambia, anyone refusing to undertake forced labour could be imprisoned for up to six months. In Southern Nigeria, men between the ages of 15 and 50 and women aged 15 to 40, were liable to undertake compulsory labour 24 days a year. Although some of the compulsory labour was paid for this was normally at rates lower than that paid to labour undertaken at the labourers' own volition.

The colonial powers also introduced various types of direct and indirect taxation. Hut taxes and poll taxes were particularly popular with colonial administrations. Taxation was seen as much more than merely a means of raising money for the administration. British and French administrators made it plain they thought that taxation would force Africans to work and so help in the economic development of the colony. In areas where there were substantial numbers of white settlers, demands were frequently made for an increase in taxation so that Africans would have to sell their labour to settlers in order to obtain the money to pay taxes. On the whole, before the First World War colonial administrators moved cautiously in the area of direct taxation. There was always the fear of African armed resistance to the implementation of direct taxes. British fears became even greater with the Sierra Leone Hut Tax Wars of 1896, provoked by Governor Cardew's decision to impose a direct tax on houses. Britain tried to manage with indirect taxation. For instance, plans to introduce a hut tax in the Gold Coast in 1897 were abandoned. The administration determined to survive on indirect taxes on cocoa and gold mining, and duties on imports. Direct taxation was not introduced to the Gold Coast until 1936.

Partition almost inevitably meant an increase in taxation in Africa. Colonial administrations needed officials and whether these officials were African or European they had to be paid, housed, and given transport around the country. A military force was needed to ensure that, in the last resort, taxes were paid. This force inevitably consumed some of the revenue that it had made sure would be collected. Taxes and customs duties were also used to raise capital for developments which the colonial governments deemed necessary. These included roads, railways, harbours and bridges: the very communications infrastructure which ensured crops a route to market, which in turn brought about even more revenue for the colonial administration.

French colonial government

The French practised assimilation only in the four communes of Senegal (St Louis, Dakar, Gorée and Rufisque), where citizenship was granted to all Africans long before the colonial era. However, in Senegal's hinterland and in the other French African territories, Africans who continued to live by African law and custom remained subjects. Association, or paternalism, was the dominant French colonial philosophy and practice. Yet in some areas indirect rule was practised. Marshal Lyautey, who administered Morocco from 1912 to 1925 with the title of Resident-General, exercised his power through the traditional rulers—the 'tribal leaders' and the leaders of local branches of Sufi orders. Indirect rule was also practised by the French in the Sahara desert lands of the Maghrib and West African territories, from Morocco to Tunisia and from Mauritania to Chad.

A major feature of French colonial administration was federalism. Federalism was physically possible because French conquests from Senegal to the Congo were linked in a continuous block of land. The thinking behind it was partly military and partly political. The difficulty of defeating Samori Toure had highlighted the need for united military command. The concept of *France d' Outre-mer*, or Overseas France, and the desire by Paris to subordinate the colonies closely to the metropolitan government made federation desirable. Like the Portuguese colonies, the French colonies were regarded as an integral part of the home country. France had no plans, not even long-term ones, for the creation of self-governing colonies. The French colonies were regarded as administrative units rather than countries, and were federated with one another according to the convenience of Paris. French West Africa became one federal administrative unit. In 1895 Senegal, Soudan (Mali), Guinea and Ivory Coast were placed under a Governor-General in St Louis. Dahomey was added to the federation in 1899, and Mauritania and Niger in 1904. The Federation was reorganized in 1904 with a Lieutenant-Governor. In French Equatorial Africa, the colonies of Congo, Gabon, Ubangi-Shari (Central Africa) and Chad were united with a federal capital in Brazzaville.

Federation was one reflection of France d' Outre-mer. Another was the right of Algerian and Senegalese representatives to sit in the French National Assembly in Paris—a right that symbolized their ultimate political equality with whites, but not their right to self-government. African representation in the National Assembly proved to be a failure. There was no parity of representation in proportion to the population, and very few African delegates sat in the Assembly. Those who did, like Blaise Diagne of Senegal, served French rather than African interests (see Chapter 9). The Assembly had very little interest in Africa or the colonies generally. Very few Africans were qualified to vote in National Assembly elections. As late as 1937, out of 15 million Africans in French West Africa only 80,500 were French citizens and so entitled to vote, and 78,000 of these had acquired citizenship because they were born in one of the communes·in Senegal.

Despotism was another strong feature of French colonial government. The French colonies were administered by decree of the French president. The parliament of the Third Republic had the right to pass laws for the colonies, but rarely did so. Ministerial despotism was paralleled by the local despotism of administrators. All colonial law was administrative law. There was no legislative or statute law in the French colonies. The highly centralized chain of command is illustrated in the diagram on the following page.

French administrators had considerably greater judicial power than the British colonial officers. All criminal cases were tried by them and customary law was ignored, except in civil cases. French administrators freely used the *indigenat*, a decree of September 1887 which allowed them to arrest and punish African subjects, (though not citizens) without holding a trial.

Like the British, the French ruled as far as possible through chiefs, but in rather different ways. Unlike the British, the French eliminated traditional rulers who had more than purely local authority. Initially the French replaced kings who had resisted their invasion by more pliant men, but abolished the kingships as soon as the 'collaborators' began to assert independent views. In Dahomey King Behanzin, who had led the resistance to the French occupation was deposed and exiled. He was replaced by a French stooge, Agoli-Agbo, who was in turn deposed in 1900 for trying to assert his independence of the French by opposing direct taxation. No successor was appointed. At the break-up of the Tokolor empire Aguibu, a brother of Emperor Ahmadu and an ally of the French, was appointed king. But in 1902 Aguibu was retired and the kingship abolished because he sought to exercise some traditional prerogatives. In the Congo, Makoko's successor as paramount chief of the Bateke opposed the claims of the new chartered companies who later came to exploit the colony. He was arrested and died in custody in 1892.

The French opposed African kingship because kings were seen as obstacles to colonial despotism. At the canton and village level the French used the traditional political system because the local rulers were considered much less of a threat to French control than kings. In Dahomey many of the surviving members of the royal family even held office in the local colonial administration. Yet the way in which the French used local traditional rulers had the effect of undermining their traditional authority with the people. The French forced them to become agents of colonialism and this turned the people against them. The canton and village chiefs were used as agents to collect taxes, control forced labour, ensure compulsory cultivation and recruit soldiers. They were mere servants of the French. Unlike chiefs in British Africa, French African chiefs could not try criminal cases or even present grievances. They were not properly paid and consequently resorted to extortion. Moreover, they were forced to be despots because the least delay with taxes or in the carrying out of orders was considered their responsibility, and they would be arrested, imprisoned and flogged for failing to perform their duties. The people, therefore, ceased to give allegiance to the traditional local political rulers and turned instead to the spiritual leaders in the community.

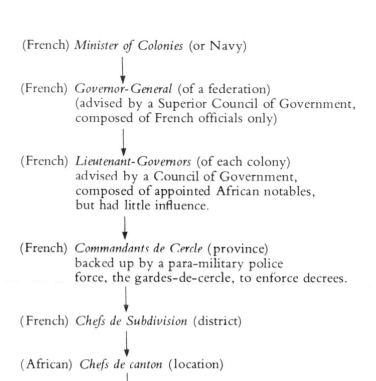

(French) *Minister of Colonies* (or Navy)

(French) *Governor-General* (of a federation)
(advised by a Superior Council of Government,
composed of French officials only)

(French) *Lieutenant-Governors* (of each colony)
advised by a Council of Government,
composed of appointed African notables,
but had little influence.

(French) *Commandants de Cercle* (province)
backed up by a para-military police
force, the gardes-de-cercle, to enforce decrees.

(French) *Chefs de Subdivision* (district)

(African) *Chefs de canton* (location)

(African) *Chefs de village* (sub location)

The British generally built their administration on indigenous
political institutions, though they were not always successful, most
notably in south-eastern Nigeria, and they were more responsive to
local situations than were the French. The French were more logical
and consistent than the empirical and pragmatic British, but they
were less successful in keeping their colonial subjects under control.
There were far more armed rebellions in French West Africa than in
British West Africa, especially in the First World War, when
hundreds of thousands rose up against the hated *indigenat* and
military recruitment. There were even protest migrations from
French West Africa to British territories, to escape the harsher French
rule. Africans migrated from French Dahomey to British Nigeria,
from French Ivory Coast to British Gold Coast, from French
Senegal to British Gambia, and from French Guinea to British Sierra
Leone and even to Portuguese Guinea.

The French reduced traditional slavery but introduced a new form
of slavery on a massive scale: forced labour (see page 120). Forced
labour was commonly used by French administrators. General
Gallieni created *villages de liberté* in 1887. Freed slaves were settled in
them, but they were made to work for the French administration and

army. Forced labour was then extended from the 'villages of liberty' to all villages in French Africa.

British colonial administration in Nigeria

A study of British administration reveals not only the strengths and weaknesses of indirect rule, but also the marked differences between the French and British use of traditional African authorities. While the French generally undermined traditional rule and had little time for indigenous chiefs the British determined to rule through traditional channels as the Foreign Office's 1891 instructions to Sir Claude MacDonald, Commissioner and Consul-General of the newly-created Oil Rivers Protectorate clearly shows.

> It is not advisable that you should interfere unduly with tribal government; the chiefs should continue to rule their own subjects and to administer justice to them; but you should keep a constant watch so as to prevent injustice and check abuses, making the chiefs understand that their powers will be forfeited by misgovernment... You should be careful, however, not to arouse discontent by attempting too abrupt reform.

(From: C. W. Newbury, *British Policy towards West Africa. Select Documents 1875–1914*; Oxford, 1971, page 263.)

There were fundamental differences between British indirect rule and French 'association'.

South-east Nigeria

In 1891 Macdonald introduced a *warrant chief* system in the Niger delta and the system was later applied to Igboland as it was gradually occupied by Britain. The authority of warrant chiefs derived from the *Warrant* or certificate of recognition given to them by the colonial government. Macdonald and his successors, Sir Ralph Moor and Sir Walter Egerton, built up the warrant chief system as a system of indirect rule. However, the warrant chief system was a notorious failure because indirect rule could not be built successfully upon the types of government of the south-east Nigerian peoples. In the village republics of central Igboland, the city-states of the Niger and Cross River deltas, and amongst the riverain Igbo political authority was widely decentralized among lineages, age grade, secret and title societies, and diviners. There were no 'chiefs' of either villages or clans. There were village councils but generally no centralized political institutions for a clan although there were a few exceptions.

The Aro clan of the Igbo had a general council of its village-groups, but the Aro council was only a council. There was no single Aro leader and no bureaucracy. Heads of Igbo, Ibibio and Ijo lineages presided over lineage or village councils, but they were arbitrators, not executives. Legislative, executive and judicial functions could only be carried out by the whole council. Even the riverain Igbo states and the delta states, which had more centralized political institutions, were unsuitable for an experiment in indirect rule. The rulers of these states were not autocrats. Amongst the riverain Igbo, the Obi of Onitsha was a chairman of the general assembly, a kind of Speaker of the Assembly, with little more than ceremonial functions to perform. The househeads in the delta states were not autocrats. Househeads, apart from the founders, were democratically elected and could be democratically deposed.

Not surprisingly, the British experienced great difficulties in appointing warrant chiefs. Some of the appointees were court clerks and messengers, who had been to mission primary schools and become literate in English, but whose family origin or personal character made them totally unsuitable. Many were appointed because they had served the British in some capacity, perhaps as guides. Others were chosen simply by accident, because they were picked out from a crowd of elders by a British officer. For example at Oraukwu in Onitsha a British officer is said to have surveyed the assembly and called out two brothers who were 'huge and person-able' and who had brought chairs to sit on while others were either standing or sitting on the ground. The British set up councils of chiefs, most of whom were not even village heads. Those who were village heads were often given authority over villages where traditionally they had no authority at all. In cases where the people were allowed by the British to elect warrant chiefs they very rarely elected traditional leaders. Rather, they elected men with some western education who could stand up to the harassment and corruption of certain clerks in the Native Courts, who often abused their position by making false arrests and extorting bribes from people.

Only a system of democratically elected councils could have provided a sound basis for colonial administration in south-east Nigeria. However, although this was suggested by some farsighted colonial officers, it was too progressive an idea for an early colonial regime. Lugard made the warrant system worse when he tried to strengthen it after he became Governor-General of Nigeria in 1912. Instead of scrapping the system he tried to bring the south into line with the indirect rule system in Northern Nigeria and establish uniformity in 'Native administration' throughout Nigeria. Lugard's 1914 Ordinance sought to model Southern Nigeria on the adminis-trative system of Northern Nigeria, where local conditions were markedly different.

Yorubaland

Indirect rule was applied with some success in Yorubaland. The Yoruba had well-developed kingship and chieftaincy institutions on which the British could build a system of indirect rule. The basis of the system was the protectorate treaties of 1893 with the traditional Yoruba rulers, the councils of chiefs set up in the late 1890s and the sub-imperialism of successive Alafins of Oyo.

The protectorate treaties gave the British residents little more than consular powers. The residents were able to play a greater role in pushing political, economic and social innovation after the setting up of councils for Ibadan in 1897, Oyo in 1898 and Ilesha and Ekiti in 1900. The councils were presided over, before 1901, by the residents and after 1901 by the paramount rulers, Council members were the traditional ministers and clan-heads of the paramount ruler. For example, the Alafin or his chief palace official presided over the Oyo council and the members were mainly the Alafin's traditional councillors. The function of the councils were legislative, administrative and sometimes judicial. Council members ensured that new laws were carried out. Cases were heard, though largely by the resident. The resident's other duties were settling disputes between chiefs and making tours of inspection to ensure loyalty; but it is remarkable how much he left in the hands of the council.

The councils in Yorubaland were certainly not rubber stamps for the British. Ibadan council debated the abolition of tolls for three years, from 1903 to 1906, before it agreed on the measure, but then only on the understanding that the Lagos government would provide compensation. When the British Cotton Growing Association requested a grant of 15,000 acres of land to establish cotton plantations the council gave it only 5,000 under difficult terms and the grant was not taken up. Thus Ibadan council successfully defended the position of its peasant producers.

The British allowed so much latitude to traditional political leadership in Yorubaland that they made some rulers more powerful than they had been in the pre-colonial era. In Western Yorubaland, for example, a number of *oba* and *bale* who held minor positions in pre-colonial times were elevated to the ranks of crowned oba, and gained wider powers and larger areas of jurisdiction. These men were masters of 'survival politics' and were appointed because they were pro-British. Yet the real experts in survival politics were the alafins of New Oyo in central Yorubaland.

In 1895 Oyo had been bombarded by a British force in order to encourage the alafin to accept British sovereignty less grudgingly than he had been doing. Thereafter Alafin Adeyemi changed his policy. He decided to cooperate with the British in order to win control over lesser chiefs. Lawani succeded his father as alafin when Adeyemi died in 1905. During his reign Captain Ross arrived as the first district commissioner in Oyo, in 1906. Ross, who served in Oyo for the next twenty five years, was a strong supporter of the alafin's authority and of Oyo sub-imperialism. In 1909 Ross gave full backing to Lawani when the alafin expelled the American Baptist missionary, Pinnock, who had preached against the alafin's 'oppression'. It was significant that not even such a man could challenge the alafin's authority. However, it was during the reign of Lawani's son, Siyanbola Ladugbolu (1911–4) that the alafin's supremacy over other paramount rulers was achieved. When in 1912 the Bale of Ibadan died, the popular and favourite candidate was Situ, the army commander, but Ross arranged for the alafin to appoint the candidate. Ladugbolu selected Situ's rival, Irefin, thus asserting Oyo sub-imperialism over Ibadan.

Northern Nigeria

The classical system of indirect rule, which Lugard described fully in his book *The Dual Mandate in Tropical Africa* (1922), was the system Lugard and others applied in Northern Nigeria. Lugard had insufficient men and money to administer the vast new Protectorate, established by Britain in Northern Nigeria, but the Fulani emirs possessed large numbers of trained and experienced officials for the administration of justice, the maintenance of order and the collection of taxes. Therefore Lugard enlisted the emirs as partners in government, but there was no question that the British were senior partners. The emirs were allowed to rule the people, but they were under the supervision of British residents attached to their courts, and the residents took their orders from the High Commissioner (later Governor). The Empire of Sokoto was destroyed as the Emir of Gwandu and the Sultan of Sokoto were reduced from the status of paramount rulers to that of provincial rulers like the other emirs. They could no longer receive tribute from other emirs or play a part in their selection. The High Commissioner assumed these functions.

Lugard favoured indirect rule of an interventionist nature, to prevent stagnation in the emirates. The status of slavery was abolished. Christian missions and mission schools were established, though Koranic laws and Islam were not interfered with. The complicated Fulani system of taxation was replaced by a single tax levied on each village. Although taxes were collected by the emir's officers and were paid into the emir's treasuries, a fixed proportion of their revenues was transfered to the central British administration and used to finance services like health, agriculture and railways. There were careful checks on the emir's spending. A system of Native Treasuries for the emirates, with preparation of proper budgets and checking by residents, was set up. To avoid or reduce extortion regular salaries were paid to emirs and other members of Native Authorities.

Lugard has been blamed unfairly for encouraging conservative tendencies in Northern Nigeria. On the contrary, he hoped that traditional rulers and society in the north would constantly adapt to modern change. His successors in Northern Nigeria, Girouard and Bell, favoured non-interventionist indirect rule. When Northern and Southern Nigeria were amalgamated in 1914 Lugard hoped unification would help modernization in the north as southern port customs revenues would provide more funds for the north's development. He even wanted to include the emirs' budgets in the General Budget of Nigeria; but he was opposed by Governor Temple of Northern Nigeria who feared such a measure would lessen the emirs' autonomy. Lugard did not get his way. In the inter-war period the emirs became increasingly dictatorial as the residents intervened rarely in the emirs' rule. The northern Nigerian emirates opposed modernization or progress of any kind—political, economic or social. Nigeria became increasingly polarized between a progressive south and backward north. Moreover, the system of government favoured such a polarization. The amalgamation of 1914 created a colonial federation of two largely separate territories. There was a Governor-General in Lagos but also a Lieutenant-Governor for Northern Nigeria in Kaduna and a Lieutenant-Governor for Southern Nigeria in Enugu. Many government departments were not centralized. This division of north and south Nigeria in colonial administration proved to be a crucial factor leading to and encouraging separatism in later Nigerian politics.

British administration in Sierra Leone

The replacement of Creoles in the administration of Sierra Leone after the war of 1898 marked the end of Anglo-Creole partnership in government, business and missionary enterprise in West Africa. Governor Cardew blamed the outbreak of the Temne-Mende War of Independence, not on the hut tax and extortion by colonial chiefs, but on the Creoles who had warned him that revolt might follow a hut tax. After the war Creoles were kept out of the interior or protectorate administration so that they could not influence interior communities with radical western ideas like representative government. In the colonial administration, Creoles were replaced on their death or retirement by whites. In 1892 as many as 50% of senior civil service posts were held by Creoles, but by 1917 the proportion had fallen to only 10%. Cardew's policy became general throughout British West Africa. In 1902 African doctors (almost all of them Creoles) were excluded from government medical service. By 1911 there was not one Creole left in the judiciary or executive council of any British West African colony.

In the interior the chiefs collected and handed over to the government the hut tax. Apart from this the chiefs ruled in the traditional manner and relied on income, such as tribute, from traditional sources. In practice, therefore, the protectorate government was a very loose form of indirect rule. A clear system of indirect rule on the Nigerian model, with Native Treasuries in the Mende and Temne chiefdoms, was not introduced until 1937.

British administration in East Africa

Uganda

Lugard, the first British administrator in Buganda, favoured the introduction of indirect rule in Uganda. By 'Uganda' Lugard meant 'Buganda'. He recognized the role of the kabaka and his chiefs in the new protectorate. Later administrators, like Special Commissioner Sir Harry Johnston in the famous 1900 Buganda Agreement, confirmed and defined the functions of the traditional Baganda rulers within Buganda. Yet in the end, indirect rule was not implemented in Uganda, either in Buganda or in the non-Ganda areas ruled for the British by Baganda agents. The fact that the agents of the British were not white does not necessarily mean that the British practised indirect rule in Uganda. The colour of the colonial administrators was less important than the nature of their powers and functions and the work they did.

The basis of British administration within Buganda was the 1900 Agreement, which introduced considerable modifications to the traditional Baganda political system. The Agreement strengthened the special position of Buganda within Uganda as a reward for the loyalty of the Christian leaders to Britain. The Baganda were no longer allowed to receive tribute from neighbouring communities, but their gains more than offset their losses. Buganda's recent annexation of several counties from Bunyoro was confirmed. The kabakaship remained and the kabaka retained the power to appoint chiefs. Buganda was given a parliament called the *lukiko*, whose members were the three regents (for the infant Kabaka Daudi Chwa), twenty senior chiefs and sixty-six notables nominated by the kabaka. The lukiko was allowed to spend funds without supervision from the British. No further direct taxation, in addition to the existing hut and gun taxes, was to be imposed on the Baganda without the consent of the kabaka and the lukiko.

It should be noted, however, that these measures did not amount to autonomy for Buganda. The kabaka's powers were considerably weakened. He was deprived of his main sources of income—tribute and taxation—because all tax collected in Buganda was now to be merged with the income of the entire Uganda protectorate. The British had thoroughly subjected the kabaka to themselves by deposing Mwanga in 1897 and appointing in his place an infant and three pro-British regents. Moreover, the land tenure reform of the 1900 Agreement destroyed the traditional royal patronage system. In 1919 Daudi Chwa complained that even his own subjects were beginning to regard him as 'merely one of the British government's paid servants'. The lukiko resembled the kabaka's court but it was essentially a British-created institution. Its main function was to control the collection of colonial taxation. It was allowed to forward proposals for the approval of the kabaka and the British commissioner, but the commissioner could veto any proposals. The British had decided to use the well-organized traditional administration of Buganda rather than introduce expensive British administration; yet Buganda was to be simply one province of the British Protectorate of Uganda, subject like other provinces to the laws which the British made for the whole protectorate.

The real beneficiaries of the 1900 Agreement were neither the kabaka nor the traditional *bataka* clan-chiefs whose influence was reduced, but the pro-British Christian *bakungu* hierarchy of the *saza* (county) chiefs who had risen to prominence in the late pre-colonial period. Moreover, the bakungu chiefs after 1900 served not as old-style client-chiefs of the kabaka but as new-style British administrators. In other words, the British did not so much use the Baganda traditional power structure as reorganize it to suit their purposes.

The land tenure reform in the 1900 Agreement provided for all occupied land to be granted to the occupier in *freehold*. Freehold was a European concept. Formerly the kabaka had disposed of land which in fact was owned by the community. Now the occupied land became freehold. The Christian bakungu chiefs benefited most from the distribution of *mailo* estates of freehold land, mainly because they had the pleasant job of distributing it. Naturally the kabaka got a large share, though he could no longer distribute it as patronage. The land reform was a practical demonstration of Britain's alliance with the dominant political group in Buganda, the Christian bakungu chiefs, who were dependent on Britain in order to retain effective control of the government against rivalry from the kabaka and bataka clan-chiefs. Peasants on the mailo land now became tenants of the bakungu chiefs; thus the political power of the latter was strengthened, because they could evict tenants for political dissent. Unoccupied land became Crown land and could be distributed in any way the British administration thought fit. Much of it was made available for peasants to buy, and thousands of ordinary Baganda thus gained new, freer status. At the same time the bataka clan-chiefs lost many workers, clients and tribute-payers.

To sum up, the 1900 Agreement assured the ascendancy of Apolo Kagwa's Protestant party and completed the Christian revolution in Buganda's politics that began in 1887. The Agreement was a blow to the traditional political forces in Baganda.

The Baganda were used as colonial agents in Bunyoro, Busoga, Bukedi, Bugisu and almost all of Uganda by the British. Baganda agents were used by the British because the often segmentary societies surrounding Buganda, like the Nilotic communities of the north and the Kiga of Kigezi, had few or no political leaders resembling chiefs and no centralized political institutions. Even in Bunyoro where chiefs and centralization did exist, the British employed the Muganda agent Jemusi Miti as administrator because of Banyoro hostility to the colonial regime and the refusal of most of their chiefs to cooperate with colonialism. Men like Miti gathered tax and recruited forced labour for the British though Banyoro were sometimes used as forced labour for Baganda settlers in the disputed counties. Men like Semei Kakungulu actually carried out colonial conquest for Britain (in east Uganda). Thus Baganda agents were used by the British administration in newly occupied areas. Over each Muganda agent there was a superior British officer. The British fairly quickly replaced the Baganda agents when the local people were considered to be ready to replace them. In some cases they were replaced when the local people showed persistent resistance to them and the British wanted to avoid an armed revolt. An example of this was seen in Bunyoro after the Kyanyangire passive resistance in 1907 (see Chapter 9).

The various kings of Uganda such as those in Toro and Ankole who signed protection treaties with the British, had no real power under the colonial regime. On one occasion King Kasagama of Toro was fined a thousand shillings and forced to write an apology and show public humility for organizing the sending of an 'impertinent' letter to a European provincial commissioner. In these 'special status' kingdoms the traditional rulers possessed only ceremonial privileges.

The bakungu chiefs in Buganda and the Baganda agents in the rest of Uganda were not avaricious men who threw in their lot with the British for the sake of loot, nor were they simply Christians who identified their future with the fortunes of their white co-religionists. There was a positive side to the work of the Baganda chiefs of the early colonial period as they introduced schools, enforced progressive measures like campaigning against sleeping sickness, by moving people from the lake shore, saving the quality of the embryonic Uganda cotton crop by decisive action, and spreading new crops around the country (like bananas, coffee and Irish potatoes in

Kigezi). The Baganda chiefs at this time were instruments of progress, and the British were fortunate in having such an able group of men to work for them.

Kenya

The British had to create chiefs throughout Kenya, except in Wanga, where Nabongo Mumia was king. The British turned Mumia's tiny local state into a regional one by inventing Wanga sub-imperialism and using Wanga men as colonial agents throughout Buluyia and in parts of Luo country. Elsewhere in Kenya the British appointed as chiefs outstanding individuals who had no traditional authority over their people.

Mumia had been an ally of Britain in establishing colonial rule in western Kenya. Between about 1904 and 1927 he was the virtual ruler of North Nyanza District. Wanga agents throughout the district owed their appointment to Mumia and were either his relations or his followers. In 1909 Mumia was appointed Paramount Chief of North Nyanza as a reward for his colonial service. The position was not a traditional one, because only a small area of Buluyia had been tributary to Wanga. Mumia's authority really rested on two of his responsibilities: he was appeal judge in all 'native cases', and had power to settle boundary disputes. Ultimately, however, the Wanga agent system failed, because after the First World War there was a reaction by subject peoples and by 'mission boys' who wanted their own men as chiefs. Wanga men were gradually replaced, as the Baganda were in Bunyoro.

In Ukambani the British soon realized the pitfalls of appointing as chiefs men who, in a chiefless society, made up the rules as they went along. The first Kamba colonial chiefs looked on their work as an opportunity to amass wealth. They were paid commission on any amount of tax they collected, and often collected more than they should have done. Chiefs' courts were established in Ukambani in 1908. The chiefs set their own scale of fees. In imitation of the European magistrates' courts they imposed fines of livestock, but they usually kept the animals for their personal use, not for the government. Two Kamba government chiefs who did particularly well out of their duties between 1900 and 1910 were Musau wa Mwanza who in the period built up a herd of 8,000 cattle and Nthiwa wa Tama who acquired fifteen wives.

K. R. Dundas, a reforming district commissioner, was so appalled at the corruption in the Kamba chiefs' courts that in 1910–11 he utilized the traditional *nzama* or councils of elders as courts. He hoped to strengthen genuine traditional institutions in a chiefless society. This was a rare experiment in British colonial Africa. But it failed for the obvious reason that it was impossible to graft colonial laws and practices onto a traditional democratic institution. The elders were very reluctant to impose unpopular colonial measures such as handing over tax defaulters to the white man and sending young men to work outside Ukambani. Nor were they prepared to abandon the spirit and practice of customary law, with its emphasis on reconciliation and compensation in 'criminal' cases, in favour of the fines and imprisonment which the British administration demanded in such cases. Many elders refused to attend meetings of the nzama under the new dispensation. In any case, Dundas' enthusiasm for traditional African institutions and practices soon brought him into disrepute with the local white settlers and his official superiors, who 'exiled' him to be in charge of Kismayu in Somali country.

Elsewhere in Kenya the British had more success in finding outstanding individuals who could serve as chiefs; but they never really found men who were fully subservient. Karuri wa Gakure of Kikuyuland is a case in point. Karuri was born in about 1849. He was not a Kikuyu but a Dorobo, but he rose to power in Kikuyuland as a result of his skill in divination, his trade with the Swahili and his alliance with the European trader, John Boyes, who supplied him with guns and ammunition. In 1900 Karuri became a colonial chief in his home area. He helped the British conquer the surrounding Kikuyu areas, and in 1912 he was appointed Paramount Chief of the northern Kikuyu land unit. Karuri was illiterate but he saw the need for progress. He was an efficient tax collector and helped in the building of roads, bridges, schools and a factory. He was not a collaborator. In 1910 he led protests at land alienation and succeeded in restricting European settlement to the area east of Fort Hall (Muranga town).

British administration in Central and Southern Africa

The Lozi

The British South Africa Company was initially given a charter to rule Northern (Zambia) and Southern (Zimbabwe) Rhodesia on behalf of the British government. Its administration in Northern Rhodesia was relatively weak because of lack of manpower and because it was grossly underfinanced. Therefore in the western part of the country the Company needed King Lewanika and his Lozi chiefs as allies in the task of administration. Consequently the Lozi were used as sub-imperialists over neighbouring African communities, as the Fulani emirs, the Alafin of Oyo, the Baganda and the Wanga were used elsewhere in British Africa.

In 1897 Robert Coryndon arrived as the Company's first Resident in Barotseland (Bulozi) and in 1900 a final treaty was signed between Lewanika and the Company. The treaty allowed the Company to exercise only limited authority in central Barotseland. But Lewanika was granted general administrative powers throughout the rest of the British territory as far east as the Kafue River, and was recognized as Barotse Paramount Chief. The Company was allowed to make land grants to white settlers in Ila and Tonga country, parts of which had been under Lozi rule; but the centre of Barotseland was closed to white settlers and prospectors alike. The 1900 treaty limited the British South Africa Company's authority in a way which existed nowhere else.

The result of the 1900 treaty was that although Lewanika's country was in practice much reduced, the Lozi system of government continued to function more or less independently. Lozi chiefs had to collect taxes for the Company but they received a fixed percentage of the taxes for their own use. However, by the time he died in 1916 Lewanika had became extremely discontented at the steady European encroachment on his power. For example, in 1905 the scope of Lozi criminal jurisdiction was greatly reduced. Also, many former subject chiefs stopped sending annual tribute to Lewanika. As early as 1900, Chief Monge had declared, 'Why should I pay tribute when I am under the White Queen?' Indirect rule gradually gave way to direct Company rule as Lewanika's authority declined.

Khama

In the Bechuanaland Protectorate indirect rule was employed at first. In 1885 Sidney Shippard, a Cape Colony judge, was appointed Resident Commissioner. Shippard did not interfere with Khama's rule of the Ngwato or the rule of the other Tswana communities by their rulers. But something approaching direct rule was established by the 1891 Order in Council which set up full-scale British administration with assistant resident commissioners, magistrates, police officers, courts of law, and so on. Since European courts could hear purely African cases the British government had almost complete powers of administration and legislation, but in practice after 1891 Khama still ruled in the traditional manner. Technically he was a colonial chief under direct rule. Yet right up to his death in 1923 Khama was in reality a king. He saw himself not as a colonial administrator but as an independent ruler in alliance with the British government which not only protected the Ngwato from the Boers and the British South Africa Company, but also helped him against his traditional internal rivals. The European administrators allowed Khama to conduct himself as an independent ruler because he saw eye to eye with them on most matters. His aim of 'improvement'—

the spread of Christianity and the development of agriculture and trade—was identical with theirs.

Khama actually increased the power of the Ngwato monarchy in the community by using British officials in his struggle against internal rivals. When his ambitious son Sekhoma tried to get Khama to retire as chief and give way to him in 1898, Khama had him exiled until 1921, when he held his 50-year jubilee. Many lesser chiefs or headmen opposed Khama's westernizing innovations, so he placed control over the various territorial districts in the hands of either local non-Ngwato headmen on whom he could rely, or men sent directly from his capital. Khama resembled the centralizing autocrats of the period of the Mfecane, rather than a colonial chief.

South Africa: Afrikaner self-government and the Union

In the Second Anglo-Boer War Britain inflicted a military defeat on the Afrikaners (Boers). British troops occupied the Afrikaner republics of the Orange Free State and the Transvaal. But in a breathtaking political reversal, within a few years the Afrikaners were self-governing once again and in political control of the whole of South Africa.

The War of 1899–1902 destroyed the Afrikaner republics. At the end of the war the British High Commissioner, Milner, tried to destroy the Afrikaner identity through his education programme. He ordered mass schooling for the ill-educated Afrikaner children in government schools where English was the medium of instruction. The Afrikaners had been divided at the end of the war into *Bittereinders* (bitter-ends who opposed surrender) and *Hensoppers* (hands-uppers who had surrendered), but Milner's education programme reunited them. The Afrikaners were also roused by the importation of Chinese workmen to work in the mines on the Rand, and the fear they would be 'swamped' by a large Asian population.

By a quirk of fate the Afrikaners were saved by a dramatic change in British politics. At the end of 1905 the Conservative government gave way to a Liberal government in Britain and in 1906 the Liberals won a general election with a huge majority. Liberal policy was to conciliate the Afrikaners and to enlist their cooperation in creating a united, self-governing pro-British South Africa. In 1906 the Liberals granted responsible self-government with dominion status to the whites of the ex-Afrikaner republics. Then in 1907–8 the Afrikaners won by election what they had lost on the battlefield: control of the political future of South Africa. Afrikaner nationalist parties won the whites-only polls in the Transvaal in 1907 and the Orange River

Colony in 1908. In the Transvaal the victorious party was *Het Volk* (or 'People's Union') led by ex-generals Louis Botha, a farmer, and Jan Christian Smuts, a lawyer. The Afrikaners had been expected to lose the Transvaal election but it was found that *Uitlanders* (non-Afrikaner whites on the Rand) did not outnumber the Afrikaners. The numbers of Afrikaners and uitlanders were about equal, but Het Volk won easily because the uitlander vote was split between three rival parties. In the Orange River Colony the victors were *Orangie Unie* (or 'Orange Unity') led by Fischer and Hertzog. After the 1908 election in Cape Colony a pro-Afrikaner government representing the *Afrikaner Bond* was set up, though the Prime Minister was the English-speaking John X. Merriman. Only in Natal, where few Afrikaners lived, did English-speaking whites remain in power. The Afrikaners, dominating three of the four white self-governing colonies in South Africa, were now ready to cooperate with the Liberal government in Britain to create a Union of South Africa, because they felt confident they could dominate such a Union.

In 1908–9 a National Convention at which only whites were represented was held to draw up a draft constitution for the Union. The Afrikaners won several major victories at the Convention. The non-white franchise in the Cape was restricted to the Cape. The Afrikaners of the High Veld ensured agreement on this restriction by allying with the extremist English-speaking Natal settlers against the white liberals of the Cape. The white settlers of Natal, the Orange Free State and the Transvaal believed Africans could never attain the level of white 'civilization' and insisted on totally separate political, economic and social arrangements for whites and blacks. Secondly, the Convention agreed that no non-white could be elected from the Cape to the Union parliament. Thirdly, the franchise for Union elections was weighted in favour of rural constituencies, an arrangement which favoured the rural Afrikaners over the urban English-speakers. Fourthly, the Afrikaners ensured a strong unitary constitution instead of a loose federal one: a strong Union would help to cement white unity against the blacks and would make it easier for the central government to act more promptly and effectively in suppressing African risings like the recent revolt by Bambata in Zululand. The British government also favoured a strong unitary government in South Africa that would relieve it of the burden of sending imperial troops to suppress African risings.

African protests against the draft Constitution were ineffective and unavailing. However, a small number of western-educated Africans did manage to establish the South African Native National Congress and stir up the beginnings of modern African nationalism in South Africa.

The early years of the Union, from 1910 to 1914, were crucial in the establishment of Afrikaner political control of South Africa. Afrikaner political unity was in sharp contrast to the political disun-

ity of the English-speakers. The separate provincial Afrikaner political parties (Het Volk, Orangie Unie and the South African Party in
the Cape) united as the South African National Party, which formed
the first government of the Union in 1910. The SANP's leader,
Louis Botha, became the Union's first prime minister. The English-
speaking community in contrast, was split into three mutually an-
tagonistic political groupings, based on rivalry between the Cape
and Natal and rivalry between the employers and labour. The Prog-
ressives of the Cape, led by Jameson, formed the nucleus of the later
Unionist Party. The Natal settlers were generally hostile to the idea
of Cape domination of English-speaking politics. Two of their
Union parliament members joined Botha's Cabinet, only four
joined the Unionists, and the majority remained Independents.
There was also the Labour Party of English-speaking artisans, led by
Colonel Creswell. It refused to cooperate with the Unionist Party,
which was seen as the party of employers. To Africans these quarrels
between Europeans seemed irrelevant. However, the objective conditions which would enable Africans to make effective protest
against white supremacy had not yet come into being. The black elite
was still too small and the black urban proletariat was still in the
making.

German rule

Germany's approach to the administration of her colonies was essentially pragmatic. In Togo the Germans used local chiefs and headmen
as the agents of their rule. The problems faced by the Germans were
similar to the problems faced by Britain in eastern Nigeria: there
were no real district chiefs and political authority was highly fragmented. In areas such as the Lome district the Germans imposed
artificial chiefs on the people and gave them greater power than had
been enjoyed by anyone in the pre-colonial era. They collected taxes,
provided labour for the roads and exercised judicial power in petty
civil cases. On the whole the Germans encouraged the continuation
of the existing system of local justice in civil cases. However, cases
involving educated Africans or Europeans as well as all criminal
cases were heard by the local administrative officer. It was possible to
appeal to the German administrator from the local courts but the
administrator often had great difficulties in understanding the in-
tricacies of local law. At the beginning of the twentieth century the
administration commissioned a study of local Ewe law with the hope
that it could be codified. This was the first attempt in the colonial era
to codify local law but the new code was never issued as the Germans
were ejected from Togo in the First World War.

The same pragmatic approach to administration can be seen
in East Africa. Throughout most of Tanganyika the Germans em-

ployed literate Swahili-Arab akidas and jumbes for the collection of taxes and the recruitment of labour. Needless to say, many societies objected strongly to the imposition of Swahili-Arabs and it was one of the factors in the outbreak of the Maji Maji uprising. In the west of the country, however, in what is now Ruanda and Burundi, indirect rule was applied as there already existed in those areas an indigenous centralized system of government. Direct rule was also applied in South West Africa although Germany did recognize a number of chiefs and attempted to use them to spread German rule. As in Togo chiefs were given positions which they had not enjoyed in the pre-colonial era. The recognition of paramount chiefs for the Herero and Nama are clear examples: neither of these societies had been ruled by paramount chiefs before the arrival of the Germans.

The Congo Free State

The Congo (now Zaire) was totally different to the other European colonies in Africa in that it was the personal possession of one man. Leopold attempted to supervise every detail of the Congo administration but in practice this was impossible. However, what did develop was a highly centralized system of government. The central government of the colony was in Belgium where all major decisions were taken. In the Congo itself was a Governor-General, who was assisted by a vice-Governor General, four directors in charge of different government departments and a Commander-in-Chief of the *Force Publique* (the local army). Eventually the colony was divided into fourteen districts, each with a commissioner, and the districts were subdivided into zones, *secteurs* and *postes*. All decisions had to be referred to a higher official: 'an arrangement ideally contrived to multiply correspondence and to paralyse effective action (Ruth Slade).

The greatest criticism of Leopold's administrative system can be made over his decision to use as state officials men who were employees of concessionary companies. These men, on the one hand, were supposed to investigate cases of exploitation and ill-treatment of Africans by commercial companies on behalf of the government while, on the other hand, as employees of a concessionary company, they needed to obtain maximum output from Africans. Inevitably in this situation exploitation was more important than protection, particularly as the company employees were paid on the basis of their production of rubber, ivory or some other raw material. In the eastern Congo Leopold even came to an agreement with Tippu Tip which made the Arab slave and ivory-trader the Governor of Stanley Pool. In 1891 the government signed a contract with Tippu Tip for the provision of 2,600 men to work on the Lower Congo Railway. They were supposed to be free labourers but in reality the Congo government had become involved in the slave trade. It is hardly surprising that the legal system, which in theory was set up, never really functioned and that, in practice, any European-administered corporal punishment to Africans as he felt fit. In many cases the punishments administered were most brutal and as we shall see in Chapter 7 provoked massive criticism from missionaries working in the Congo Free State.

As we end this chapter, one thing is quite clear. Whatever the theory of government applied to their colonies by the European administrators, all of them were determined to make the administration pay for itself within a short period of time. It is equally clear that theories rapidly gave way to the reality of ruling huge areas with relatively few expatriate officials. Africans were involved in one way or another in the administration of the new European colonies even though they were not a part of the political decision-making process.

7
The colonial economy

Overview

It is impossible to generalize satisfactorily about the effects of the colonial economy on Africa. Did expanded European economic enterprise between 1885 and 1914 lead to the development or the exploitation of Africa? Answers to this question have usually been given on a political rather than an economic basis. Two points are, however, fairly clear. First, both economic growth and exploitation took place in the African colonial economy, not just in the continent as a whole or even within the same region but even in the same locality. It is important to distinguish between widely varying regional and sub-regional patterns of growth and exploitation. For example, Elizabeth Isichei has shown that within south-eastern Nigeria, while the expansion of European trading firms into the interior ruined the delta middleman traders, and the men of Arochukwu suffered economically from the destruction of their oracle by the British army, new colonial administrative towns like Aba and Owerri were presented with new economic opportunities. Secondly, many areas of Africa were left untouched by the new colonial economy. They remained firmly within the orbit of traditional low-productivity local economies for a long time after the establishment of colonial rule, and even throughout the colonial period. However, this kind of lack of development is not necessarily the same thing as exploitation. Modern development often went hand in hand with exploitation. Railways, for example, helped economic growth because they made it easier to export cash crops and minerals and reduced transport costs. For instance, a head load from the coast of Ghana to Kumasi which had cost 26s. 6d. cost only four shillings by rail. Yet the railways also assisted exploitation because they allowed European cotton goods and iron tools to be sold in the interior much more cheaply than those of African manufacture and many African craftsmen, especially weavers and blacksmiths, lost their livelihood.

It has often been claimed that Europe exploited Africa by deliberately failing to industrialize the continent. However, in reality, there were a number of powerful factors which prevented industrialization including a lack of local capital and skills, low local incomes to buy goods and an undeveloped infrastructure. Africa could only industrialize after expanding its domestic market and purchasing power: this it could do after first supplying the world market with agricultural produce and other raw materials. European businessmen were not bound in any conspiracy to prevent Africa from industrializing: they were concerned with making profits. Once local incomes rose and the infrastructure was developed they were quite prepared to industrialize Africa. Before the First World War local economic factors did not encourage such developments.

It is proposed in this chapter to examine economic growth and exploitation in the colonial economy with reference to regional and territorial case-studies.

The colonial economy in West Africa: a general regional survey

A. G. Hopkins, in *An Economic History of West Africa* (1973) has shown that colonialism brought impressive economic growth in West Africa. There was 'substantial growth in the value and volume of overseas trade'; and in 'colonies which developed export crops . . . there was a rise in both living standards and in government revenue for the development of ports, railways, roads and education'.

In the period between 1900 and 1913 West Africa pulled out of the late nineteenth century economic slump (the worldwide Great Depression of 1875–1900). The main consequences of this trend were the easier financing of development projects, like railways that were essential to economic growth, and the encouragement it gave to more Africans to enter the export market. During this period both expatriates and Africans were involved in the development of the transport network, the distributive system, and money and banking, while the Africans made major contributions to increased production.

Colonial economic policy before 1914 was underdeveloped. Joseph Chamberlain did talk about developing the tropical estates of the British empire, but before 1914 there was little expenditure except on railways. West African colonial governments before 1914 were too busy with 'pacification' to begin to concentrate on more positive activities.

The period from 1880 to 1914 was the great age of railway building in West Africa. The railways of West Africa were built primarily to facilitate the export of cash crops and minerals. No clearer evidence of this can be found than in German Togo where the lines were actually named after the products they were built to carry: iron line, palm-oil line, cotton line and coconut line. In the Gold Coast the railway helped to stimulate cocoa production; in Northern Nigeria it was groundnuts. Strategic considerations entered into the decision to build as did administrative convenience, but these were not generally of prime importance in West Africa. Builders were, however, determined that the railways of one colony should never join to those of the colony of a rival European power. The result was a variety of different gauges which have made it impossible to develop an integrated railway system for West Africa.

The Senegal railway was begun in 1881 (and finally joined to Bamako in 1923). In the Gold Coast the Sekondi-Kumasi line was completed in 1903. In Nigeria the railway moved inland from Lagos in 1896 and reached Kano, 711 miles away, in 1911. The Freetown-Pendembu line in Sierra Leone was completed in 1906, the Lome-Atakpame line in Togo in 1913, and the Conakry-Kankan line in Guinea in 1914. From around 1900 West African harbours were substantially modernized and enlarged to enable them to handle the increased volume of produce brought by the railways. However, before 1918 very few all-weather roads were built in West Africa because only slow, expensive and heavy models of the motor-car, a recent invention, were available at the time.

Expatriate commercial houses expanded between 1885 and 1914 and became dominant in the distributive system of West Africa. They soon began to amalgamate into sizeable companies that could defeat competitors, like the *Compagnie Française de l'Afrique Occidentale* (CFAO) founded in 1887. The Niger Company lost its royal charter in 1900 but continued to trade on a large scale, until it was bought by W. H. Lever in 1920. The advantages of creating larger firms were numerous. They could more easily establish branches in the interior, finance stocks over a long period, withstand sudden fluctuations in trade and buy more cheaply by placing bulk orders. But did the large European firms exploit Africans? And did they curb African enterprise?

European firms did exploit Africa and Africans in a number of ways. They transferred abroad a large proportion of their trading profits and expatriate salaries instead of investing the money in West Africa. They paid low prices to African producers and low wages to their African workers, and they charged high prices for imported consumer goods. They curbed African enterprise inasmuch as they trained very few Africans for responsible positions and many firms trained none at all. On the other hand the large European firms did not destroy the African middleman firms. At the outset of the colonial period outstandingly able African rivals like Jaja and Nana Olomu were removed but in general after 1900 there was actually an increase in the number of African middlemen handling goods for large European firms. Africans as well as expatriates took advantage of the new economic opportunities and the vast increase in trade presented by colonial rule.

African mercantile firms, however, did decline around the turn of the century. The inherent weakness of these firms was the main reason for this. Ineffective accounting, excessive giving of credit, lack of suitable provision for succession on the deaths of owners, and fragmentation of business and property under traditional rules of inheritance, were as important as European price-fixing and high rate-fixing in driving them out of business.

African peasant farming played a major role in the growth of the West African economy up to 1914. Peasant farming was able to cope with major innovations, such as the growing of new crops for export. Surplus land was available and so West Africans did not have to choose between growing new crops and growing essential food. Exports of palm products recovered from the 1880–1900 slump, and expanded after 1900. By 1910 the Gold Coast cocoa industry had become the largest in the world. By 1914 groundnuts had become a very important export from Northern Nigeria.

European plantation agriculture failed to develop in West Africa, except on a small scale in the Ivory Coast and Dahomey and only in any degree of importance in German Cameroons. The reason was not the climate. After 1900 West Africa was no longer the 'White Man's Grave' it had been in the nineteenth century; malaria was under control because of the use of quinine. Moreover, the tropical climate and malaria failed to keep European planters out of the Cameroons, where by 1913 there were 58 plantations covering 75,000 square miles and employing 18,000 Africans, or out of the French Congo or the Belgian Congo. What kept white planters out of West Africa was the success of African peasant producers in developing the production of export crops in the nineteenth century. Existing African enterprise made European enterprise hardly necessary.

A major feature of the early colonial economy in West Africa was the readiness of Africans to migrate vast distances in order to work. Over 4,000 Nigerians went to work on the railways in the Gold Coast in the year 1901 alone. Thousands of Igbo migrated to Fernando Po to work in Spanish plantations. Between 1892 and 1897 over 3,000 Yoruba left for the Congo Free State. The Mossi from the Upper Volta moved south to the cocoa plantations and gold mines of the Ivory Coast and the Gold Coast. Soudanese (Malians) annually travelled to Senegal for seasonal work in the groundnut fields. Each year this export of manpower from Upper Volta and Mali amounted to some one million men. These migrations were not forced nor were they new. They predated the colonial era, though the need to pay tax increased the number of migrants.

In spite of the positive innovation and economic growth in the early colonial period, an essential aspect was forced labour. The colonial authorities immediately abolished the internal slave trade and soon afterwards the status of slave, but they introduced a new kind of slavery: forced labour.

Forced labour was extensively used in the building and maintenance of roads. The French used forced labour to build the Dakar-

Bamako railway and in Nigeria the British employed many forced labourers on railway construction. The French made wide use of forced labour in cultivation of crops on European-owned plantations, such as banana plantations in Guinea and cocoa and coffee plantations in the Ivory Coast. One of the worst examples of forced labour in West Africa was in the Cameroons, where the Germans rounded up men in the high plateau that was free of the malarial mosquito and forced them to work in the mosquito-infested plantations of the lowlands, where 10% of them died of malaria.

The colonial economy in the Gold Coast

The transformation of the Gold Coast's economy between 1890 and 1914 was a success story for African peasant production. At the same time the Gold Coast in this period provides a model example of colonial economic exploitation.

Between 1880 and 1895 the Gold Coast was the world's leading rubber-producing country as peasant farmers cashed in on the world's first rubber boom, which followed the development of the rubber tyre in Europe and North America. Rubber helped to overcome the effects of falling palm oil prices in the late nineteenth century, though it remained second to palm oil in the Gold Coast's exports. In the late 1890s the rapid development of rubber plantations in Malaya and Sumatra caused a sharp decline in the Gold Coast's rubber industry, and the Gold Coast turned to cocoa to maintain its economic growth.

Between 1892 and 1911 exports of cocoa from the Gold Coast grew from nothing to 40,000 tons, making the colony the world's leading cocoa exporter. The colonial government played a part in this achievment by making seeds and plants available, but the real innovators were the cocoa farmers on their smallholdings of one to five acres. The leaders in the cocoa farming revolution were the migrant farmers in the south-east, who began to move in the 1890s from the Akwapim ridge to virgin land in Akim Abuakwa, determined to find a replacement for less profitable palm products. The migrants used their 'traditional' social structure to develop cocoa farming. They utilized long-established patterns of cooperative enterprise to finance the migration and buy land. To start with, the migrants used cheap family labour, but after 1900 turned increasingly to hiring outsiders as labourers. The results of the cocoa farmers' efforts may be summarized in the following table of the value of cocoa exports:

Year	£
1901	43,000
1902	95,000
1907	515,000
1914	2,194,000

Thus the cocoa revolution contributed to substantial economic growth in the Gold Coast. On the debit side, however, was the fixing of cocoa prices at low levels by European combines which controlled the export trade. In 1914 some cocoa farmers held back their crop and demanded higher prices. But the protest was not well organized and failed (though protests in the 1920s and 1930s proved to be more effective). Therefore, much of the profit from cocoa farming was made by a few British businessmen in the export trade who resold the cocoa at disproportionately higher prices in Britain and other parts of Europe. Another weakness in the Gold Coast economy was over-dependence on the cocoa crop.

Gold was another of the natural resources of the Gold Coast that was exploited by expatriates at maximum profit for themselves. The impulse for increased gold production was the extension of the Sekondi railway to Tarkwa in 1901. Growth in the gold trade was considerable, as the following gold export figures show:

Year	£
1897	22,000
1902	97,000
1903	255,000
1907	1,165,000
1914	1,687,000

Europeans benefited far more than Africans from the development of gold mining. The mines passed into European hands and most were consolidated under the Ashanti Goldfields Corporation. The European companies paid their workers very low wages, less than African cocoa farmers paid their workers. Yet the colonial government neither imposed income tax on the companies nor taxed their profits. Not surprisingly, the low wages caused difficulties in recruitment, especially of underground labour. Chiefs in the Northern Territories were ordered to find recruits for mine work, and when men failed to offer themselves the chiefs felt forced reluctantly to select them.

The colonial economy in Nigeria

In Nigeria, as in the Gold Coast and other West African colonies, the period before the First World War saw considerable growth based largely on peasant production of new export crops, alongside European control of the export trade. British rule provided conditions in which farming and trade expanded in the years up to 1914. In Yorubaland a boom in production and trade followed the introduction of peace and the abolition of tolls. Cocoa was first cultivated in Yorubaland in 1899 on an experimental 'model farm' at Ibadan, and its production had become widespread amongst the Yoruba by 1914. The Yoruba farmers became active, too, in cotton production for the British Cotton Growing Association, which set up fifteen buying stations in Yorubaland by 1911. In Igboland, as in Yorubaland, enterprising African traders took advantage of the new economic conditions. For example, Omu Okwei (1872–1943), a prominent woman trader in Onitsha, developed before 1914 a flourishing business selling palm produce to the Niger Company and retailing imported goods. By 1914 she was obtaining credit of up to £400 under the trust system. After 1918 she extended her operations successfully to property, transport and money-lending.

Northern Nigeria also played its part in the enormous export expansion. In 1920 over one million pounds worth of groundnuts were exported, but the foundation of this achievement had been laid before 1914. The railway from Lagos reached Kano in 1911 and as early as 1913, 19,300 tons of groundnuts valued at £175,000 was exported. The British government favoured production of cotton in the north, and tried to persuade the Hausa to grow it in greater quantities. But Hausa farmers and traders preferred groundnuts to cotton. Cotton was less profitable, needed more labour, exhausted the soil more quickly, and, needless to say, could not be eaten during a buying slump.

As in the Gold Coast, mining activity in Nigeria was dominated by expatriates. Coal mines were developed at Enugu in Igboland to provide fuel for the new railways. Labour recruitment resembled forced labour. Before 1914 Igbo warrant chiefs were paid so much for every labourer supplied, so they forced the people to work in the mines. This led to a revolution against the chiefs in the Enugu area in 1914. Many of them were driven out of their towns and the West African Frontier Force was called in to 'restore order'.

The colonial economy in French West Africa

The economies of Senegal and Ivory Coast tended to grow in the same pattern as those of the Gold Coast and Nigeria: agricultural expansion based on innovation by peasant producers. Other areas, in particular Dahomey, were subject to rigid state control of production; consequently there was little room for African initiative as producers or entrepreneurs, and little or no economic growth took place.

In Senegal the production and export of groundnuts continued to rise between 1885 and 1914 at an annual average rate of growth of 8.8%. In 1884–5 export of groundnuts reached 45,000 tons. In good years before 1914 the figure passed 200,000 tons. The original initiative shown by African groundnut producers in the interior from the 1850s was given a boost from the 1880s with the building of the railway, which encouraged an extension of the area of cultivation. The increase in production led to changes in its organization. Firstly the Wolof, Fulani and Serer developed cooperative organizations and modified traditional agricultural practices. Secondly, much more use was made of migrant labour from the upper Senegal and the upper Niger.

Agriculture in Senegal was promoted almost entirely by African initiative, in order to satisfy the demands of the international economy; but it was also promoted in ways detrimental to the long-term benefit of the country's economy. The over-emphasis on groundnuts led to a dangerous dependence on one crop, and even to a decline in the production of food crops. Rice was increasingly imported, from French Indo-China (Vietnam). Between 1906 and 1915 the annual average figure for imports of rice from Indo-China to French West Africa was 29,000 tons, and nearly all of it went to Senegal. Similarly, in British Gambia over-reliance on groundnuts let to imports of rice from India. In the Ivory Coast cocoa and rubber production expanded considerably before 1914. As in the Gold Coast, migrants led the way in developing and expanding cocoa-farming. At first Dioula migrants from the forest itself moved into new land and started cocoa-growing. Because of the wars of resistance from 1891 until 1918 Ivory Coast cocoa production developed more slowly than the Gold Coast's. However, by 1901 Ivory Coast had surpassed the Gold Coast in production of rubber.

In contrast to colonies like Senegal and Ivory Coast, Dahomey's economic growth declined under French colonialism. The French carried on the Dahomeyan kingdom's rigid state control of production. As before the conquest, Dahomeyan farmers were ordered to plant and sell crops, labour on public works and enlist in the armed services. They were given detailed instructions on what crops to cultivate, and where, when, and how to sow, harvest and store them. The farmers had been willing enough to cooperate with their own government, but they were unprepared to cooperate with an alien regime, especially in view of the low prices they were paid for their crops by European companies. Within a few years of the conquest the great trading families of Dahomey had been ruined by the French trading companies. The old Dahomeyan bourgeoisie formed by these families sank back into the peasantry from which their ancestors had raised themselves during the period of Dahomey's pre-colonial greatness.

Leopold II and the Congo Free State

The activities of Leopold II's agents and of the concessionaire companies in the Congo Free State were amongst the worst examples of colonial exploitation.

The Congo Free State was recognized by the European Powers and the United States on Leopold's assurance that he would end slavery and the slave trade. The King of Belgium kept his promise to end these evils but he introduced immediately a new evil, one that was greater in its effects on the Congo. In order to attract private capital Leopold granted land and mineral rights to European companies, most of them based in Belgium, covering vast areas of the Congo.

In 1886 Leopold made a contract with the *Compagnie du Congo Pour le Commerce et L'Industrie* (CCCI) which agreed to build a railway round the lower Congo rapids from Matadi to Leopoldville (Kinshasa). In exchange the company could claim 1,500 hectares (about 5 ½ square miles) for every kilometre of line constructed. The lower Congo railway alone resulted in the alienation of more than 3,000 square miles. Similar contracts were made with two other companies to build railways to Lake Tanganyika and to Katanga (Shaba). Many other companies were granted concessions to exploit inland from river banks and far into the interior. Leopold himself took over and managed large areas of Crown land. The areas he leased to private companies were also exploited by himself indirectly because he leased them on a profit-sharing basis.

The only way the companies and Leopold could make profit was to force the Africans to work for them. Africans were therefore forced to give European agents rubber or ivory as a levy or tax. There was a great demand for rubber especially between 1895 and 1905 following the invention of the pneumatic rubber tyre for bicycles and motor-cars. Wild rubber in the Congo brought enormous profits for European companies. Leopold got a profit on rubber alone of over £3 million between 1896 and 1905. The Concessionaire Company started with a paid-up capital of £9,280 yet made a net profit in six years of £720,000. Each share of a paid-up value of £4 6s. 6d. received £335 in dividends. The concessionary company working the Kasai region with a paid-up capital of £40,200 made a profit of £736,680 in four years.

The Africans received very small rewards for tapping rubber and handing it over to European agents. They were hardly ever paid for their work as the rubber was usually taken as 'tax'. But they suffered far more than mere financial loss. Failure to deliver the levy in rubber, food or by unpaid labour was punished by flogging, chaining, mutilation, imprisonment, the burning of villages or death. A Reuter's report in the London newspaper, *The Times*, on November 18, 1895, quoted extensively from an American missionary, the Reverend John B. Murphy:

'Each town in the district is forced to bring a certain quantity of rubber to the headquarters of the commissaire every Sunday. It is collected by force. The soldiers drive the people into the bush. If they will not go they are shot down, and their left hands cut off and taken as trophies to the commissaire. The soldiers do not care who they shoot down, and more often they shoot poor helpless women and harmless children. These hands, the hands of men, women and children, are placed in rows before the commissaire, who counts them to see that the soldiers have not wasted the cartridges.'

Faced with the demand to collect rubber or hunt ivory and pay it as tax, the Africans of the Congo had insufficient time to cope with the major task of cultivating food and fishing, and of continuously fighting the forest to prevent it winning back cleared land. African farmers were forced to abandon villages and flee into the forest to escape from company agents and punitive expeditions. The neglect of farming and fishing led to starvation, famine and depopulation. The 1911 census recorded 8,500,000 people, but it was estimated that the population had fallen in twenty years by two-thirds from over 20 million.

Conditions and atrocities in the Congo were exposed in 1900–1 by the British consul at Kinshasa, Roger Casement. His report was published in 1904 as a British government state paper. Casement showed that free trade hardly existed in the Congo, that the country was the private property of one individual, the King of the Belgians, and that the Free State was colonial enterprise of the worst kind. Faced with earlier criticism by American missionaries, Leopold had successfully diverted attention from the real nature of his activities by resorting to a brazen public relations exercise. In 1896 he had set up a Commission for the Protection of the Natives. However, he had no effective answer to Casement's report, which created an international outcry. Under increasing international pressure and public opinion at home the Belgian government took over the Congo from the king in 1908, and the Congo Free State became the Belgian Congo. The government take-over brought little immediate change. The government inherited from Leopold the contracts with the concessionaire companies and left them in possession of their vast territories. Leopold's and the companies' soldiers, the very men who were guilty of the appalling atrocities that had been committed, were recruited into the *force publique*, the military force which the Belgian Congo inherited from Leopold. The worst abuses ended only with the collapse of the rubber boom on the world market between 1906 and 1910, a period when the Congo's rubber also ran out.

After 1900 Belgian and British mining companies began to exploit the mineral wealth of the Congo Free State. In 1900 the *Comité Spécial du Katanga* (CSK) was created by an agreement between the Congo Free State and the concession company, *Compagnie du Katanga*, to manage jointly the assets of the two associates. Four members of the CSK's six-member board were appointed by the State, and two by the company. Shortly after its foundation, the CSK made an agreement with Robert Williams, the founder of a British company called Tanganyika Concessions Ltd (TANKS). Williams agreed to undertake prospecting in Katanga (now Shaba) on behalf of the CSK. The CSK and TANKS would each put up half the necessary capital in any subsidiary companies to be created; profits would be split 60% to the CSK and 40% to TANKS. Subsidiaries were soon set up. In 1902 the *Compagnie du Chemin de Fer au Katanga* was created, and four years later the *Union Minière du Haut Katanga* came into existence. Prospecting of mineral deposits lasted from 1906 until 1911, when a copper mine began production. In 1912 production was 2492 tons. Five years later, production had reached 27,462 tons. Therefore Katanga was on the way to becoming Africa's major mineral-producing area north of the Witwatersrand.

The colonial economy in French Equatorial Africa

De Brazza established French rule in the north Congo basin with the minimum use of force and the maximum use of negotiation and discussion. As Governor of the French Congo from 1882 to 1898 the former explorer presented himself as an obstacle to the exploitation of north central Africa. De Brazza always looked on France's imperial mission in Africa as a humanitarian exercize. He regularly defended Africans against abuses by European traders. He held up Marchand's expedition from Brazzaville to Fashoda in the Sudan by refusing to press-gang porters and extort supplies from Africans for the expedition. De Brazza was dismissed in 1898 for trying to hold up the economic exploitation of French Congo. By then French shareholders, including leading Third Republic politicians, were gripped by a frenzy of greed for the imagined wealth of the French Congo on the north bank of the river.

With De Brazza out of the way, the French government imitated Leopold's system of grants of land and local authority to large concessionaire companies. It hoped by this means to obtain quick profits and reduce the large annual deficits in the budgets for the region. In 1899 thirty-year concessions were granted to forty companies, covering almost 70% of French Equatorial Africa in Congo, Gabon, Ubangi-Chari (Central Africa) and parts of Chad. One company, the *Societés des Sultanats du Haut-Oubangui*, received 140,000 square kilometres. Conditions of the concessions provided that full ownership of the land would be conceded if there was a harvest of rubber on twenty feet per hectare in five years, or cultivation or buildings covering one-tenth of the area. In exchange, the companies were to pay into the colonial budget an annual rent plus 15% of their profits. The companies were allowed to establish administrative or military posts in their domains. In practice, however, colonial police were placed at the disposal of company agents.

The concessions entirely ignored the indigenous political organization of the African population. The European companies held monopoly rights over trade and organized themselves in a syndicate, *L'Union Congolaise*, which effectively destroyed African enterprise. The companies made hardly any investment in agriculture, forestry or mining, preferring to concentrate on extorting rubber from the people and on the import and export trade. Africans were often not paid, or were paid almost nothing, for their rubber. Impressment of porters was common, whether carried out by companies or by the administration. Women and children were frequently taken as hostages to force men to submit to porterage. Men acting as porters or as forced labourers on roads and farms suffered starvation, flogging, and death from brutality and disease. The colonial administration was severely undermanned; therefore, it was hardly in a position to exercise control over company agents when the latter abused their power, as they did frequently.

The Gaud-Toque affair of 1905 revealed something of official attitudes towards French Congo. In 1903 Gaud and Toque, two psychopathic colonial civil servants, tortured and murdered black prisoners in horrifyingly brutal circumstances. Ex-Governor De Brazza was sent out to make an official investigation, and wrote a full report. Gaud and Toque were tried, found guilty, and sentenced to five years imprisonment, but were released after two years. De Brazza's report was suppressed by the French government which feared its publication would damage French prestige.

One of the main effects of French rule in Equatorial Africa after 1899 was depopulation. In 1900 the population of French Equatorial Africa was estimated at 15 million people. In 1913 various estimates put the figure at 10 million, 9 million and 5 million. The 1921 census recorded 2,860,868. But whatever the accuracy or inaccuracy of the figures, the general opinion of administrators and missionaries was that the population declined by about two-thirds between 1911 and 1921. French colonial rule and the activities of the concessionaire companies were compounded by the devastating world-wide influenza epidemic which followed the First World War. Less cultivation resulted in cleared land reverting to forest and a return of the tsetse fly and sleeping sickness, a killer disease. Forced labour also separated spouses for long periods and thereby reduced the birth rate.

The Portuguese colonial economy, 1890–1914

In theory, the Portuguese adopted new policies for the exploitation of their African colonies after the Scramble. The Portuguese government wanted to develop the colonies on a pattern of white settlement and African labour that was expected to bring profit for the Crown in the form of surplus revenue. Contract labour replaced both slavery and forced labour, and an influx of white settlers and chartered companies transformed the prazos in Mozambique. In practice, however, there was little real change and the African was still regarded primarily as a worker for Europeans. This situation was considered by the Portuguese as morally justified: the African should be 'civilized' by being 'made to work'. Settlers regularly abused so-called 'contract' labour: workers were held indefinitely, and often treated worse than slaves, because the employer felt less obligation to them than he would to his personal property. In any case the prohibition of forced labour in the new labour code of 1878 was ignored in the interior of Angola where settlers were not inspected. Other codes of 1899 and 1911 were also reforms on paper which were not widely implemented.

Perhaps the worst case of abuse of contract labour was the shipping of thousands of Angolan Africans to the cocoa-producing islands of Sao Tome and Principe. These contract workers were actually bought in the interior of Angola, brought in chains down to Benguela, registered as contract workers, and sent to the islands, from whence they never returned. These happenings were first exposed by a Governor of Portuguese Guinea, Judice Biker, who described the long working hours, the poor diet, the brutal treatment and the high mortality rate of the contract labourers in the moist and malarial infested islands. The matter came to international attention with the publication of *A Modern Slavery* (1906), a book written by an English journalist Henry Nevinson. The book roused British and American opinion against Portuguese contract labour.

The British chocolate firms Cadbury, Rowntree, and Fry, and the German firm Stollwerck, agreed to boycott Sao Tome cocoa in a concerted campaign organized by William Cadbury, who actually visited the islands to see for himself what was going on. But the boycott made little difference as Sao Tome cocoa continued to be sold to other firms.

Some Portuguese fought hard to get reforms carried out, but they failed. The Governor-General of Angola resigned in 1912 because he failed to suppress forced labour. At the same time the Governor of Mossamedes in southern Angola was dismissed by the Lisbon government partly for his opposition to forced labour. The famous Governor-General of Angola from 1912 to 1915 and from 1921 to 1924, Norton de Matos, failed in his attempts to suppress abuse of contract labour, and for his efforts to do so he was forced out of office.

In Mozambique the prazos were transformed by legislation in 1892. The prazos were to be developed into estates leased by the government to white settlers. The estate holders, or prazeros, were no longer politically independent but agents of the government, collecting tax at standardized rates, taking the census, supervising development, and resolving local disputes. A high hut tax was imposed to attract abundant cheap labour for the settlers. Chartered companies were to be the means of cheap administration to develop those parts of Mozambique away from the prazo lands. Two companies were set up and given charters.

Both the new settlers on the prazos and the chartered companies were undercapitalized. Consequently they ignored the task of development and concentrated on maximizing profits by systematic exploitation. The Africans were condemned to forced labour, in spite of legislation against it. The *Companhia do Mozambique* made men work on sugar plantations and public works projects. Women were forced to grow cotton and to sell it only to Company agents. Hardly any schools or hospitals were built as required in the Company's charter. The *Companhia do Niassa* was so poor that it came to be controlled by the Nyasa Consolidated Company, a South-African based agency that recruited labour for the Rand, Katanga, and even the Mombasa docks. Most men 'recruited' went to the Rand. After 1903 recruiting was taken over by the Witwatersrand Native Labour Association and northern Mozambique became a major source of the labour supply for the gold mines in South Africa. The Portuguese administration was intimately involved in the whole business. The supply of labourers was regulated through the port of Lourenço Marques (Maputo) and the colony administration got a fee for each labourer recruited. Portuguese officials and village chiefs were bribed to produce workers. The salaries of the labourers were low and the death rates high in the South African mines.

The German colonial economy

The various German economic experiments in their four African colonies show that however much a colonial power might invest in a territory and launch programmes of agricultural development, public works, health and education to benefit the people, these measures might be negated by accompanying exploitation and despotism.

Togo was regarded as a model colony by the Germans. The agriculture of the south of the country was rapidly developed. An agricultural college was set up to provide assistance to peasant farmers. Diversification away from a one-crop economy based on palm oil was successfully carried out. Palm products accounted for 89% of exports in 1895 but only 52% in 1911. Cotton exports rose from 14,000 kilos in 1902 to 502,000 in 1913. Cultivation of other crops like coconuts, coffee, sisal, rubber and cocoa also spread. The development of agriculture made possible a high level of taxation and of public expenditure on public works, health and education.

In public works, the Germans built a modern dock at Lome that did not have to be improved until 1968, 330 kilometres of railway for a small country of only 85,000 square kilometres and only 1,032,000 people (in the 1911 census), and the best road and telegraph systems in Africa before 1914. An extensive government medical and sanitary service was established. Many government schools were built and mission schools were subsidized. German Togo was far ahead of other West African colonies in pupil enrolment. Its 13,700 pupils in 1914 represented 9% of the age range, compared with Southern Nigeria's 3%.

In spite of these achievements Togo was not a model colony. European merchants were given exclusive rights to import and export goods, a measure which led to the destruction of the African bourgeoisie. Forced labour on public works was enforced by flogging. The twelve day's labour tax was payable annually by all adult males, and was additional to forced labour. Much land was alienated to European companies in the south. The land was bought very cheaply, and sometimes the government ordered the Africans to sell land to the companies. Finally, in 1910 the colonial administration annexed all unoccupied land on the false assumption that it was ownerless. The people of Togo felt their burdens heavily and they resisted not by force of arms, but by migrations mainly to the Gold Coast, usually at night, in small parties. Sometimes, however, migration took place on a larger scale; for example 14,000 crossed over from Misahohe district to the Gold Coast in 1910.

Unlike in Togo, where the emphasis was encouragement of African peasant-farming, in the Cameroons the Germans concentrated on developing their own plantations through concessionaire companies. *The Gesellschaft Sud-Kamerun* (South Cameroon Society) and the *Gesellschaft Nordwest Kamerun* (North-west Cameroon Society) were each given about one-fifth of the colony. Large profits were made by the companies from wild rubber and ivory, cocoa, bananas, coconuts, tea, timber, ostrich feathers, copal, groundnuts and palm oil. In 1903 in the south chiefs were required to ensure that 25 palms were planted for each old house and 50 for each new one. In 1908 a soap factory was built in Doula. Considerable progress was made in diversification of crops to avoid a one-crop economy. The rapid economic growth was unfortunately accompanied by the ruthless exploitation of forced labour. We have already seen in the introduction to this chapter, how men from the highland plateau died when sent to work in the lowland plantations.

The colonial economy in German South-West Africa was based on the South African pattern of alienation of land from the indigenous people and its distribution at derisory low prices to white settlers. The Nama, Herero and other peoples lost not only much of their land but also many of their cattle to German settler-farmers.

In Tanganyika the Germans combined encouragement of white-settler and plantation farming with aid to African peasant producers, though there was far more emphasis on African farming after the Maji Maji Revolt of 1905–7 (see Chapter 9). A Biological and Agricultural Institute was established in the Usambara Mountains at Amani, where scientists made experiments with soils, crops and fertilizers, and passed on much new knowledge to African farmers through government agents. African cash crop farming included cotton in the Rufiji area, robusta coffee grown by the Haya of Bukoba, arabica coffee grown by the Chagga of Kilimanjaro, and groundnuts in Unyamwezi and Usukuma. At the coast, farmers were encouraged to grow coconuts for a variety of products and coconut plantation owners were given government advice on cultivation and pest control. White settlers developed sisal, coffee, rubber and cotton plantations, but their activities were never of as much importance as those of African farmers. In 1914 African produce for export was greater than that from European-owned plantations. Yet in spite of this economic progress, resentment of German rule grew.

This resentment of German rule in south-east Tanganyika was based on many factors, not all of them economic, but prominent among them were forced labour, taxation and the cotton pro-gramme. The Germans used forced labour to build permanent brick administrative buildings and farmhouses in plantations. Taxation forced people to travel to distant places in forests to collect beeswax and rubber, which they could then sell to earn a few coins to pay the tax. This meant neglect of food cultivation. Moreover, failure to pay the tax resulted in severe punishment and social humiliation. A man who failed to pay was jailed and flogged in public—regardless of his adulthood or his status in society—until a relative paid on his behalf.

The cotton programme was particularly unpopular. The Germans forced the people of the south-east to grow cotton for the textile industry in Germany and to increase revenue from cash crops for the colony. Cotton was unpopular because it required hard work, considerable growing-time, picking, and protection from vermin, especially birds and wild pigs. The cultivation of cotton resulted in less acreage and time being available for food production. Thousands of people were rounded up for labour at low rates of pay on German-owned plantations and to work under *jumbes* (headmen) and European-controlled District Development Committees. The 1903–4 harvest was so poor that the workers were not paid at all. Significantly, the beginning of the Maji Maji Rising coincided with the beginning of the 1905 cotton-picking season.

The result of the Maji Maji Rising for the economy of Tanganyika was marginal improvement as far as the Africans were concerned. The forced cotton programme was abandoned—if only because of the devastation and depopulation of the area affected by the Rising and the German counter-measures. The new, reforming Governor, von Rechenberg, gave more support to African cash farming. He refused to force Africans to work for settlers and punished settlers who ill-treated their workers. The railways the Germans built with African forced labour, from Tanga to Moshi and from Dar-es-Salaam to Kigoma (which the line reached in 1914), considerably assisted the export of African cash crops. Whilst they helped to increase the profits of German import/export firms they also boosted African production.

The colonial economy in Uganda

The story of the development of African crop farming in Uganda from 1900 to 1914 illustrates how difficult it is to generalize about the colonial economy for Africa as a whole. There *was* no one colonial economy for Africa; rather, there were different economies, even within each colony. For example, the cotton programme in German Tanganyika was a disaster which led to the Maji Maji Rising, whereas in Uganda the cultivation of cotton was a success story. Uganda economically in the early twentieth century was a triumph for African cash crop farming, as in the Gold Coast, Nigeria, Senegal and the Ivory Coast. Yet, in contrast with the development of export crops in these countries where African initiative led the way independently of the colonial government, Uganda's success was a result of government direction and careful central planning.

The Uganda administration aimed to develop the country's economy in such a way that it would become self-supporting from revenue and finance its own further growth (as the Germans managed to do in Togo). Therefore the administration set up a Scientific and Forestry Department manned by experts who could advise the people on cash crop farming. The obvious product to concentrate on was cotton, which grew well in the Ugandan soil and climate. Moreover, British manufacturers were encouraging cotton-growing in Uganda because they needed alternative supplies to those from the USA. In the early twentieth century there was a shortage of cotton on the world market. The British Cotton Growers Association was unusually influential in Uganda because its agent there was a CMS missionary, K. E. Borup, who was in charge of the CMS's industrial missions. The CMS had very close connections with the powerful ruling oligarchy of Christian and predominantly Protestant chiefs in Buganda. Equally important, the katikiro or prime minister, Apolo Kagwa, realized that ivory was a wasting asset and the supply was declining rapidly. He managed to reconcile the Baganda to the replacement of the 'traditional' ivory and barkcloth trades with a cotton trade. Moreover, as a result of the 1900 Agreement (see Chapter 6) many Baganda began to develop their new freehold land along capitalist-farming lines because they were assured of permanent ownership of it. The changeover to a cotton economy in Buganda was greatly aided by the 1907 campaign against sleeping sickness. Sir Hesketh Bell (Governor 1905–10), Apolo Kagwa and the Ganda Christian chiefs persuaded one million people to move from the tsetse-fly-infested lakeshore. The migrants tended to take up cotton-farming in their new homes.

The 1908 Uganda Cotton Ordinance was the work of Bell and Kagwa. It gave the governor authority to regulate cotton production. Farmers were allowed to grow only high quality American Upland seed, which the government introduced from the Sudan. Hand-ginning was banned. The government bought up hand-gins and destroyed them, and opened three modern ginneries to ensure proper cleaning and grading. Central control and these drastic measures were necessary to obtain the highest quality for Uganda cotton and so enable it to compete successfully on the world market. They had the desired effect because in 1914–15 Uganda's cotton exports were worth as much as £369,000.

European settler farmers played only a small role in the Ugandan economy. There were about fifty of them before the First World War, and there were severe restrictions on their buying land. Land alienation was very difficult; any allocation exceeding 1000 acres had to be considered by the Secretary of State in London, and settlers had to buy it at high prices. In 1911 there were only twenty alien estates with over 2000 acres under permanent crops. The settlers had variable success with rubber but their plantations were too small, because of the difficulty in getting land. In 1914, 80% of Uganda's exports were produced by Africans.

Development of transport was a major factor in the growth of the Ugandan economy before 1914. Many all-weather roads were built in and around Kampala and Port Bell. In 1912 the railway from Jinja on Lake Victoria to Namasagali on Lake Kioga was completed. Cotton exports could now be sent to Jinja by railway before being sent by steamer to Kisumu and then by railway again to Mombasa.

Perhaps no one individual contributed more to Uganda's economic growth before 1914 than Allidina Visram who reached Kampala in 1898. Visram had been born in India in 1863 and had migrated to Zanzibar as a young boy. He led the way as Indians expanded into the interior of East Africa. He set up trading posts from Bagamoyo to Kampala and had agents along the Nile. His caravans and later the wagons he hired on the Mombasa-Kisumu Railway were laden with a great variety of goods. Visram exported first ivory and later cotton, and retailed food, kitchen utensils, clothes and furniture. He acted as a banker, loaning money and issuing cheques. Later he became an industrialist and built oil mills, furniture workshops, saw mills, soda factories and in 1914 the great cotton ginnery at Kampala. Visram died, enormously rich, in 1916. He was incomparably the most successful of the 2000 Indians in Uganda in 1914. By then, his compatriots controlled 80% of the commercial trade, and he held an enormous share of this. But Visram was not just an exploiter. He was renowned for his donations: to Namirembe (Anglican) Cathedral, the African hospital, and the Indian school at Mombasa that he founded and which was named after him. His entrepreneurial activities served to sell the products that African farmers produced, and provided employment for thousands of Africans both directly and in indirect ways.

The colonial economy in Kenya

The Uganda Railway

The Mombasa-Kisumu Railway was called the Uganda Railway because until 1902 Kisumu and almost all the land from a point about fifty miles west of Nairobi was in Uganda. The British reasons for building the railway were mainly political, but the results were mainly economic.

Lord Salisbury, the British prime minister 1886–92 and 1895–1902, regarded the railway as a means of consolidating claims to territory that had been recognized on paper in the Anglo-German Treaty of 1890. His prime concern was to establish effective British administrative control in an area which was five months' journey on foot from the coast. Salisbury managed to get public opinion, parliament and his cabinet behind the idea of a railway from Mombasa to Lake Victoria by appealing to anti-slavery sentiment. It thus became easier for him to get money out of the British Treasury, and parliament approved £20,000 for a preliminary survey in 1892. In 1892 there was a general election in Britain and the Liberals came to power, with Gladstone as prime minister. Gladstone was opposed to the proposed railway, and it was not until Salisbury and the Conservatives returned to power in 1895 that the railway was built. It was optimistically believed that the railway would easily pay its way from exports from the Lake Victoria basin, with its fertile land, large population and potential for cash crop production on a large scale.

The railway was built by British engineers and 32,000 Indian labourers, who were brought to East Africa because the local population saw no reason for its building. The railway moved inland from Mombasa in 1896. Construction was temporarily held up by man-eating lions at Tsavo near the beginning and by the Nandi near the end, but the line reached Kisumu in 1901. Various problems such as drought in the Nyika, flash floods, inadequate port facilities for unloading materials, disease amongst workers and engineering problems in such places as the Rift Valley escarpment had to be overcome.

The final cost was about £5½ million, far more than originally expected. Therefore the British parliament which had financed what was now called 'The Lunatic Express' insisted that the line be made to pay. In the first few years it made operating losses. A hut tax was introduced in 1902 to help offset the cost, but the tax led to expensive military expeditions by Britain to extend its jurisdiction over African communities who were required to pay. There was no immediate cash crop revolution around Lake Victoria. Therefore Sir Charles Eliot, Commissioner for the East Africa Protectorate (Kenya) (1900–4), made the fateful decision to introduce European settlers into what Harry Johnston had described as 'White Man's Country' because of its altitude and temperate climate. If the white settlers could develop agriculture in the highlands, freight rates on their farm produce might make the railway pay. The most significant result of the completion of the Uganda Railway, then, was the arrival of European settler-farmers in Kenya. The coming of these white immigrants changed the economic, social and political history of Kenya.

The railway had a number of important economic results. African farmers could now sell their produce outside their home areas. The result was a boom in African farming and it was largely African produce which enabled the railway to pay its way. Uganda now possessed a quick route to the coast for cotton exports. Most of the Indian railway workers returned home, but 6,700 stayed, and many traders migrated from Gujarat in India and established shops at various points along the railway. The Indians replaced the old trade in beads and wire with trade in cloth, soap, iron and tobacco, and introduced rupees as currency. Large numbers of Asians and Africans were employed as permanent staff on the railway. Towns grew because of the railway. Nairobi and Kisumu began as railway towns, and Mombasa became more important.

The political effects of the Uganda Railway were also considerable. Firstly, in 1902 the British East Africa Protectorate (Kenya) was enlarged by the transfer of Uganda's Eastern Province in order to put the whole of the railway under one colonial administration, and to put the whole of the highlands—opened up by the railway for white settlers—under one administration. Secondly, in 1905 the capital of Kenya was transferred to the railway headquarters, Nairobi, which was also near the geographical centre of the country. Thirdly, the railway made it far easier for the British to establish their authority in Kenya and to govern the country, because administrators and soldiers could be moved quickly along the railway. For example, in 1905 the British sent a large expedition by railway to suppress Nandi resistance.

White settlers in Kenya

A few settlers established themselves in Kenya before the building of the Railway. In 1896 the McQueen family walked from Mombasa to Kikuyuland. But the railway and Eliot's encouragement of settlers transformed the situation. The settlers came on the railway and exported their cash crops along it. They were a motley crowd at first. There were soldiers and fortune-seekers like Grogan; big-game hunters like the aristocrat Lord Delamere who came for sport and stayed to settle; frustrated British aristocrats who could not get land in Britain because of land shortage and because land was too expensive there; Afrikaners from South Africa whose farms had been destroyed by Kitchener and who preferred to start afresh in a new land. The 1902 Crown Lands Ordinance made settlement in Kenya attractive. It established the legality of selling, granting and leasing unoccupied land, and allowed land to be leased for 99 years at a rent of a few cents per acre. The 1915 Crown Lands Ordinance increased the length of leases to 999 years. By 1915, 8242 square miles or 4,500,000 acres had been leased to about a thousand settlers. But it was unevenly allocated. Twenty per cent of it went to five individuals or groups: Delamere (who got 100,000 acres), the two Coles, Grogan, and the East African Syndicate. Land values in the Rift Valley rose from 6d an acre in 1908 to 240d or £1 an acre by 1914. Most of the land alienated from African communities to white settlers was 'unoccupied land', which the administration had declared to be Crown Land. The administration thought it had acted in African interests and that no racial clash over land could emerge. However, the concept of 'Crown Land' in Africa ignored African land tenure, which was based on shifting cultivation. Much of

Kikuyu 'unoccupied land', for example, had been temporarily vacated a short while before the European intrusion, because of natural disasters like cattle disease and famine. Even so, many thousands of Africans were moved off occupied land to make way for white settlers: 11,000 Kikuyu were moved off land in Kiambu; 3,000 Kamba were evicted from the Mua Hills; in 1906 the Nandi were moved away from the railway by the British army; Taita, Kipsigis and Elgeyo-Marakwet were forced to move. However, the people who were moved in the largest numbers were the Maasai, who were evicted from most of their land in two stages, by the so-called 'Maasai Agreements'.

In the 1904 'Agreement' the Maasai agreed to move into two reserves, one to the south of Ngong (just outside Nairobi) and one on the Laikipia Plateau west of Mount Kenya. The British promised Lenana, the Laibon, and the other Maasai leaders that the two reserves would belong to the Maasai 'so long as the Maasai shall exist'. The Maasai were allowed to use a half-mile wide 'corridor' between the two reserves. All the rest of the land formerly used by the Maasai in their nomadic wanderings was made available for white settlement. The Maasai did not really agree to the move, but the only alternative to a voluntary migration was forced eviction. Equally the Maasai leaders did not fully understand the agreement, but they trusted the white man sufficiently to put their marks to it. In 1911 the Maasai were ordered to evacuate the Laikipia reserve and move to the less attractive southern one which was now extended to the west, because white settlers coveted Laikipia. The Laikipia Maasai moved unresistingly, in 1913, after a period of protest led by Chief Ole Gelushu of Laikipia. The Maasai could not offer concerted opposition because Lenana, the leader at Ngong, favoured the move so that he would be able to establish closer control over Ole Gelushu's group. Besides, the Maasai as a whole accepted the move, though reluctantly, because they would still have enough land to continue with their traditional way of life and largely ignore the British presence and the money economy.

The agricultural achievements of the white settlers before 1914 were considerable. They cleared and fenced much land previously only occasionally occupied by nomadic pastoralists. They pioneered many new crops. Coffee of the high quality arabica type was first planted in 1899 near Nairobi; it became important after 1910 and by 1920 was the most important crop in Kenya. Sisal was first planted at Thika in 1904, and by 1920 it had become the country's second most important plantation crop. Tea was first grown at Limuru in 1904, but it was of little importance in Kenya until the 1920s. Rubber was tapped, and was an important export before 1914. However, the leader in agricultural experimentation was Lord Delamere, on his farm at Soysambu near Lake Elementeita. He succeeded so well in growing wheat in spite of rust disease, that in 1909 a flour mill was opened in Nairobi. He imported sheep, cattle and pigs from Britain and carried out cross-breeding experiments with beasts native to the tropics. At first his animals died of diseases, but he persevered and had them studied by veterinary experts. Cures were discovered, and the foundations of the dairy, beef and sheep industries were laid.

African farming in Kenya

African produce accounted for more than half of Kenya's export trade before 1914. Most of this produce was grown by Luo peasant farmers around Kisumu to whom aid was given by John Ainsworth, the Nyanza Provincial Commissioner, between 1908 and 1914. Impressed by the success of cotton on similar land in Buganda, Ainsworth called in the British Cotton Growing Association. But the cotton programme had very limited success in Nyanza, because of a shortage of technical assistance personnel and lack of funds. The chiefs were unsure what to do, poor rains led to poor harvests and lack of profit, and initial Luo interest was lost. However, Ainsworth and the Luo did have considerable success in the growing of groundnuts, simsim and maize, all of which were carried by the railway from Kisumu to Mombasa and exported. Between 1911 and 1913 simsim from Nyanza was Kenya's most valuable export.

African labour in Kenya

Government policy in Kenya was to encourage Africans to work on European farms, but to try to ensure they were not badly treated. Many thousands of Africans, especially Kikuyu, began to work on European farms for wages in the money economy. Many Kikuyu became voluntary squatters on European farms, some in the Kikuyu highlands but most of them in the Rift Valley. The squatter movement was partly a result of Kikuyu population expansion after 1902 and the impossibility of moving into lands now occupied by Europeans. But the movement onto white-owned farms was so great that additional explanations need to be found. The need to pay the 1902 Hut Tax is an obvious one. Another is that on European farms squatters were safe from forced labour on roads or dams in their home areas. Again, many young men were anxious to escape from the restrictions of traditional life and rule by elders as well as by the new colonial chiefs. Moreover, many of the squatters lived like free tenants and some were sharecroppers.

By 1914 thousands of Kikuyu, Luo and Luyia had settled on the coast to work in coconut or sisal plantations, with the Mombasa water supply, or at Kilindini docks. The Mijikenda people of the coast disliked sustained wage labour. The men from up-country however, were willing to migrate to the coast where wages were roughly double what they were on highland farms. Not all migrants went voluntarily: some were forced to go by the new colonial chiefs, anxious to ingratiate themselves with the European administrative officers who had recently appointed them. European officers' 'strong requests' for workers were taken as orders by chiefs who sent men to the coast under threat of arrest or confiscation of their livestock.

Urban development in Kenya

The growth of Nairobi before 1914 exemplifies colonial urban development all over Africa. Nairobi was purely a colonial creation, having its origins as a railway depot. It became the headquarters of the railway and the military before it became the administrative capital of Kenya.

It was laid out along lines of racial segregation. The railway station and workshops and the town centre lay in the low-lying marshy area near the river. The African residential area was placed next to the railway, on the east side of it, but lower down. The European area was placed on the west side of the railway, on higher ground. The Asians were allotted a separate area to the north, which came to be called Parklands. The African areas were overcrowded and insanitary slums—the result of low wages, high unemployment, high rents and a shortage of low income housing. The administration provided hardly any services, not even sewage disposal and clean water, and this inevitably resulted in epidemics and deaths. Nairobi did not become an officially zoned city until after the First World War, but unofficially the pattern of residential segregation along racial lines was set before 1914. Only a few changes were made after the War, such as moving some Africans from the Asian Residential Area and from Kileleshwa in the European area.

The Asian immigrants played a major role in urban development and business enterprise in pre-1914 Kenya. The most successful individual was A. M. Jeevanjee, a builder and contractor, estate agent, general merchant, importer and exporter, and shipowner. Jeevanjee operated two lines of steamships between Bombay and Mauritius and Bombay and Jedda. He built offices in Nairobi which were leased to the administration, and in 1905 he built the municipal market in Nairobi. Apart from big businessmen like Jeevanjee, the Indian shopkeepers (named *dukawallahs*) in the villages, many of which later grew into towns, played their part in urban and commercial development. The dukawallahs were largely successful as traders because at the outset they were prepared to operate on smaller profit margins than European traders.

The colonial economy in Nyasaland (Malawi)

Malawi's considerable economic growth before 1914 based on plantation coffee and the Blantyre-Nsanje railway that was built between 1904 and 1908, was marred by four major abuses; abuses which help to explain the armed rising led by John Chilembwe in 1915.

Firstly, the tenga-tenga system of porterage for government and for trading companies was widespread between 1895 and 1914. Wages were paid in calico not cash; the food allowance was paid in calico instead of food being served; many young boys were used as porters; and there was a lack of proper night shelter. Secondly, recruitment for the Rand mines was allowed to begin in 1903, though it was stopped in 1907 and not resumed until after the First World War. There was some compulsion in recruiting; a serious danger to physical health both on the long journey and in the mines; a danger to moral health in the mining barracks; and social and economic problems in the Malawian villages deprived of their able-bodied young men. Thirdly, European coffee planters made a peak demand for African labour at the very time when village farms growing food crops needed most attention. Yet the plantations on African land were only leased by African communities to Europeans. Thus the African 'tenants' of the planters were reduced to being serfs on their own land. Fourthly, the tax rate was fixed in 1902 by Commissioner Alfred Sharpe at 6/= unless a man worked for a European, in which case it was reduced to 3/=. Thus the administration got its revenue and the planters got African labour. The missionaries supported the colonial economic pattern, though they made well-intentioned but ineffective representations for reform of abuses and higher wages for Africans.

The colonial economy in Southern Rhodesia (Zimbabwe)

The British South Africa Company in its rule of Southern Rhodesia before 1914 naturally concentrated on the exploitation of the land and labour of the country for agricultural and mining profits.

The Pioneer Column of 1890 had hoped to find another Rand, but a mainly settler-farm economy developed. Between 1890 and 1893 Rhodes' 'pioneers' each helped themselves to 3,000 acre farms. They alienated between 2 million and 3 million acres of land from the Shona, although this was mainly land not occupied by the Shona.

Each white man who took part in the invasion of Matabeleland in 1893 got a minimum of 3,000 morgen (6,350 acres) of land. By August 1894 some 5,400,000 acres—nearly all from Matabeleland—had been alienated and the Ndebele were forced to work on their own land for the new white owners.

The 1896 risings of the Ndebele and Shona ensured that the Africans would possess some land which was secure from expropriation. Rhodes made concessions to the Africans to bring the rising to an end without even greater loss of life. The British government appointed a Resident Commissioner who placed a number of restrictions on forced labour, especially on farms, and on the Company from raising its tax from 10/= to £2 in 1903. He also made sure that 'native reserves' were demarcated in 1897 and 1898. The reserves were finally approved by the British government in 1908. They were generally adequate, purely in terms of size, for that time—but not for the future. Moreover, many Africans, especially Ndebele, preferred to stay on their traditional lands even if they were occupied by white farmers, rather than move into reserves in 'foreign' country. The reserves in Matabeleland totalled 7,753,140 acres, only 17% of the total acreage of the province. Over 5 million acres lay in the remote, waterless and largely uninhabited Gwaai, Nata and Shangani areas. In Mashonaland the African reserves totalled 17,138,560 acres, about 37% of the province. By March 1899 the settlers had alienated a total of 15,762,364 acres.

Before 1914 the settlers concentrated on growing maize and rearing beef cattle to serve the growing market in mines and new towns. Maize was exported from 1911. Tobacco was less important before the First World War than it was to become afterwards. However, pre-war experiments in high quality tobacco were successful and in 1910 the first tobacco auction sales were held.

Perhaps the worst exploitation of the Africans in Southern Rhodesia before 1914 took place in the mines. In 1898 gold production was worth £20,000. Then the effects of railway building began to be felt, and production jumped as follows:

Year	£
1899	126,000
1905	1,000,000
1907	2,000,000
1914	3,000,000

Coal was discovered at Wankie in a rich seam of several hundred million tons near the surface which could be worked cheaply. Coal was essential as a fuel in the gold mines and on the railways.

Mining labour was exploited to the maximum by coordinated employer action. Wages were uniformly low, lower than in South Africa. Conditions in the mine compounds were appalling, as labour legislation on minimum standards of food and accommodation were ignored by the mining companies. Between 1900 and 1920, 18,000 black miners died from diseases in the compounds, like pneumonia, influenza and scurvy and from accidents in the mines. Strikes were common. Two famous stoppages were the 1901–2 strike in the Camperdown Mine, over reduction in pay, and the 1912 Wankie Colliery strike, over bad food and whipping. Desertion and boycotting of certain mines became so common that the administration introduced coercive labour legislation. The Master and Servants Law made it a criminal offence to break a labour contract. A pass law was introduced to limit the mobility of labour and make it easier to find deserters.

The colonial economy in South Africa, c. 1900–14

The establishment of British control of the Transvaal during the Second Anglo-Boer War led to greater burdens for non-white labour on the Rand than ever before. The mine-owners in the Transvaal, who were largely British, believed that British victory over the Afrikaners would make it easier for them to recruit African miners, many of whom had deserted the mines during the war. So at the end of the war the owners decided to cut wages from over 50/= a month to 30/= a month. Not surprisingly, recruiting figures dropped instead of rising as black miners failed to return for new contracts in the mines.

The mine-owners, desperate at this large-scale labour boycott, got the British government to recruit several thousand Chinese labourers in 1904. Wages were very low for the Chinese. African miners feared losing their jobs permanently, and so returned to work after accepting the lower wages. The Chinese then left. Not long afterwards the 1911 Mines and Works Act was passed to prevent non-whites performing skilled or semi-skilled work: this act was in effect an industrial colour bar.

After winning control of the new Union government the Afrikaners introduced the 1913 Land Act. This act did not formally introduce apartheid (racial separation) in the farming areas of South Africa; but in practice it did so. The background to the Act was the growing 'poor white' problem and the difficulty of white farmers in obtaining a cheap African labour supply. In the early twentieth century a large class of poor, landless Afrikaners emerged. Land shortage for whites had been caused by a number of factors. The land frontier that the Afrikaners had steadily extended since the first Dutch arrived in South Africa in 1652, was finally closed by Rhodes' occupation of Zimbabwe in the early 1890s. By 1900, constant subdivision of Afrikaner farms among numerous sons had caused fragmentation into small farms and even landlessness in many places. In the 1890s mineral speculators were buying up vast areas of unoccupied land just in case diamonds or gold might one day be discovered on them. Many Afrikaner farmers had lost their wealth in the rinderpest epidemics of the 1890s and the drought of 1897. And 10,000 Afrikaners had become permanently landless as a result of the war against the British. To add to the problem, after the war some impoverished Afrikaner farmers sold parts of their land to African farmers. Finally, by the early 1900s many white farmers, including many Afrikaners, allowed African squatters to live on their farms and work as sharecroppers—thus making both less land and less work available for landless Afrikaners. In the early years of the Union the prime minister, Botha, and the Minister of Native Affairs, Hertzog, travelled throughout the country urging white farmers to expel black squatters and replace them with poor whites. The white farmers ignored Botha's appeals, for economic rather than humanitarian reasons. Many other white farmers who did not have squatters put political pressure on Botha to legislate against squatters in order to ensure a cheap supply of labour on their farms. Therefore, Botha's government pushed the 1913 Natives Land Act through parliament.

The Land Act limited land sales to blacks. It also eliminated squatters, who had a choice of becoming servants of their white landlords or of leaving. Many chose to leave. Thus began a vast migration of thousands of African families with inevitable hardships and sufferings. Most of them ended up in the towns, where they found work as house servants or labourers or joined the ranks of the unemployed. The Act solved neither the problem of poor whites, very few of whom were prepared to replace Africans as squatters or work with them as manual labourers, nor the problem of a labour supply on white farms, because very many Africans left the white farms for good.

The colonial economy in Egypt and the Sudan

Purely in terms of economic growth Britain's record in Egypt and the Sudan was impressive. The two countries cashed in on the cotton boom of 1900–10, a period when cotton prices doubled. In addition, the Sudan began to be provided with a network of railways that was essential for the development of a vast territory.

Lord Cromer ruled Egypt as consul-general from 1882 to 1907. He inherited a debt of nearly 100 million Egyptian pounds and managed to service it alongside balanced budgets. He abolished many unproductive taxes and the use of the whip for tax collection. New dams were built on the Nile and old ones repaired. Agricultural production, especially cotton, rose to record levels. Egypt enjoyed a period of unprecedented prosperity, as rising prices and a rapidly growing population were more than matched by a rise in real 'per capita' income.

Cromer was a great reformer. But he was an imperialist. He abandoned Mehemet Ali's plans to industrialize Egypt, and by his encouragement of cotton-growing to bring in revenue and raise income, he turned Egypt into a satellite of the Lancashire textile industry. Cromer also encouraged the investment boom of 1900–14. Foreign capital poured into Egypt, to such an extent that by 1914 as much as 92% of the capital of joint-stock companies was foreign-owned. Thus Egypt was once more heavily in debt to foreign businessmen. In his concern with limiting 'unnecessary' expenditure, Cromer allowed almost no spending on education. He seriously weakened the state education system created by Ismail by abolishing free education and imposing high school fees.

In the Sudan, Britain built railways originally for purposes of military reconquest, but extended them for purposes of easier administration and economic growth. The railway from Egypt reached Khartoum in December 1899. In 1905 the capital was connected by rail to the Red Sea coast. Railways penetrated south of Khartoum to Sennar on the Blue Nile and westwards to El Obeid in 1911. New towns, such as Khartoum North, Atbara, Port Sudan and Kosti grew up on the railway.

Experimental cotton planting was begun in the Sudan in 1900. By 1905 nearly 24,000 acres were under cotton. An experimental pump-irrigation cotton scheme was launched successfully in the Gezira plain south of Khartoum between 1911 and 1914. Plans to dam the Blue Nile near Sennar were pushed ahead. By 1914 the British government had guaranteed a loan to the Sudan government and surveying was complete. Yet the Sudan, like Egypt, had become an economic satellite of Lancashire. Diversification of the economy was hardly considered by the British before 1914.

The Maghrib

We have already seen how European economic and financial penetration of the states of North Africa ultimately led to their occupation by one or another European power. Almost inevitably the impact of the European occupation of the Maghrib was felt in the economy of these countries. In Morocco the formal French occupation did not come until the end of our period. The same was true of the Italian occupation of Libya. These two did not formally become parts of a colonial empire until just before the First World War. The European impact on these countries was less than its impact on Algeria which was first occupied by France in 1830.

Until after the First World War Algeria relied on agriculture as the mainstay of its economy. However, two different systems began to evolve. European agriculture grew in terms of land holding and productivity, while Muslim agriculture contracted. The Muslim population in Algeria rose steadily during the latter part of the nineteenth century. However, their holdings of cattle and sheep in 1900 were only 75 per cent of what they had been in 1865. There was also a decline in Muslim cereal production as a result of the loss of land. This is turn helped to bring about the partial famines of 1893 and 1897. With the advent of European settlers and the loss of land, many Muslim farmers became share-croppers, who cultivated land owned by Europeans, and gave up a fifth of the produce in return. Others became agricultural labourers with no land at all. It has been estimated that by 1900 when Muslims made up about 90% of the population in Algeria, they owned only 37% of the country's wealth.

While the Muslim sector of the economy declined, the European sector expanded. There was a great inflow of settlers between 1860 and 1900. Much of the best land in the country was taken by the settlers. There was a vast increase in the amount of productive land, and such areas as the Mitidja plain, near Algiers, which had been swampy and malarial, were developed. The European agricultural sector accounted for the increase in cereal production from 520 million kilogrammes to 1880 million kilogrammes between 1850 and 1910. Vine growing on a large scale began in 1880 and the plantation growth of tobacco was also boosted.

However, a number of warning signals stand out. Despite the increase in European farming, food production failed to keep pace with population growth. The serious imbalance between Muslim and European agriculture grew rather than declined. There was almost no opportunity for the primitive Muslim system to evolve. The owners lacked the training and the capital to bring about change even had they wished to do so. Similar disparities between settler agriculture and Muslim agriculture also became obvious in Tunisia before the First World War.

The Muslim population of the colonised countries was unable to find employment in industry and mining in sufficient numbers to offset the lack of opportunity in agriculture. Traditional crafts only occupied about 50,000 town dwellers in Algeria in 1880, and about 25,000 in Tunisia in 1910. In Morocco the number was probably about 100,000 in 1910. However, this was but a small proportion of the total population. Heavy industry did not develop in the Maghrib until after the First World War, and only became significant after 1965.

Iron mining was begun in Algeria in 1880 and about one million tonnes per year was being produced by the First World War. Phosphate mining began in 1910. Iron production began in Tunisia in 1900 and lead in 1905. Morocco had no significant mining operations before the First World War. As with agriculture, so with mining: European capital dominated the industry, and took most of the profits. The Muslim population provided a relatively poorly-paid labour force. Nonetheless in the Maghrib, as in other parts of Africa, the developments in agriculture and mining, which primarily benefited Europeans, brought about the development of a communications infrastructure, and helped to integrate Africa more closely with the modern world economy.

8
The African religious response

Islam and European colonialism

Overview

The spread of European rule in Africa helped the spread of Islam—though this result was certainly not intended. European missionaries in late pre-colonial West and East Africa had certainly been alarmed at more successful Islamic missionary activity in many African societies, from the Asante and the Yoruba to the Baganda and the Yao. The establishment of colonial rule made conditions for Christian proselytization considerably easier; but Islam spread more rapidly than Christianity in many of the new colonies, especially in West Africa. Islamic as well as Christian missionaries took advantage of the colonial peace and the improved communications to spread the news of their Book.

In northern Africa and the northern part of the West African savanna, where Islam was already the dominant religion, the spread of European rule had the effect of strengthening Islam. Modernized forms of Islam were often developed; Muslim leaders realized that the Islamic modernist tradition provided better possibilities for resisting European cultural encroachment. The Mourides of Senegal developed groundnut-growing as an imaginative response to the colonial economy. The Egyptian cultural revival was dominated by modernists like Shaykh Mohammad Abdu, a liberal theologian, who combined a rationalist approach with interpretation of the Koran.

A number of factors assisted the rapid spread of Islam between 1890 and 1914. Colonialism led to the break-up of many traditional social structures, and people turned to religious movements as an anchor. This is certainly a factor in the growth of Mouridism. It is a factor, too, in the rise of Christianity. Yet in the areas where Christianity and Islam were in competition, Africans often turned to Islam for their security rather than to Christianity. Islam, unlike Christianity, allowed polygamy and was thus in accordance with a vital aspect of African culture. Islamic missionaries were almost always Africans and could understand the spiritual and social problems of their converts more easily than European Christian missionaries. It was much easier to become a Muslim than a

Christian. It required but a simple affirmation to follow the Prophet Muhammad, while Christianity demanded a much deeper initial understanding. Islam had the advantage over Christianity that it could not be identified with the colonial master's culture. The population in Lagos was attracted strongly to Islam, partly as a form of protest against the powerful colonial presence in their midst.

Islam spread particularly rapidly in the southern savanna lands of West Africa—in areas like Senegambia, Guinea, northern Asante and northern Yorubaland. One of the factors that helped this consolidation of Islam in the savanna was labour migration. Many Mossi Muslims from Upper Volta, who went to work in the cocoa farms and mines of the Gold Coast, spread Islam to their work-mates and hosts, who had been followers of African traditional religion. Many traditionalists migrated to work on the groundnut farms of the Muslim Wolof of Senegal, and embraced the religion of their employers. In a number of places the colonial conquest opened up formerly rigid traditionalist communities to the influence of Islam. For example, the Hausa state of Kebbi in Northern Nigeria had been traditionalist in religion until the coming of colonialism broke down Kebbi's barriers with its neighbours; then Muslim preachers poured in. The same thing happened to the traditionalist Bambara in the French Soudan (Mali).

In a number of communities.the colonial authorities actively discouraged Christian missionary activity in order not to arouse Muslim hostility; and so they gave a boost to the consolidation of Islam in these areas. In strongly Muslim Northern Nigeria, Church Missionary Society missionaries were active from 1900 to 1914. However, they made hardly any converts—only 20 in the whole of Zaria district, for example. Lugard, the Commissioner from 1900 to 1907, did not prevent missionaries working in Northern Nigeria—unlike Cromer who forbade them to work in the Arabic northern Sudan—but he prevented them working in areas where there would be any open opposition to them. He had promised the emirs he would not interfere with Islam, and he feared that revolts might be unwittingly stirred up by Christian missionaries. Lugard's successor, Governor Girouard (1907–10), allowed more autonomy to the emirs and more indirect rule than Lugard had done, and was totally opposed to Christian missionary activity in Muslim areas. Girouard was succeeded by Sir Hesketh Bell who continued Girouard's policy. When Lugard returned to Nigeria in 1912, he continued the strong pro-Islamic policies of Girouard and Bell. Britain followed a similar policy of discouraging Christian missionary activity in heavily Muslim areas in the northern Gold Coast, the interior of Sierra Leone and in the Gambia. The French adopted the same approach in the Muslim areas under their rule.

The Muridiyya

The emergence of the Muridiyya (or the Mourides) showed that Islam could serve as a modernizing force in Africa's economy. The Muridiyya was founded in about 1886 by Ahmadou Bamba (c. 1850–1927). Its doctrine could be summarized as 'reward in heaven for labour on earth'. There were few religious demands on followers. Ahmadou was not strict on prayers; more important was the amount of groundnuts a man produced and the regular payment of tithes to the marabouts of the movement. From the early 1890s the Muridiyya made many converts in the groundnut regions of Senegal, notably among the Wolof. Young people were attracted away from their home villages to set up pioneer Mouride villages for cultivation of groundnuts.

The Muridiyya greatly helped the French colonial economy and economic growth in Senegal. The French administration even agreed to have a special railway branch line built to Touba, the holy city of the Mourides. The Muridiyya also helped the marabouts who led the movement, because they gained wealth from tithes and from marketing their followers' crops. The ordinary people who joined the Muridiyya not only gained economic benefits from groundnut farming but the movement also provided them with an ordered social organization to replace the disruption caused by French colonialism.

What was the political significance of the Muridiyya? In the early 1880s Bamba was a follower of Lat-Dior-Diop but the Muridiyya was a new form of resistance based on adaptation to French rule. Bamba never openly challenged French rule after 1886, but he exploited the colonial situation to gain economic and political benefits. He was deported for a long time, and after his return to Senegal he was held under house arrest. After Bamba's death, however, the Muridiyya became politically conservative, and its marabouts came close to being mere agents of the French

Islam in East Africa

Islam made considerable, but uneven, progress among East Africans in the early colonial period. The period opened unpropitiously for Islam in one important area: the Muslim party was defeated by the Christians in the military and political struggle for power in Buganda, first in 1889–90 and then in 1893. Thereafter Islam made little further advance in Buganda, though it managed to consolidate its hold on the 10% of Baganda who adhered to it.

The onset of colonialism assisted Islamization among the Yao of southern Tanganyika, northern Mozambique and southern Malawi. In the 1870s and 1880s, many Yao rulers had become Muslims under the influence of, and in identification with, their coastal trading partners. In the 1890s Islam spread rapidly downwards from the rulers to the Yao masses as a result of the activities of itinerant Muslim preachers. The reasons for this sudden mass conversion to Islam are not clear, but it seems likely that it was a reaction to the growing threat of European occupation.

Islam made a number of advances in German-ruled Tanganyika. Many of the African personnel in the colonial administration were Muslims, and this fact led a large number of local Africans to embrace Islam in order to gain status and social prestige by association with the rulers. The Germans employed Muslim Sudanese and Swahili soldiers, Swahili akidas and jumbes in their administration, and Swahili domestic servants. The black Muslim subordinates of the Germans were the men the African villager came into contact with and was influenced by. Islam played a role, though not the major one, in the Maji Maji Rising (see Chapter 9). Muslim preachers were active among the Ngindo who fought in the Rising and who saw Islam as an anti-European movement and became eager converts. The defeat of the Rising was a temporary blow for the spread of Islam, but the greatest period of Muslim expansion in the country was yet to come: during the years of the First World War and immediately afterwards.

Christianity and colonialism

Christian missionary work over vast areas of sub-Saharan Africa between the European Partition of Africa and the First World War was greatly helped by the colonial presence. The European political occupation removed many of the dangers and difficulties of mission-ary work in Africa, by improving communications and imposing a new kind of law and order. The southern Sudan is a clear example of this. The early Catholic mission of the 1850s had failed because of local wars and an inability to cope with tropical diseases. The British occupation of the southern Sudan in 1898–9 paved the way for Christian advance into the non-Muslim south. Catholics set up a mission at Lul among the Shilluk in 1900, and eight missions in the Bahr al-Ghazal between 1904 and 1912. American Presbyterians established themselves among the Nuer on the Sabat River from 1902. In 1906 the CMS set up a station at Malek among the Dinka.

European missionaries in Africa were strong supporters of European political control in general, but they often supported African grievances against the colonial administration, settlers and European companies.

The views of the humanitarian missionary colonialist, John Mackenzie, the first Deputy Commissioner in British Bechuana-land, are perhaps typical of many missionaries. In some ways

Mackenzie was progressive. He opposed keeping Africans in reserves, as in Natal, on the grounds that it denied them any hope of advancement in a westernized economy. He opposed the Afrikaners' division of society into citizens and non-citizens simply on grounds of colour. He disagreed with Afrikaners and Englishmen, like Rhodes, who believed Africans were racially inferior to Europeans. However, Mackenzie thought that Africans were culturally inferior to Europeans. He regarded Tswana traditional government, law and social customs as barbaric and the Tswana to be inferior to Europeans until they had adopted western civilization. Yet the cultural colonialism—the total replacement of African civilization by European civilization—advocated by Mackenzie was inevitably intertwined with political and economic colonialism. Mackenzie realized this. He knew that cultural colonization on a large scale could only be achieved after political colonialism had been established and economic colonialism had broken up a communal African society. Mackenzie believed that once African communal society had been broken up and many traditional customs abandoned it would be easier to spread Christianity.

The European missionaries in early colonial Malawi provide a clear example of how white missionaries as a whole were strong supporters of political and economic colonialism in spite of their opposition to certain administrative measures and to certain practices of white settlers. Porterage, labour on coffee plantations and recruitment for South African mines were all opposed. The Reverend Alexander Hetherwick of the Blantyre Mission objected to the administration's decision to allow recruiting for the Rand mines. He wanted security of tenure for African tenant-farmers on plantations and better working and living conditions and higher wages for African workers. He did not question the necessity of Africans working for European plantation owners, believing that such work was beneficial to both settler and African. Likewise, in German East Africa, German missionaries consistently opposed exploitation of Africans by European settlers but never questioned the duty of Africans to work for settlers and the policy of the administration in imposing taxation at a level that would encourage Africans to go and work for settlers.

In Leopold's Congo Independent State there can be little doubt that some of the sternest critics of the administration were the missionaries. In 1890 Grattan Guinness, the director of the Regions Beyond Missionary Union, reported on cruelty to Africans at a meeting in London of the Aborigines Protection Society and in the May 1891 issue of the magazine 'Regions Beyond' referred to the burning of African towns and villages. American and Swedish missionaries revealed examples of cruelty in succeeding years while in 1899 William Morrison of the American Presbyterian Mission publicized the use of cannibal soldiers by the state and the removal of several thousand Baluba to Luluabourg to supply forced labour. Reports by missionaries of the situation in the Independent State helped to keep alive the campaign against the abuses perpetrated by Leopold's agents.

There is little doubt that throughout the rest of Africa missionaries, while accepting European colonialism, were highly critical of abuses of Africans. There can be little doubt also that many Africans clearly distinguished between the missionaries and the 'new' Europeans who arrived during the colonial era. During the revolt of Abushiri in 1888 against German rule in Tanganyika missionaries were treated with unfailing courtesy, while colonial officials were regarded as being justifiable targets for attack.

Christianity under colonialism: its spread

Overview

The establishment of political colonialism and the development of communications in the colonial economy made Christian mission work in Africa much easier. In North Africa missionary enterprise was almost totally unsuccessful, because either Orthodox Christianity amongst the Ethiopians and a section of the Egyptians or Islam amongst most of the other peoples had been thoroughly entrenched for centuries and were undergoing spiritual renewal in the early colonial period. In West Africa Christianity spread more rapidly among coastal communities, though over the region as a whole Islam spread faster in the southern savanna and northern forest communities. In West Africa Christianity, as the religion of the colonizer, suffered in comparison with Islam.

Christianity's greatest success before 1914 was in Igboland, where local conditions were probably more congenial to Christian mission work than anywhere else in West Africa apart from the already Christianized coast of Sierra Leone. In East Africa Christianity spread more rapidly in Uganda and Kenya than Tanganyika where it had to face competition from Islam. In Central and Southern Africa, where rivalry from Islam was negligible, Christianity made considerable progress. The spread of Christianity (and Islam) could be regarded as part of the enlargement of scale brought about in Africa as a whole by colonialism—an enlargement of scale in political units, in economic growth and in a wider religious world-view. The traditional High God, so remote in the generally local nature of traditional life, seemed in the early colonial period to take on the more active role commonly associated with the lesser spirits.

One important qualification is necessary to this general picture of the spread of Christianity in sub-Saharan Africa in the early colonial period. The vast majority of Africans up to 1914 and for a long time thereafter did not become Christians (or Muslims) but remained true to African traditional religion. Generally, with the exception of a few areas like Ivory Coast, Igboland, Buganda and Malawi the spread of Christianity was fairly slow after the colonial occupation. Before 1914 most Christian mission stations in Africa were still passing through a pioneer phase when the Gospel met with indifference from the local people who were satisfied with their own conception of God and his purpose. Many missions, as in the pre-colonial period, remained self-supported plantation villages for people who had cut themselves off or had been cut off from traditional life. Typical of them was Kikuyu Mission just outside Nairobi, a self-supporting agricultural estate of 3,000 acres that would require another generation to pass before it made significant impact on the surrounding community.

Igboland

The largest response to mission work by European churches in West Africa before 1914 was in Igboland, where 18,500 Christians were counted in 1910. The Igbo adopted Christianity with extraordinary enthusiasm, though negative as well as positive factors were involved. Being a Christian provided a certain measure of immunity to forced labour and porterage imposed by the administration. Missionaries regularly secured exemption for their converts, especially those who had been to school. But it would be incorrect to say that the Igbo accepted Christianity as the lesser of two evils. The positive factors in their acceptance of the Church were more important than the negative ones. The most positive factor was the intense desire of the Igbo for western education. Igbo eagerly went to mission schools to get the white man's knowledge, as the means for attaining higher status in society as clerks, teachers or engineers. Enrolment increased rapidly; in 1899 there were in Igboland only seven western schools with 334 pupils. By 1906 the numbers had increased to 24 schools and 2591 pupils. Western education was also adopted by the Igbo as a weapon to fight colonialism. The period before 1914 was too early for them to regard education as a means of acquiring nationalist ideology to challenge British supremacy. In this early period education helped in an immediately practical way: if a village sent its sons to school they could acquire the foreign language skill and experience of the white man's world that were necessary to get the better of the oppressive Native Court clerks—the locally identifiable representatives of the colonial power.

The nature of traditional Igbo society provides a clue to their readiness to adopt Christianity. Igbo society was communal in many ways, but it was intensely and unusually competitive and mobile for an African society. Status and rank were achieved, not inherited. Moreover, there was considerable freedom of choice in Igbo society. Therefore, Igbo began to compete with one another to obtain the white man's skills and knowledge. The missions realized very early that the key to success in spreading Christianity was the mission village school. The Catholic missionaries—Holy Ghost Fathers led by Bishop Shanahan—won the battle against the Protestants for Igbo converts because they were far readier to concentrate their resources on education.

The Catholics adopted but the Protestants declined the Government proposal to introduce industrial education. As a result the Catholics attracted larger numbers to their schools because from the beginning instruction was in English not Igbo, whereas the Church Missionary Society resisted the use of English until much later. The Igbo looked on English as the passport to success in colonial society.

One must not, of course, overlook the spiritual reasons for the acceptance by many Igbo of Christianity. It was a religion which showed them a god who was concerned about them, who freed them from the fear of offending ancestral spirits and numerous distant gods and who offered them forgiveness of sins. This spiritual response to Christianity was echoed by many in East, West, Central and Southern Africa.

Christianity had less impact among the Yoruba west of the Niger than among the Igbo east of the river. In Yorubaland Christianity had to compete not only with Islam but with the even stronger Yoruba traditional religion which had already adapted itself to urban life before the coming of Christian missionaries. Yet even among the Igbo the traditional religion remained the strongest force in the spiritual life of the people. In 1914 only one Igbo in fifty was a Christian.

Uganda

In the whole of Africa only Uganda became a largely Christianized society between the beginnings of the European Scramble and 1914. In 1894 the Catholics had only five mission stations in the country, all of them in Buganda, but in 1914 they had 41 stations and 149 European priests throughout Uganda. The Anglicans of the Church Missionary Society had 37 white clergy and many more stations than the Catholics. In Buganda, the 1911 census revealed that out of a population of 660,000 as many as 282,000 declared themselves to be Christians. The two main factors that led to this success for Christianity in Uganda were the work of African Christians and the constructive and disruptive effects of the establishment of European political control.

We have already seen (Volume 1) how receptive the pre-colonial

Baganda were to Christianity, and how during the temporary withdrawal of the White Fathers at the end of Mutesa's reign Christianity took root under the aegis of Ganda Catholic evangelists. After the setting up of British administration, African Christians continued to lead the way in the Christian revolution; most of the new European missionaries who came to Uganda from 1893 did so at the urgent request of gatherings of African converts. Christianity was so popular with the Baganda partly because it was a status symbol, the religion of the new ruling class. But it would be incorrect to discuss the Christian revolution in Buganda—even in this colonial period—purely in terms of secular motives. Faith in Christ was obviously genuine among the overwhelming majority of converts.

In 1893–4 Christianity 'took off' in Buganda with the growth of reading houses. In one year, the number of Protestant countryside churches or reading rooms jumped from 20 to 200—the majority being in the care of unpaid volunteers. The reading house movement was inspired originally by George Pilkington, a CMS lay missionary, but the Catholics soon followed suit, and the movement was African-led and organized.

The constructive aspect of British colonialism that materially assisted the expansion of Christianity in Buganda from 1893 was the establishment of peace within Buganda and in the south-west of Uganda. The disruptive aspect was the Buganda land settlement after the war of 1892, which led to the dispersal of communities and the weakening of ancient beliefs and customs. In such circumstances social and religious innovation took root.

The Christian revolution spread from Buganda to south-western Uganda after 1894. In Toro Christianity became associated with the king Kasagama, an ally of Buganda and Britain against Bunyoro which had dominated Toro for centuries. Christianity spread in Ankole after 1900, assisted by the introduction of the Kiganda system of county and district chieftaincies and of Christian Baganda chiefs as colonial agents. The Baganda chiefs who went to Ankole took with them their followers and relations and made a considerable cultural impact on the Banyankole people. The cotton kanzu and European coats replaced skins and bark-cloth, roads were made and stone houses were built. But above all the Baganda introduced churches and schools to the Banyankole. Significantly, the Banyankole soon developed a thirst to learn Luganda, the language of administration and of the local Bible translations, just as the Igbo and taken up the learning of English as the route to success. In the extreme south west Christianization was largely the result of the work of Apolo Kibebulaya, famous as 'the apostle to the pygmies', but in fact the evangelist to various communities in south-west Uganda and parts of neighbouring Congo.

Despite the rapid spread of Christianity in early colonial Uganda, there was remarkably slow progress in the training and ordination of African clergy. Between 1896 and 1914 the number of African clergy in the Church of England in Uganda rose from 3 to 33. This may seem a high figure, and it certainly was if compared with Anglican ordination of Africans elsewhere, even including Sierra Leone, but it is a tiny figure set against the 100,000 Ganda Anglicans. Progress was even slower in Uganda for the Catholic Church. It had only two African priests by 1914.

Christianity under colonialism: its impact on African society

New values

The impact of Christianity on African society between 1885 and 1914 was far wider and deeper than would seem from the simple increase in the number of Africans who professed their belief in a new religious faith. To Africans, Christianity was far more than a religion: it presented itself also as a new and revolutionary social ethic.

Christianity as it was brought to Africa in the late nineteenth century was steeped in individualism. The individual African who became a Christian now saw the reason for his existence in his relationship to God rather than his family, clan or wider ethnic group. The solidarity of communal society was also broken up by the division between Christians and non-Christians, and by divisions among Christians themselves.

It was necessary for an African Christian to adopt a new social and economic outlook. If he abandoned polygamy or steadfastly refused to take a second wife he abandoned the basis of prosperity in the traditional economy and of prestige in the traditional society. It was important for him, therefore, to learn a trade or take up cash crop farming as compensation. More than that, he needed to make financial profit in the new colonial economy in order to pay the government tax and his children's school fees, as well as giving to the Church.

Missionaries built and ran hospitals partly out of a spirit of humanitarian service but also as an assault on the values of traditional society. The medical mission came to be regarded as an essential and integral part of the Christian community in its fight to destroy the influence of the 'witchdoctor' in African life. It was, of course, essential that the African Christian who could no longer turn to the traditional diviner should have access to medical help. Mission hospitals opened in the 1890s at Livingstonia in Malawi and at

Lovedale, the great Protestant missionary training centre in Cape Colony, South Africa. In 1903 Lovedale began to train African girls as nurses. In Nigeria a number of medical missions were opened before 1914, including the CMS Iyi Enu Hospital near Onitsha, the Baptist Hospital in Ogbomosho, the Wesleyan Guild Hospital in Ilesha, and the Sacred Heart Hospital of the Society of African Missions in Abeokuta. However, it was in schools rather than hospitals that missionaries made their greatest impact on African society before 1914.

Missions and education

The Christian missionaries built and maintained schools and devoted a great deal of their time, energy and limited financial resources to them. The missionaries used mission schools to spread the Christian message. Christianity is a religion of a book: therefore the spread of the Church inevitably went hand in hand with the spread of literacy. The missionaries used schools to attack some aspects of African society and its values and customs, such as polygamy and divination. However, the mission schools did far more than destroy; they began the modern African educational system. While the forces of colonial government, capitalism and trade were often creating havoc, the missions were building a new culture on the scene of destruction. Thus they performed an early 'nation-building' role in recent African history.

Among the positive achievements of missionaries in the field of education was the preservation of African languages, often against the wishes of their converts. In spite of their lack of training the missionaries made a major contribution in African linguistics in order to translate the Bible into African languages. In so doing they often produced new languages which could be read and written, and often spoken, over a wider area. For example, Union Ibo is a synthesis of three widely different dialects. The New Testament was published in this new composite language in 1909, and in 1913 T. J. Dennis' whole Bible in Union Ibo was published. In German East Africa the use of Kiswahili as the language of education effectively elevated the coastal tongue into a national language even more than its use in administration did. Before the colonial period Kiswahili had been widely used as a lingua franca, but its use in German mission schools spread its standard and literary form throughout the country. In southern Uganda, African missionaries developed Luganda as a literary language based on religious publications. Everywhere in sub-Saharan Africa missionaries published a whole range of religious literature in the vernacular, including the Bible (starting with the New Testament), catechisms, hymn books, primers, material for readers, and even newspapers (generally monthly).

Some missions provided a variety of schools and educational courses. In 1894 the Livingstonia Mission in Malawi opened a school near the Manchwe Falls on Mount Nyamkowa, and later named it the Overtoun Institution. Overtoun had an elementary school, a middle school, a teacher training section, commercial courses to train clerks, store-keepers and telegraphists, medical courses to train nurses and theological courses to train ministers. The Henry Henderson Institute set up at the Blantyre Mission in the south in 1909 had a similar wide range of schools and courses. The children educated in mission schools were often from an impressively wide range of social backgrounds. Buganda, the classic example of conversion from the top, naturally established schools for the sons of chiefs: exclusive boarding schools like King's School at Budo, for Protestants, and St Joseph's College at Kisubi, for Catholics. In Southern Nigeria, the classic example of conversion from below, slave children went to school. Thus the unprivileged were able to advance as council and court clerks and ministers of religion.

Mission education, however, in spite of its successes, had its negative aspects and its limitations. The knowledge that it imparted rarely went beyond the 'three Rs' of Reading, Writing, and Arithmetic, with special emphasis on Religious Knowledge and character training. In Nigeria, for example, the Protestant churches were extremely reluctant to introduce an educational system that would prepare their converts for professions outside the church. There were very few facilities for education beyond primary school level. An exception was the United Presbyterian Mission's Hope Waddell Institute in the Niger delta, with its industrial and secondary education departments. One has, of course, to remember that in Europe before the First World War secondary education was enjoyed by only a small minority.

A paradoxical result of mission education was that, in spite of its assault on African culture and its provision of a basic minimum of lower-grade clerical personnel to serve the colonial system, it began the undermining of this system. Eventually the mission-trained western-educated elite of Church pastors and teachers in largely mission schools would make a significant and, in many colonies, major contribution to the struggle for racial equality and political reform. Already before 1914 such an elite had reached an advanced state of formation in Sierra Leone and the Gold Coast. Casely Hayford had already conceived the idea of a National Congress of British West Africa by 1914, and would have called it to meet earlier than 1920 (when it did meet) if the First World War had not broken out. Mission students could not help drawing obvious inferences from their lessons. One of them was that if all men were equal before God they could be equal in this world, too. Thus the Bible played its part in the emergence of African nationalism. In another sense, too, Christian mission teaching helped the development of nationalism:

although denominationalism brought disunity among Africans, Christianity also brought some unity in African society. Christianity was a world religion, not an ethnic one; it united people of different clans and ethnic communities, especially in boarding schools. Thus mission education was beginning to equip African societies with the means to challenge political colonialism.

African independent churches before 1914

Overview

Between 1883 and 1914 the Independency movement in the churches in Africa got under way as African Christians broke away from European churches to form independent African churches. What drove the African converts to this drastic form of protest against mission churches?

In the first place, the details of daily life in the European churches influenced many Africans to leave. The first generation of converts often enjoyed close contact with their missionaries. However, in the second generation such contact was reduced. The days were over when white missionaries supported 'Ethiopianism', that is, Afric-anization of the church in Africa at all levels. From the 1880s onwards, European missionaries were increasingly reluctant to Africanize the priesthood immediately, let alone promote African priests to bishoprics. In the European-run churches there were no full African bishops after Crowther until the Second World War. Africanization was regarded as a long term project. All this was not entirely the fault of mission churches: the period of training to become a clergyman was too long for many Africans and the Catholic demand for priestly celibacy effectively ruled out many from even beginning to train.

Independent churches came into existence in Africa before the colonial era. The first one was a branch of the African Methodist Episcopal Church of the USA and was established in Sierra Leone in 1820. Thereafter many small independent churches grew up among the Sierra Leone recaptives, such as the African (Igbo) Baptist Church in the 1840s. Then in the 1890s the Afro-American Bishop Michael Turner visited South Africa to ordain African bishops and pastors, an act that provided a tremendous boost in Independency in South Africa, and in Central and East Africa to which it spread from South Africa. In West Africa, however, the independent Church movement of the late nineteenth century developed under its own inspiration.

Independent churches in South Africa

Not all the independent churches that arose in South Africa were influenced by the churches of the black diaspora. The first fully established independent church in South Africa was Nehemiah Tile's Thembu Church in eastern Cape Colony, formed in 1883 when Tile broke away from the Wesleyan Methodist Church because his involvement in the politics of the Thembu chiefdom was unacceptable to the missionaries. Tile had become the close adviser of Ngangeliswe, the Thembu paramount chief, and had, by means of petitions, questioned the justice administered by European magistrates. The Thembu Church expressed the political grievances of the Thembu at rule by the European minority of the Cape, at the hut tax and pass law, and at the settlement of Afrikaners in north Thembuland. In 1891 Tile died but his Church lived on. It underwent a change, however. It spread from the Thembu to neighbouring ethnic communities like the Gcaleka. It lost support among the Thembu when in 1894 the paramount chief Dalindyebo returned to the Wesleyan fold, but it became stronger among the Gcaleka who called it the Tilite, not the Thembu, Church. The Thembu/Tilite Church was untypical of other South African independent churches which placed little or no reliance on political protest.

The conditions of South African life gave a powerful impetus to Independency: the colour bar, loss of land to white settlers and the disruption of African life by the growth of a migrant labour economy. The 1890s saw a series of breakaways from parent European-dominated Churches: Anglican, Presbyterian, Methodist, Lutheran and others. But two other factors strongly influenced the growth of Independency in South Africa: the black diaspora and events in Ethiopia. In the 1880s missionaries from the African Methodist Episcopal Church of the USA arrived in South Africa. In 1892 Mangena M. Mokone of Pretoria was partly inspired by them to found the Ethiopian Church. In 1896 James M. Dwane, who had visited the USA, became leader of the Ethiopian Church and affiliated it with the AMEC. In 1900 Dwane rejoined the Anglican Church but carried only a minority of Ethiopians with him.

Ethiopia's victory over the Italians at the Battle of Adowa in 1896 greatly inspired many black South African Christians, who looked on Ethiopia as an African empire and a Christian community that proved that Africans could run their own affairs. Thus Ethiopia helped to inspire Ethiopianism. By 1913 there were 30 different Ethiopian Churches in South Africa. The differences in language, culture and customs of the different African communities helped to cause division within the independent churches. Since 1913 divisions have multiplied, some of them as a reaction to white rule and others as a result of ethnic differences amongst Africans.

Independent churches in Malawi

1898 marked the end of the period of initial primary resistance to the establishment of colonial rule in Malawi. Thereafter African political activity generally took the form of Independency. The background to the formation of African churches in Malawi was a general set of grievances common to any colonial country—such as land alienation to white settlers and land companies, collection of hut tax, and forced labour—in addition to slow African involvement in European-dominated churches. Between 1898 and 1914 a number of Africans were appointed to responsible positions in the Church. In 1898 Johanna Barnaba Abdallah, a Yao and author of *Chikala cha Wayao* (History of the Yaos), was ordained an Anglican priest. Augustine Ambali was ordained in 1906 and Leonard Kamungu in 1913. The Presbyterians made seven African deacons at Blantyre in 1898, appointed five Africans as elders in 1903, and in 1911 ordained two African ministers: namely, Harry Kambwiri Matecheta and Stephen Msoma Kundecah. The Church of Scotland mission at Livingstonia ordained two ministers in 1914. For some, the Africanization of the church was proceeding too slowly. This became one of the factors in the growth of Independency.

The four dominant figures in Malawian Independency before 1914 were three Africans: Eliot Kamwana, Charles Domingo and John Chilembwe, and a radical European, Joseph Booth (1851–1932), who believed in 'Africa for the Africans'. Booth was deported from Malawi in 1903, but he still managed to influence events there by correspondence from South Africa, and by contacting Malawians in the mining centres of South Africa. In his correspondence to Kamwana, Domingo and Chilembwe and his personal instruction to Malawian miners he won them over to beliefs like Watch Tower and sabbatarianism.

Kamwana left the Livingstonia Mission in 1901 as a protest against the introduction of school fees. In 1909, encouraged by Booth, he began to spread the teachings of the millenarian Watch Tower Bible and Tract Society (Jehovah's Witnesses), prophesying the imminent Second Coming of Christ and the end of British rule and taxes. He gained 10,000 adherents among the Tonga around Livingstonia. Before the end of the year the administration arrested Kamwana and deported him to Chinde in the south. Kamwana was unable to return to the north until 1937, but he maintained his influence over his followers by correspondence and receiving visitors. The Watch Tower movement, far from collapsing, actually spread into Zambia, Zimbabwe and Tanganyika.

Charles Domingo, a prospective Church of Scotland minister, completed a course at Lovedale in the Cape, finished his theological training in 1900 and was licenced in 1902. In 1908 he left the Livingstonia Mission and in 1909 joined the Watch Tower, but became a Seventh Day Baptist in 1910. The Seventh Day Baptists rejected monogamy as incompatible with African civilization, but they accepted many facets of western civilization, especially western education. The desire for independent schools, free from missionary influence, was the driving force behind the sudden upsurge in the movement in northern Malawi in 1910. Domingo appealed to Booth and other white benefactors outside the country for money for teacher's salaries and for books and other educational materials. But Booth was poor himself, money and materials did not arrive, and most of the Seventh Day Baptist schools closed down. Almost all the Tonga members left to rejoin the Watch Tower movement, though the Ngoni members tended to remain Seventh Day Baptists. Domingo and the Seventh Day Baptists did not openly oppose colonialism. They were not vigorous protesters like Kamwana and the Watch Tower. Kamwana was a pacifist and totally opposed to armed resistance to colonialism. John Chilembwe, however, was not only a prominent independent churchman but the leader of an armed rebellion against colonial rule.

Chilembwe was a Yao from Chiradzulu, and a student at the Blantyre Mission of the Church of Scotland from about 1890. In 1894 he became Booth's house servant, and a member of Booth's self-supporting Baptist Church at the Zambesi Industrial Mission at Blantyre. Booth took Chilembwe to the USA with him in 1897, to enable his intellectually brilliant servant and pupil to study. In 1898 Chilembwe enrolled as a student in the Virginia Theological College and Seminary, and was supported financially by black American Baptists. Chilembwe returned to Malawi as an ordained minister in 1900. He devoted himself to developing his own independent Baptist mission station, and putting into practice contemporary black American ideas of black improvement. Chilembwe built a church and schools, developed a farm and introduced a strict hygiene programme. European clothing was made compulsory and alcohol was banned. In 1909 he helped to establish the Natives' Industrial Union. Before the First World War Chilembwe gave little indication of the radical direction in which he would turn in 1915.

Independent churches in West Africa

The reasons for the establishment of African churches in West Africa in the early colonial period were varied. In 1884 the Germans colonized the Cameroons and the pioneer British Baptist missionaries there were forced to withdraw and hand over to a German mission. One section of the African members of the church refused to submit to the German missionaries and set up the United Native Church. In 1888 the African Baptists seceded from the American Baptist Mission in Lagos because the local missionary attempted to override the autonomy of the local congregation. In 1891 the United

Native African Church was formed in Nigeria by breakaway Yoruba Anglicans and Methodists. The new church was Anglican in its doctrine but permitted polygamy. In 1901 the African Church (nicknamed Bethel) was formed out of a majority of members of the Anglican Breadfruit Church of Lagos, whose laity demanded more choice in the government of the Church. Nigeria became a flourishing field for Independency, and by 1917 there were 14 independent Churches in the country.

The greatest of the Nigerian independent churchmen was Mojola Agbebi (1860–1917). Agbebi was born David Brown Vincent, but assumed his African name in 1894. He was born at Ilesha in Yorubaland, the son of a Yoruba ex-slave who had been liberated by the British Navy and settled in Sierra Leone, had become a CMS Minister and had been posted to Yorubaland. Agbebi's mother was of Igbo origin. From 1895 to 1898 Agbebi underwent training at the CMS Training Institution at Ibadan, where he set a record for his marks in Theology and Sacred History. He was expelled from the Institution, and after trying out both Methodism and Catholicism he joined the American Baptist Mission. From 1888 he was prominent in the breakaway African Baptist Church. He established close co-operation with later independent churches such as the United Native African Church (1891) and the African Bethel Church (1901). Agbebi became the President of the African Baptist Union of West Africa, which spread along the coast to Sierra Leone and the Congo, and had set up 20 churches and schools by 1903.

Agbebi wanted an African church, based on African culture and expressing the African personality. Strongly influenced by Blyden, Agbebi believed that before Christianity could truly take root in Africa the most thorough research should first be undertaken into African culture and particularly African religions. Then once some understanding of African religion had been achieved it should be transformed into an authentic African Christianity. Agbebi completely rejected the widespread contemporary view that the more Europeanized an African convert made himself then the more Christian he became. From 1894 until his death Agbebi never wore European clothes, even when he was in Britain and the USA. He wanted hymns and tunes to be composed by African congregations, not to be introduced by the missionaries. Agbebi believed the culture of the Church must be Africanized and that only African personnel could achieve this task satisfactorily.

Agbebi was not anti-European. He did not believe African-ness in the Church was incompatible with close co-operation with disinterested white organizations who were prepared to give aid with no strings attached. He was a great believer in education. His churches placed a very strong emphasis on education, and his model farm-school at Ijebu combined literary education with agricultural studies. Agbebi was also a political nationalist and pan-Africanist of note. He denounced the British conquest of Yorubaland and the European Scramble for Africa in general. He attended the 1911 Universal Races Congress in London.

The most successful of all independent African Church leaders, judged in terms of the number of converts made, was the Liberian Protestant evangelist William Wade Harris. In 1910 Harris saw a vision of the Archangel Gabriel, as a result of which he arrived in the Ivory Coast in 1913 to convert people who had already rejected French Catholic missionaries. Harris was a breathtakingly inspiring preacher, he tolerated polygamy and he was not associated with the hated French colonial regime. Within a short time he made between 60,000 and 100,000 converts. He was expelled from the Ivory Coast in 1916 when some of his followers expressed nationalist political feelings and spread rumours that the French were about to leave. Yet Harris preached obedience to the colonial government, and the destruction of fetishes and traditional sacred groves. His Church survived his expulsion and in the 1920s there were about 40,000 adherents.

African traditional religious movements: survival and adaptation

African traditional religions remained the religions of the overwhelming majority of Africans before 1914, in spite of the spread of Islam and Christianity. Traditional religion not only survived. It also adapted to colonialism and played a prominent part in resistance to European rule. The armed rebellion of the Ndebele-Shona in 1896 and the Maji Maji Rising, as well as smaller-scale armed resistance movements like the Nyabingi in Uganda and Rwanda, were dominated by new traditionalist cults or old ones transformed.

An example of a new traditionalist cult that arose in response to European colonialism but did not take the form of armed revolt was the cult of Mumbo among the Luo and Gusii of Western Kenya. Mumboism is also a prominent example of passive resistance to colonial rule (see Chapter 1) and illustrates the continuing vitality of traditional beliefs. It originated from an ancient spirit-possession cult among the Luo around Lake Victoria and took a new form among them just before the First World War. The Luo believed that Mumbo was a large sea snake in Lake Victoria and a god. Possession of Mumbo's spirit was a gift reserved for only a select few, who were reputedly given powers of prophecy and healing by Mumbo. In 1913 a certain Onyango Dunde of the Seje clan in Alego on the northern side of the Kavirondo Gulf received a call to preach to the Africans that Mumbo was their God; that crops would grow naturally without people working; that daily sacrifices of cattle, sheep and goats should be made to Mumbo and that these animals would be replaced by new ones which would emerge from the lake; that Africans should abandon their European and Christian habit of wearing clothes and let their hair grow and never wash; that all Europeans were about to leave soon. Mumboism promised an imminent paradise on earth while at the same time it offered active resistance to colonialism.

In 1914 Mumboism spread across the Kavirondo Gulf to the Luo of South Nyanza and the neighbouring Gusii. In South Nyanza a Mumbo prophet, Mosi Auma, was arrested and sentenced by the colonial administration to three years imprisonment for 'witchcraft'. Mosi was a Luo from Kabondo on the border with the Gusii; they became convinced he was a true prophet in September 1914 when Germans from Tanganyika drove the British out of Kisii town. Thousands of Gusii became Mumboites overnight and tried to destroy all physical evidence of European imperialism by sacking Kisii and the nearby Christian mission stations of Nyanchwa (Seventh Day Adventist), Nyabururu and Asumbi (both Catholic). The British retook Kisii quickly, but Mumboism did not die. It grew stronger from 1916 onwards as a catalyst for opposition to forced labour in the First World War. The inevitable famine and following pestilence resulting from widespread Mumboism occurred in 1919, and then Mumboism declined among the Gusii. It continued intemittently among sections of the Gusii until 1954, when it was banned, and among sections of the Luo up to the end of the colonial period.

9
The African political response to colonialism: early forms of political nationalism

Overview

'Nationalism' is a word with different meanings at different times and in different places. It is usually associated with a struggle for self-determination, whether political, economic or cultural. This chapter is concerned with African political nationalism before 1914, and the forms which it took.

At the beginning of the colonial period there was 'traditional nationalism', or primary resistance, as African states and peoples resisted the foreign invasion. Almost everywhere this was defeated. It passed through two stages: initial primary resistance to the imposition of colonial rule, (described in chapters 2-5) and post-pacification primary resistance (described in the first part of this chapter), which generally took the form of armed rebellions. These armed rebellions were frequently forward-looking. They were mass movements which cut across ethnic boundaries, and were led by revolutionary and millenarian figures, but the rebellions were essentially traditional and non-western in their character. Then towards the First World War the beginnings of modern nationalism could be discerned in the secondary resistance movements of western-educated elites. Secondary resistance was important in two ways. Firstly, it did not assert political self-determination as a practical early goal, but advocated reforms in the colonies. Thus in its earlier stage modern African nationalism was associated with the struggle for greater racial equality rather than with the battle for political independence. It was not until after the Second World War that modern elitist nationalism became modern mass nationalism. Secondly, the secondary resistance served as a link between the traditional nationalism of primary resistance and the modern mass nationalism of the struggle for independence.

Armed risings

The Chi Murenga: the Ndebele–Shona Rising of 1896–7

The British South Africa Company's administrators and settlers believed that, having occupied Ndebele country, they could concentrate on exploiting the land and labour of Southern Rhodesia without fear of any serious African protest. The Company men made two false assumptions. One was that the Shona were grateful for their arrival in 1890 because it brought an end to Ndbele raiding. The Shona, despite the end of Ndebele raids, had far more grievances against the Europeans than they had against the Ndebele. The second false assumption was that the Ndebele were cowed by their heavy military defeat and the death of their king in 1893. In fact, the Ndebele kingdom was not totally destroyed and demilitarized in 1893. Between 1893 and 1896 the Company was unable to control the Ndebele effectively beyond Bulawayo and the main roads. The Ndebele might have no king, but their regiments had not been broken up and they maintained an effective local military administration under the indunas.

These two false assumptions led the Company and the settlers to act, as Ranger has pointed out, as if 'Africans did not exist as a factor in the local balance of power'. Rhodes himself was only interested in extending British power further northwards, and was unconcerned about administration and African welfare. Yet both the Ndebele and the Shona were ready to rise against the Company.

The Ndebele objected to the loss of their independence and to their being given only the same rights as the other African peoples whom they had conquered in the past. The Ndebele also resented the loss of their cattle, many of which had been confiscated by the Company at the time of occupation, while others had been killed by a rinderpest epidemic. Thus many Ndebele were impoverished. Further reasons for Ndebele resentment were the Company's methods of recruitment of labour and the power of the police (many of whom were Shona) who often mistreated people. Generally, the Ndebele had lost so much in 1893 and afterwards that they felt they had nothing to lose from further armed resistance. The only questions among them were not whether to revolt but when, and who to proclaim king. The older indunas favoured Umfezela as the new king but the younger men wanted Nyawanda. The opportunity to rise against the Company came early in 1896 with the defeat of the Jameson Raid by the Afrikaners of the Transvaal. Jameson and the Company's white police were captured and interned in the Transvaal by the Afrikaners. Thus most of the Company police officers were out of

Ndebele country, leaving the European farms unprotected. The Ndebele rose in revolt.

The Shona also resented Company rule. The Shona at first believed that the Europeans had come for a short period, but when they found that they had come to stay and to rule they greatly resented their loss of independence. They also objected to the Company's bad administration, which led to abuse of police power and forced labour on European farms. Moreover, the Company had stopped the Shona from trading with the Portuguese and had obliged them to buy goods from the Company whose prices were higher.

The Rising began in March 1896 when the Ndebele regiments launched attacks on Europeans in isolated farms. The settlers then retreated into the towns which were besieged by the Ndebele. The Shona joined in the Rising in June, partly out of opportunism, as it appeared the Ndebele might be succeeding. The British were besieged in Bulawayo and the British relief force sent from the Cape had not yet arrived. But the Shona joined in for another reason too: the influence of their traditional religious leaders.

The priests of the Mwari High God cult exercised considerable influence over the Western Shona and the Ndebele in pre-colonial times. The priests were originally Venda or Kalanga rather than Shona, but they were traditionally linked with the Rozwi rulers of the Shona. After the Ndebele conquest in about 1840 Mzilikazi and later Lobengula turned to the Mwari priests for guidance in time of crisis. The chief priest of the cult in the 1890s was Mkwati, a Shona ex-slave. His assistants were Tenkela, a woman, and Siginyamatshe. Mkwati not only gave his blessing to the Ndebele Rising but encouraged the Shona to join in, and he took a leading part in directing attacks against the Europeans. Thus Mkwati helped to make the Ndebele Rising an inter-ethnic Ndebele-Shona Rising. Moreover, because he was a religious rather than political leader, Mkwati was able to get the non-Ndebele peoples in Ndebeleland, like the Holi and Kalanga, formerly victims of Ndebele imperialism, to join the Rising. Mkwati played a key role in transforming the Chi Murenga of 1896, from a war by the Ndebele regiments into a mass rising of large sections of the whole population.

It would be unwise, however, to exaggerate the importance of Mkwati in the Chi Murenga. He did not control the Ndebele indunas, nor even many Shona. Many influenced by the Mwari cult did not resist and some sections even collaborated with the British. Perhaps only 30% of the Shona resisted, and not all of these were western Shona under Mkwati's influence. Many were inspired to join the revolt by the spirit mediums Kagubi and Nehenda. Kagubi dominated the rising in his home territory in the Salisbury area in north-east Mashonaland, far from the areas influenced by the Mwari cult. The spirit mediums, like the Mwari priests, helped to make the Chi Murenga a mass rising, but they did not co-ordinate their activities with the Mwari priests. Thus in a number of ways the armed resistance of the Chi Murenga only partially succeeded in solving the problem of scale and overcoming African disunity.

The British relief force with its machine guns and howitzers soon defeated the Ndebele, who then realized that they had little hope of regaining their independence. Moreover, Khama of Bechuanaland and Lewanika of Barotseland helped the British. At the end of 1896 the Ndebele indunas negotiated peace terms with Rhodes in the Matopo Hills. The Shona and the religious leaders fought on. The Shona retreated into the caves in the hills where they applied their experience of skilled defence in rocky or wooded country, perfected by forty years of resistance to Ndebele raids. Some of the Shona defensive positions were so impregnable that even British artillery attacks were unable to overcome them, and many caves were only captured after they were dynamited. An outstanding example of Shona resistance of this kind was Makoni's defence of Gwindingwi in August and September 1896. Eventually, however, the Shona resistance was overcome in 1897. Mkwati died in 1897, possibly killed by Shona. The mediums, Kagubi and Nehenda, were captured and executed in 1898.

Many Ndebele and Shona were killed in the rising and trade and agriculture were disrupted, but it would be incorrect to think that Africans gained nothing by their resistance. Rhodes negotiated a peace settlement with the Ndebele to cut the war short, partly because of the back-breaking expense to the Company and partly because of his fear of a revocation of the Charter and an assumption of direct control by the British government. At his famous indaba with the Ndebele indunas, Rhodes conceded recognition of the Ndebele leaders as salaried officials and spokesmen for their people within the colonial administration. A regular system of procedures was established to check ill-treatment of Africans. It was not much, but it was far more than the Ndebele would have got without a rising.

The British government was alarmed by the Rising. Although the British South Africa Company kept its Charter, fear of further rebellion led the British government to withdraw over-provocative measures, like the 1903 increase in hut tax from 10/= to £2 a year. The Colonial Secretary set the tax at £1 a year with a delay in collection.

Many of the Shona turned to the missionaries after 1897 in an attempt to master European methods and perhaps turn them to advantage later. Some Shona, however, continued military resistance for many years. Mapondera led a rising from 1900 to 1903 from Portuguese territory, conducting raids into south Mazoe and the Mount Darwin area. Eventually the Portuguese mounted an expedition against him and he surrendered himself to the British authorities. In 1903 Mapondera was jailed for seven years but he died in prison after a hunger strike.

Prolonged armed resistance in the Ivory Coast, 1900—17

The Ivory Coast became a French colony in 1893 but the colony was not effectively extended to the interior until the defeat of Samori in 1898, and the occupation of Baoule country in the forest in the south between 1898 and 1900. By 1900 most of the country was dotted with French posts.

The Baoule had resisted invasion in 1898–1900, but from 1901 to 1917 they rebelled against French rule. They were motivated by opposition to the 1901 head tax, the building of the railway into the interior from 1904 and the taking of land for it, and forced labour on the railway and roads. The Baoule dominated the resistance which spread to most of the colony and became a countrywide war of independence.

Governor Angoulvant, who arrived in the Ivory Coast in 1908, countered the guerilla tactics of the Baoule and their allies by destroying villages and herding the captured people into larger settlements guarded by the French army. Thus the people were prevented from giving support to the fighters. Thousands died in the armed resistance, including women and children who hid in the forests and suffered starvation rather than be captured by the French forces. There was famine when 100,000 guns were confiscated by the French from Africans who were thus unable to hunt for meat or to defend their farms against wild animals. Massive fines were imposed on the people who mortgaged the coming harvest to pay them. Two hundred and twenty leaders of the resistance were deported to Port Etienne on the Mauretanian coast or to Dahomey, where most of them died of disease.

By 1915 the French were apparently in effective control of the interior, but in 1916 the Baoule rose again, and were crushed with immense difficulty. In 1917 the Agni, who had had enough of the French 'civilizing mission', migrated as a body into neighbouring Gold Coast to escape French reprisals for a revolt.

The Asante Rising of 1900

The Asante were not reconciled to British rule after the arrest and deportation of Prempeh in 1896 (see Chapter 2). They were determined to regain their lost independence at the earliest oppor-tunity by force of arms, having—as they thought—been tricked into not fighting at the time of the British occupation. Therefore under their military leaders they began secretly to store arms in the early years of British rule.

The Asante were determined on war, but it was the British who provoked the Rising of 1900, even though they did not want war. In 1900 Governor Hodgson of the Gold Coast demanded that the Asante chiefs surrender the hidden Golden Stool and announced that he had the right to sit on it. Hodgson mistakenly thought that the stool was the symbol of the asantehene's power, and that the Asante would submit to anyone who possessed it and sat on it. The Governor did not know that the Stool was never sat on, and that the Asante believed that it contained their vitality or life-force and that through it they were united with their ancestors and their God. Hodgson did not understand Asante culture and his misconceptions about the Stool resulted in war. The Asante in their turn misunderstood the British. They believed Hodgson wanted to annihilate them by robbing them of the Golden Stool, and they rose up in a rebellion of unusual desperation. The Asante Rising of 1900 was inspired by a remarkable woman, Yaa Asantewaa, the Queen Mother of Edweso state, and led by General Kofi Kofia.

In the early stages of the rising Governor Hodgson was besieged in the British fort in Kumasi, which was successfully defended by machine guns. At the beginning of the rising Hodgson had detained many Asante leaders in the fort, thus weakening the leadership of the rising. Nevertheless, starvation and disease forced Hodgson to lead part of his force to break out of the fort. The Governor fought his way through to Manso Nkwanta, a southern division of Asante that was friendly to Britain. Hodgson's retreat was considerably helped by the defection of Bekwai from the Asante union to Britain. In 1891 the bekwaihene, Kwaku Sei, had been humiliated by Prempeh in a Great Council debate, and he was determined to prevent an Asante victory and a possible return of Prempeh in 1900.

Kofi Kofia defeated and beat back three British relief expeditions under Carter, Wilson and Burroughs, by using skilled forest warfare tactics. But eventually the resistance of the Asante collapsed when they ran out of ammunition, and they had to face a much stronger fourth expedition led by Willcocks, who had plenty of machine guns and artillery and well-trained British African and Indian (Sikh) soldiers. Willcocks defeated the Asante at Aboaso. Yaa Asantewaa was captured, and joined her king who was transferred with his party from Sierra Leone to the Seychelles, where he would be too far away to inspire another rebellion simply by his near presence. In 1900 Asante was declared a Crown Colony. Prempeh was not allowed to return to Asante until 1924. He was reinstated in 1926 as asantehene with no powers but only ceremonial functions and died in 1931.

The Maji Maji Rising

The Maji Maji Rising was the most important anti-colonial rising in East Africa between the initial European occupation and the 'Mau Mau' War of the 1950s. It covered a large area—most of south-east Tanganyika south of a line from Kilosa to Dar-es-Salaam—and overcame many problems of scale. It united many separate ethnic communities in a single movement. It was a mass revolt, involving not merely soldiers of traditional armies but the whole people, including women and children, who supplied food to the soldiers, gave them shelter and acted as a courier service between them. Maji Maji was also a forward-looking revolt dominated by a new kind of leadership, charismatic and revolutionary religious prophets rather than hereditary and conservative traditional political leaders.

What factors encouraged diverse ethnic groups to unite in one rebellion? Before the colonial period the people of south-east Tanzania had considerably widened their horizons from their experience of the Ngoni invasions and the growth of long-distance trade with the east coast. Trade in particular had stimulated the emergence of new social and communal relationships between people of different societies, and during the colonial period the older patterns of mutual co-operation and contact continued.

More important, however than any other unifying factor in the Rising was the Kolelo snake god cult, a spirit-possession and witchcraft-eradication cult that passed rapidly over clan and ethnic boundaries and swept diverse peoples into a unity which overrode suspicions and allegations of sorcery. Like Mwari, the Kolelo cult involved priest-interpreters of an oracle. The normal preoccupation of the cult was with fertility and the land; but it was transformed in the years before the rebellion to a prophetic and millenarian belief in the reversal of the existing order by divine intervention.

The Kolelo cult was transformed from a purely religious to a political movement, because of the nature of German colonialism in Tanganyika. The economic causes of the Maji Maji Rising have been considered in the study of the colonial economy, (see pp. 156–7) but taxation, forced labour and the cotton programme were not the only grievances of the people. Social and political causes were also important. Amongst the social causes were the activities of German Christian missionaries, who got the administration to burn the sacred huts of traditional priests on the grounds that these were havens of 'witchcraft'—though often the traditional priests were strong opponents of witchcraft. The Ngindo were particularly incensed by the abuse of their women by mercenary soldiers in the German army. Then there were the motives for rebellion of the Ngoni, the most powerful of the societies of south-eastern Tanganyika. The Ngoni sought revenge for the Boma Massacre of 1897, when their political leaders and generals had been treacherously imprisoned or shot by the Germans (see pp. 53–4). Moreover, the Ngoni had been the dominant political and military group of the region before the German occupation and felt keenly the reduction of their status to that of ordinary subjects. Chabruma, the Ngoni king, had a personal reason for fighting the Germans because they had given protection to a young Ngoni man who had seduced one of his wives. Above all, the Ngoni and other ethnic groups desired political freedom and the restoration of their lost independence.

The man who inspired the Rising was Kinjikitile Ngwale, a Kolelo priest or spirit medium at Ngalambe. Kinjikitile was a man of imposing personality and eloquence. He mocked Europeans with names like *utupi nkere* (red potters's clay) or *liyomba lya masi* (ugly fish of the sea), no doubt to help his hearers overcome their superstitious awe of the white man. He instilled strict discipline among his followers, prohibiting witchcraft and looting, two common local evils. From late 1904 he began secretly to give *maji maji* or magic water, as war medicine to men of the Pogoro, Matumbi and Ngindo communities. Some came to receive it at Ngalambe but most had it taken to them by Kinjikitile's assistants. The water was supposed to give protection against the white man's bullets, but its real significance was as a symbol of unity. The water was given to all who wanted it, not just to a single clan or group of warriors. Thus it inspired a mass rising that was also inter-ethnic. Later the water was sent to the Zaramo, Benzi, Ngoni and others.

The Maji Maji Rising began in July 1905 when the Pogoro of Kitope refused to pick cotton. A spontaneous rising broke out over a wide area and the Germans were caught completely by surprise. Plantations, missions, administration bomas and Swahili shops were attacked. Several German planters and missionaries and many government officials (akidas and jumbes) were killed, though some jumbes joined the rebellion, such as the Ngindo chiefs Abdallah Mapanda and Omari Kinjalla. The coast town of Samanga near Kilwa was sacked and burnt. In September the Ngoni belatedly joined the rising, though by that time reinforcements from Germany and German-hired Zulu, Sudanese and Somali mercenaries had arrived. Thus Chabruma involved himself in the united inter-ethnic resistance that Mkwawa had farsightedly proposed to him in 1891, but which the Ngoni leader had then opposed. However, the Ngoni had learnt no new military tactics. In pitched battles they charged heroically at the German machine guns. At the Battle of Uwereka half the Ngoni soldiers were killed, while the Germans lost none.

After Uwereka the Maji Maji fighters settled down to two years of guerilla resistance, employing ambushes, night attacks, moving from place to place and attacking the German forces without warning. The Ngoni (who finally adopted realistic tactics) and the hill-dwelling Matumbi kept the struggle going. However, Chabruma was assassinated in 1906 by an Ngoni rival, and resistance slackened. In 1907 resistance was beaten into total submission by ruthless German suppression. Many leading fighters were executed by hanging, including Kinjikitile and Mputa Gama, the paramount chief of the southern Ngoni. Thousands of villagers were killed or died from starvation when their homes and farms were burnt as part of the German scorched earth policy, which the Germans adopted because they could supply themselves readily from the nearby coast.

The immediate aftermath of the Rising was famine and depopulation in south-east Tanganyika, and 75,000 Africans died. Thousands of survivors who had no seeds for planting new crops after the war, migrated to the coast in search of food.

The Germans defeated the Rising largely because they destroyed the means to resist. They also had modern weapons like machine guns and howitzers. The Matumbi had 8,000 guns but nearly all of them were old-fashioned; their arrows inflicted more casualties. Spears were universally used by the Maji Maji fighters but proved next to useless. The Maji Maji soldiers had no military unity and no single military strategy. Except for the Ngoni, each community had many leaders who did not as a rule co-ordinate military operations. There was little co-ordination between the Ngoni and other peoples. The unity of the movement was a unity of faith rather than practical military organization.

The Maji Maji movement successfully united the peoples within the area of the Rising. However, it failed to spread to a wider area than the Rufiji river basin. Large powerful communities like the Hehe and Nyamwezi did not join it. Some African groups supported the Germans. Some of the Hehe fought on the German side because their traditional enemies the Ngoni, Pogoro, Mbunga and Sagara joined the Rising. Chief Kiwanga of Mahenge joined the Germans in 1905 in gratitude for their help against Mkwawa in the 1890s.

What did the Maji Maji revolt gain for the African peoples of Tanganyika? Firstly, the German administration introduced a number of reforms. The new Governor, Rechenberg, encouraged African cash-crop farming, allowed Africans to choose not to work for German settlers, and punished settlers who mistreated African workers. He also replaced a number of traditional chiefs by western-educated young men from mission schools—though less to improve African conditions than to break the traditional leadership. In general however, German rule improved as German administrators and settlers were now dominated by fear of another Maji Maji.

The most positive result of the Rising, however, was that the people learnt two lessons from its failure: the importance of unity if freedom were to be attained, and the futility of resorting to armed resistance against a colonial power possessing vast military capacity. After the Maji Maji Rising educated Africans in Tanganyika turned to self-improvement and constitutional protest, which led to TANU and eventually independence.

The Nama and Herero Risings

The Herero of South West Africa had begun the colonial period by allying with the Germans against their local enemies. But in January 1904 they broke out in a spontaneous revolt led by Samuel Maherero, an erstwhile collaborator who was turned by the increasing misfortunes of his people into one of colonial Africa's most heroic resistance leaders.

By 1903 the Herero were feeling the full effects of more direct German occupation as the white settler population steadily increased. The Herero were losing their land to settlers and railway companies. Many of their cattle died in the rinderpest epidemic of 1897 and their remaining animals were being lost to German traders. For a long time German traders had sold goods on credit to Africans, but the 1903 Credit Ordinance gave creditors one year to collect debts, after which debts would be declared invalid. The inevitable result was the seizure of African cattle as traders tried to settle debts within the year. As Maherero pointed out in a letter to Governor Leutwein on the causes of the war, German traders 'went so far as to pay themselves by, for instance, taking away cattle by force-two or three head of cattle to cover a debt of one pound sterling'. The timing of the outbreak of the Herero Rising coincided with a German expedition against the Bondelswart people. Consequently Herero country was relatively free of German military units in January 1904. Over a hundred men—settlers and soldiers—were surprised and killed. There was no opposition to Europeans as such only Germans were attacked; Afrikaners, British and even German women, children and missionaries were spared. The railway from Swakopmund to Windhoek was cut in several places and telegraph communications were broken. The Herero besieged German settlements and garrisons and remained on the offensive until June 1904.

In the second phase of the war, the German Governor, Leutwein, and General Von Trotha, having obtained reinforcements, managed to suppress the Rising. The Herero were decisively defeated at the Battle of the Waterberg, but lost far more people in the retreat that followed, as the Germans pursued them relentlessly and carried out a massacre. Von Trotha ordered that, 'Inside the German territory every Herero tribesman, armed or unarmed, with or without cattle, will be shot.' Von Trotha waged a war of extermination, driving the Herero into the Kalahari Desert to the east where thousands starved to death. Thousands of women and children were held in prisoner-of-war camps where most of them died of scurvy or the effects of forced labour. By the time of the December 1905 armistice only 16,000 Herero survived out of an original population of 70,000.

Maherero and about a thousand followers succeeded in crossing the Kalahari, and were given refuge by Tswana chiefs in British Bechuanaland.

The Herero failed to win support from other African communities in their revolt. In January 1904 Maherero had sent letters to the Nama leader, Hendrik Witbooi, via the Rehoboth chief Hermanus van Wyk, proposing a military alliance against the Germans. However, Van Wyk handed the letter over to the Germans. It is doubtful, though, whether Witbooi would have co-ordinated action with Maherero if he had received the letter. When the Nama did rise in revolt in October (two months after Waterberg) it was largely as a result of extreme German provocation.

The Nama shared the same grievances as the Herero—loss of land and cattle—but their resort to armed resistance was a response to the German plan to disarm and disperse their community. Nama resistance lasted much longer, until 1909, because the Nama were more skilled than the Herero at guerilla tactics in the desert. Witbooi was killed in battle in October, but leadership was taken up by Jakob Morenga, half Nama and half Herero, who had been educated in Europe. He attracted followers from many different ethnic communities, though the focus of his support remained Nama. He had been resisting the Germans since 1903, even before the Herero revolt. Morenga was killed in 1907 by British police inside Bechuanaland, and inter-ethnic resistance died with him. Leadership was assumed by a Nama chief, Simon Cooper, who emphasized Nama nationalism. He continued resistance until 1909, when he agreed to stay out of South-West Africa in return for a large bribe.

The Nama suffered almost as badly as the Herero from German military reprisals and herding into prison camps. Half of them died. Only 9,800 Nama were alive in 1911, compared with 20,000 in 1892. In the post-war 'native policies' the Herero and Nama lost all their land. The survivors were condemned to years of forced labour and many of them were deported to other parts of the colony. Originally freemen, landowners and ranchers, the Herero and Nama were turned into landless labourers for German settlers.

Why did the Germans over-react to the Herero and Nama Risings? It was not simply because of the greed of their settlers or the brutality of their soldiers. The Risings were seen in Germany as a national emergency and the mighty German military machine was unleashed on the Herero and Nama cattle-farmers. Even the Socialist leader August Bebel declared, 'This is the worst crisis we Germans have faced since 1870.'

The Zulu Rising of 1906

The Zulu Rising of 1906 was a response to harsh and unjust laws and unimaginative actions of the government of Natal. The Zulu had never become reconciled to the loss of political independence in 1879. In 1889 the new chief, Cetshwayo's son Dinizulu, had led a rebellion which the British had crushed. Dinizulu was deported to St Helena and allowed to return in 1898, but only as a local headman. In 1897 the British government handed over Zululand to Natal and white-settler control. The Natal government introduced so many anti-African laws that the Zulu could not cope with them. The most unpopular of the new laws was the 1905 poll tax of £1 per head, introduced to increase revenue and to force more Africans to work for whites. Other measures were the alienation of land to white settlers and consequent overcrowding in the Zulu reserves, an increase in rents for Zulu tenant farmers on white – owned land, and harsher labour laws. The Zulus despaired of using constitutional means to redress their grievances because civil servants had lost contact with their chiefs.

Early in 1906 a small local rising—mainly a protest against the poll tax—took place, and two white officials were killed. This event involved members of an independent African Church, Mzimba's African Presbyterian Church, which had been spread in Natal by John Sibiya. But most of those involved were religious traditionalists, who had begun their protest by a spate of animal killing at the end of 1905 (an action similar to the Xhosa cattle killing of 1857). The panic-stricken Natal government now provoked a more widespread rising by over-reacting: declaring martial law, calling in imperial troops, sentencing to death a dozen leaders of the revolt in a military court, and then—despite a warning from the imperial government—actually carrying out the executions. The European troops and settler militia also confiscated large numbers of sheep and cattle from the Zulu, burnt many Zulu homes, and inflicted mass floggings on hundreds of villagers. The over-reaction by the white settlers was a result of their general consciousness of being heavily outnumbered by non-European peoples—not only Africans but even Asians outnumbered Europeans in Natal in 1900—and their general fear of an African insurrection. However, their over-reaction brought on the revolt they feared. The result of the executions and other punitive measures was Bambata's Rising.

Bambata was a minor induna of the Zondi section of the Zulu who had been deposed by the government. He rebelled spontaneously and organized a defence in the fortress-like Nkandla mountains. Bambata had no clear plan of action, but he appealed to Zulu national feeling and a number of Zulu leaders joined him. One was Mehlokazulu of the Qungebe people, a prominent commander in the Anglo-Zulu War of 1879. He seems to have been influenced to rebel mainly by the poll tax. Another was Sigananda, the 97 year-old chief of the Cubea, a mat-carrier for Shaka and a close follower of Cetshwayo, and therefore a link between pre-colonial African imperialism, initial primary resistance to European imperialism and post-pacification primary resistance. Sigananda was also influenced by the poll tax but largely by a government order to arrest Bambata, his guest, and hand him over. The laws of hospitality forbade that, but Sigananda would be treated as a rebel by the government if he did not comply. He felt he had nothing to lose and joined Bambata. Indeed, the government fanned the flames of the rising by forcing neutral chiefs to act against the rebels and treating them as rebels if they did not. Moreover, the white militia attacked the Zulu indiscriminately, including clans loyal to the government. Members of Faku's group, guarding river fords against Bambata, were attacked by the militia and retreated to the Nklanda forest to join Bambata.

Although not a single white woman or child was harmed by the rebels, the Rising was ruthlessly suppressed. Bambata, Mehlokazulu and many others were killed at the Battle of Mome Gorge where hardly any prisoners were taken. Throughout the war only 30 whites were killed but over 3,000 Africans died—many of them innocent victims of indiscriminate search and destroy tactics.

After the suppression of the Rising the Natal government held a show trial to try to prove that the resistance had been inspired and organized by Dinizulu, who was arrested in 1907 and put on trial for treason in 1908. Bambata had used Dinizulu's name and support, but no evidence could be produced to implicate Dinizulu in rebellion. In the judgement of 1909 he was acquitted of most of the charges but sentenced to four years' imprisonment for harbouring Bambata.

In the aftermath of the Rising the Natal government made a token effort at reform. In 1908 a bill was introduced, allowing for the appointment of four white members to represent African interests in the legislative council, but it was not enacted. In 1909 a Council of Native Affairs was set up, but its membership was restricted to whites and its functions were only advisory. The African reaction to the defeat of the Rising was to oppose the white man by new methods, no longer by arms but by education and modern political organization, and no longer by local uprisings but by concerted country-wide action.

The Giriama Rising

The Giriama are the most populous Bantu-speaking community on the Kenya Coast. A chiefless society, the Giriama institution of government was the *Kambi*, the council of clan elders. In the early colonial period the Giriama were not effectively administered. Their country is to the north of Mombasa and far from the railway. Little influenced by Christian missions they struck tenaciously to their traditional beliefs and customs, and proved very reluctant to pay tax and perform labour for the government or for wages in Mombasa.

Then in 1913–14 an Assistant District Commissioner, Arthur

Champion, began to impose effective colonial rule by attempting to take a census and by marking out the boundaries of appointed headmen. Huts of those who took to the bush to escape the hut-counters were destroyed. In return the elders refused to meet Champion and he was intimidated by parties of armed Giriama.

The government response was to move the Giriama who lived north of the River Sabaki, and were the strongest opponents of the government, to the south of the river into less fertile land. The objectives of this move were punishment; to give the vacated land to white settlers; and to overcrowd the Giriama reserve, thus forcing Giriama men to work on the new white farms. In order to weaken the hold of traditionalism on the Giriama, the government decided to transfer the site of the *Kaya*, the central shrine of the Giriama where senior elders of each clan met and formed a high court of appeal, from its hill fortress to a more accessible place where it would be more under the control of the district commissioner. When the Giriama refused to move the Kaya, the government dynamited it and open war broke out.

The outbreak of the Giriama-British War coincided with the outbreak of the First World War. The Giriama did not rise against the British in order to help the Germans. Their rising was a natural outcome of British policies since 1913. But the World War certainly distracted the British in their war against the Giriama, who were thus able to keep the war going for a year. The Giriama used guerilla warfare in the forests. They suffered much loss of life and destruction of property, but they secured a negotiated peace in 1915 and a number of concessions: the fine they had to pay was used for development; their leaders were not deported; they were allowed to resettle north of the Sabaki River. Thus the Giriama, like the Basuto in 1881 and the Ndebele in 1896, won concessions by taking up arms against British imperialism.

Giriama resistance in 1914–15 was led by traditional religious leaders, the priestess Me Katilili wa Menza and her son-in-law Wanje wa Mwadarikola, who toured the clans administering an oath of unity. The Giriama, like the Nandi and Maji leaders, used traditional religion as a unifying anti-colonial force. The Giriama saw Me Katilili as the reincarnation of Mipoho, an earlier prophetess who had promised to return and drive out the white man.

John Chilembwe's Rising

Chilembwe's revolt against the Nyasaland administration in 1915 is the first example in black Africa of secondary resistance led by a member of the western-educated elite rather than by traditional authorities, and inspired by new motives pointing the way to modern mass nationalism. But the revolt was too unorganized and limited in scope to be successful or to be considered an example of new secondary resistance methods.

For some years before the Rising Chilembwe had become increasingly aware of the grievances of his fellow Africans. He came to regard as un-Christian and sinful the mistreatment of African squatters on the European plantations—especially the Magomero estates near his mission—the low wages and the flogging at Magomero, the increasingly rigorous collection of government tax, and the lack of action by either government or settlers to alleviate the distress caused to Africans by the famine of 1913. Then came the World War and the recruitment of Africans into the British army. To Chilembwe this was the last straw. He saw no reason why Africans should die in a white man's war. Chilembwe's campaign against recruitment led the government to attempt to arrest and deport him. The rising was largely an ill-prepared response by Chilembwe and his followers on his mission station to this attempt.

When the Rising started Chilembwe began to formulate a forward-looking political programme for the future. He planned to create a nation: not to restore the fortunes of the traditional communities but to build an inter-ethnic modern independent African state, though he would use the help of those Europeans, such as teachers, who were prepared to accept African leadership. Chilembwe was forward-looking in another way, too: he was a millenarian, and expected an imminent Second Coming, though to his way of thinking there was no contradiction between the end of the world as he knew it and the creation of an African government: both were ideal.

Chilembwe's Rising was largely, however, a rebellion of despair. He does not seem ever to have believed it would succeed. Like John Brown, who tried and failed to stir up a slave revolt in the USA in 1859, Chilembwe courted martyrdom. Mwase, a chronicler of the Rising, reports that Chilembwe said, 'Let us then strike a blow and die', and actually referred to John Brown. When the Rising began, Chilembwe prepared no line of defence and failed to fortify his mission station. The Rising attracted little support and only 800 took part in it. Only three Europeans were killed. Chilembwe spent most of the Rising meditating on a hill top, expecting the imminent coming of the Kingdom. He was shot while attempting to escape although he put up no real resistance to his pursuers.

Chilewbwe's Rising came too soon because by 1915 an educated mass base on which a modern mass nationalist movement could be built was still lacking. Chilembwe's significance was therefore that of a martyr who could serve as inspiration for a later generation of nationalists.

Non-violent resistance

The Kyanyangire

The *Kyanyangire* (refuse) revolt in Bunyoro in Western Uganda in 1907 is a classic example of how non-violent resistance might achieve as much as, or more than, might be won by armed resistance. It was untypical of many post-pacification revolts in that it was led by traditional chiefs. Moreover, it was a revolt less against the European overruler than the Ganda sub-imperialists.

The defeat of Kabalega and his capture in 1899 did not mark the end of Banyoro resistance. In 1900 many of Kabalega's loyal officials had themselves confirmed as colonial chiefs, partly to preserve their privileges but also to be in a better position to fight for the restoration of the Lost Counties taken by Buganda in 1894. It was these men led by one of Kabalega's favourites, Paulo Byabachwezi, who inspired the revolt of 1907.

The British made the mistake in Bunyoro of adding insult to the injury of the 'Lost Counties' by placing Ganda chiefs in Bunyoro from 1901. A Muganda saza chief, Jemusi Miti, was put in charge of reform of the administration. Miti did his work well, but most of his Ganda subordinates were arrogant and greedy. In 1902 the young king, Kitahimbwa, was deposed by the British for opposing the Ganda take-over of the administration. He was replaced by the pro-Ganda Duhaga II.

The 1907 revolt was planned in strict secrecy. Byabachwezi insisted on no violence. A peaceful delegation of thousands led by the Banyoro chiefs demanded the removal of Baganda chiefs from Bunyoro. This peaceful protest to the British administration was reinforced by intimidation of Baganda in Banyoro, who were arrested on trumped-up charges or whose harvesting was interfered with. Many of the Baganda chiefs and their followers took refuge in the British post at Hoima and others fled to Buganda.

The British reaction was to reinstate all the Baganda chiefs and arrest 53 Banyoro chiefs at a baraza, just to show that Bunyoro was a conquered country. But the Banyoro leaders were soon released or given light prison sentences or fines, and concessions were made. The Ganda chiefs remained in their positions, in order to show British authority, but no new ones were appointed after 1907 in order to avoid another revolt. Gradually the Baganda chiefs were replaced by Banyoro. The Banyoro were given control over the tombs of the Kitara kings in the Lost Counties. Finally, Bunyoro's land was divided among the chiefs between 1907 and 1914 in a land settlement akin to Buganda's in 1900.

Gandhi and Satyagraha in South Africa

Mohandas (later Mahatma) Gandhi, perhaps the greatest nationalist leader in modern world history, began his political career and first practised his revolutionary political ideas on the African continent. Gandhi was born in Porbandar, India, in 1869. He qualified as a lawyer in London and practised law for a time in India. Then in 1893 he came to South Africa where he was hired by the wealthy Indian trader Abdulla of Pretoria in a law suit. Gandhi stayed on. He was so shocked by the racial discrimination against Asians and Africans in Natal and the Transvaal that he decided to help organize the Indians to fight it. He formed the Natal Indian Congress and became its Secretary. At this stage of his political development Gandhi operated at the level of peaceful constitutional protest and petitions but this approach achieved nothing. His work in organizing the Indian Ambulance Corps in the Second Anglo-Boer War won the South African Indians some medals but nothing else.

After a brief visit to India (1901–2) when he made contact with the Indian National Congress, Gandhi returned to South Africa and settled in Johannesburg as an Attorney in the Transvaal Supreme Court. He now developed his philosophy and practice of non-violent passive resistance. The spark for action was the 1906 Asiatic Registration Bill in the Transvaal state legislature, proposing compulsory registration of every Indian—man, woman and child—above the age of eight; and requiring Indians to produce registration certificates at any time or place, even in their own houses. Gandhi organized a Passive Resistance Association to put into practice the principles of satyagraha (firmness in truth). Gandhi's new movement boycotted and picketed the permit offices, and only 500 out of 20,000 Indians registered. When Gandhi was imprisoned, many Indians deliberately got themselves arrested to join him. An impressive feature of this well-organized civil disobedience was Hindu-Muslim unity. But the bill became an Act and was not repealed.

Gandhi won a victory, however, after the 1912 Indian coalminers' strike at Newcastle in Natal. When he was arrested for organizing a strikers' protest march there was an outcry in India led by the nationalist leader Gokhale. Viceroy Hardinge intervened and the new South African Union government set up a Commission of Inquiry. The results were abolition of the £3 tax on indentured labourers, and a new law which meant that all that was required for an Indian to enter South Africa was a domicile certificate bearing the holder's thumb-print. Gandhi left South Africa for good in 1914 to resettle in India. He did not provide a solution for the Indian question in South Africa; and he failed to establish political co-operation between Indians and Africans. The significance of his South African experience is the training it gave him for Indian politics.

Early elite nationalism

In the period from about 1890 to 1914 the nationalism of the western-educated African elite was transformed in British West Africa. The elite could no longer look forward to the creation of self-governing states as they could in the heyday of assimilationist ideas and practice (from c. 1850 to c. 1890). Instead the best the elite could hope for after 1890 was reforms within the colonial system. They formed new nationalist associations to agitate for reforms. At the same time elite movements working for similar policies of colonial reform were arising in Senegal, South Africa and North Africa.

A number of general factors inspired the growth of nationalist associations in the British West African territories before 1914. These included the extension of British colonial control; colonial land policies such as declaring unoccupied land to be Crown land, and concessions to white plantation and mining companies; the failure of many African businesses to compete successfully with large European firms, the reduction of the role of African missionaries; and the forcing of the westernized elite out of the colonial civil service in the four British territories.

This last factor was perhaps the most vital. It was no longer possible for a western-educated black West African to follow a career like Africanus Horton's. Horton, together with another Sierra Leonian, William Davies, had reached the rank of Lieutenant-Colonel in the British Army Medical Service and had published the results of detailed research on tropical diseases. In his book *West African Countries and Peoples* (1868), Horton had looked forward to early independence for the British West African colonies. Right up to his death in 1883 he retained his faith in British good will. Had he lived longer that faith might have been shattered. In 1902 Africans were excluded from the West African Medical Service and condemned to a separate service with lower salary scales. Thus senior African doctors would not be in a position to give orders to junior white doctors.

The demands of the British West Africa elite tended to reflect the interests of their class rather than the aspirations of the population as a whole. They pressed for more educational facilities, especially universities, more places in the legislative councils for educated Africans, more positions in the colonial civil service, and policies of economic development that would allow the African commercial entrepreneur (generally a member of the westernized elite) to compete with European business enterprise. The elite assigned no political role to the vast peasant majority. They believed that the best thing the peasants could do was either to cease to be peasants by becoming educated and joining the elite, or by remaining peasants and retaining their traditional culture, serving as model museum pieces for elite Africans who could idealize them. It is not true however, that the elite did not care for the peasants, as the activities of the Aborigines Rights Protection Society in the Gold Coast shows.

The ARPS was formed in 1897 to fight the Crown Lands Bill of that year, whereby the Gold Coast government would be given the right to administer the country's public land (including unoccupied land) 'for the general advantage'. Although the British intention was not to seize land, but to regulate the sale of land by chiefs to concessionary companies, the ARPS opposed the Bill because African rights of ownership would no longer be automatically recognized, thus creating a loophole for possible alienation of land in the future. A delegation of predominantly western-educated Fante chiefs went to London and persuaded Colonial Secretary Chamberlain to cancel the scheme. During the agitation of 1897 a crucial role was played by the Reverend Attoh Ahuma's *Gold Coast Methodist Times*. The ARPS was also successful in delaying implementation of the 1911 Forest Bill (to establish forest reserves in unoccupied lands) until 1927.

The agitation in defence of unoccupied lands in the Gold Coast led to a flowering of cultural nationalism in literary form. Casely Hayford's *Gold Coast Native Institutions* was published in 1903, and was followed by Sarbah's *Fanti Customary Laws* (1904) and *Fanti National Constitution* (1906), Hayford's *Ethiopia Unbound* (1911) and *The Truth about the West African Land Question* (1913), Attoh Ahuma's *The Gold Coast Nation and National Consciousness* (1911) and N. A. Adaye's *Nzima Land* (1913). The aims of these books were to inform the western-educated of the history, customs and laws of their country, to keep up pressure on the government over the land question, and to help unite the people in a common nationalist purpose. One chapter in Ahuma's book was headed *The Difficult Art of Thinking Nationally*, a difficulty compounded by the existence of numerous communities with a variety of languages and differing laws and customs. In his 1903 book Casely Hayford had expressed his vision of unity between the coast people and the Asante. The ARPS, however, never tried to develop into a common political movement for all the Gold Coast people, and remained largely a Fante ethnic organization.

Casely Hayford was the most persuasive advocate of African national consciousness in early twentieth century West Africa. Born in 1866 into a prominent Christian Gold Coast family, he was educated at the Wesleyan Boys High School in Cape Coast and at Fourah Bay College, Sierra Leone. He then trained as a lawyer in Cambridge and London. In 1897 he was active in the ARPS protest against the proposed alienation of land. He became a student of traditional society, and a strong advocate of African rights against a

British colonial administration that increasingly interfered with them. Casely Hayford was more than a Gold Coast nationalist who sought Fante-Asante unity. He was also a pan-Africanist. In 1914 he made plans to call a National Congress of British West Africa, but the First World War intervened and it did not meet until 1919–20.

Nigerian elite nationalism before 1914 centred on Herbert Macaulay's People's Union of Lagos, founded in 1908 to protest against government attempts to expropriate Yoruba land in Lagos and impose a water rate that would help to provide improved facilities for Europeans. Macaulay, a grandson of Bishop Crowther, was born in 1864, gained a degree in civil engineering, and expressed his nationalism in vivid prose in the Lagos newspapers. Ultimately his Union degenerated into a conservative social club.

Black elite politics in Senegal

Blaise Diagne, a Serer by origin, came first in his class in the St Louis Secondary School. After twenty years' service in the French Colonial Service all over Africa and the Caribbean, this symbol of successful assimilation stood as a radical anti-administration candidate in the 1914 election for Senegal's seat in the French Chamber of Deputies (National Assembly) in Paris. Diagne's victory in the election marked the beginning of modern nationalist politics in French West Africa.

Diagne's victory was a triumph for his eloquence and for the hard work of his Young Senegalese Party supporters, mainly clerks and teachers. He campaigned for total equality of Africans with Frenchmen at a time when French Governors in Senegal were trying to restrict the privileges of African French citizens in the communes and prevent their promotion in the civil service. Diagne wanted to break the domination of the Bordeaux traders and their agents who fixed the price of groundnuts, and put forward election candidates to further their own interests in the French parliament. He won the support of the Lebou, the indigenous inhabitants of Dakar and Rufisque, by supporting their complaints against land expropriation. He received considerable financial support from the Mourides of the interior, although they could not vote because they were Muslims and lived outside the Communes. Diagne won because of a split vote among his six European opponents.

Diagne was a nationalist because although he wanted reforms within the French empire, and not complete independence, he strove for the total equality of black and white. He was also a pan-Africanist, regarding himself after his election as a representative of all the people of French West Africa. For some years he remained radical. In 1916 he won, in the French parliament, the right of French citizenship for all Senegalese in the communes and their exemption from forced labour and the indigenat. In return, however, for this concession for the coastal Senegalese, he served as France's major recruiter for black soldiers for the First World War. 180,000 Senegalese were recruited for the French Army and 60,000 were killed. After 1919 Diagne became a pillar of the French colonial establishment and a defender of forced labour.

Black elite politics in South Africa

African nationalism as it developed in South Africa from 1912 was different from Afrikaner or English nationalism in that it transcended ethnicism. It was based not on a common language and culture but, in Leo Kuper's phrase, on 'a shared historical experience of subordination'. Moreover, unlike Afrikaner and English nationalism it advocated inter-racial co-operation.

The South African Native National Congress was created at a conference in Bloemfontein in 1912, and renamed the African National Congress in 1923. It was set up so that the black elite—the chiefs and the western-educated intelligentsia—throughout the new Union of South Africa could act together to defend African rights more easily, especially after the creation of the Afrikaner dominated Union of South Africa in 1910. The Congress was not a mass movement and contained no representatives of the peasants or the new urban proletariat. Letsie II, Paramount Chief of Lesotho, was elected Honorary Governor of the Congress. The government was invited to send a representative to open the conference. The methods of the new organization would be strictly constitutional. Thus, it was hoped to remove the colour bar, by educating whites about the need to do so. One prominent black South African leader John Tengo Jabavu, actually opposed the Congress because he thought its aims were too radical. Also it might threaten his own position as the leader and spokesman for Africans.

Jabavu was the most outstanding product of mission education in the eastern Cape. One of the first Cape Africans to get a degree, Jabavu founded a newspaper, *Imvo Zabantsundu* (African Opinion), in 1884. But he was not a nationalist. He believed justice could be obtained for his people only if they attained his own high standard of westernization.

In contrast to Jabavu were the leaders of the Natal black elite. Dr Pixley Ka Izaka Seme, originally a Zulu nationalist, returned from studies in Oxford, London and America a qualified barrister and a convinced African nationalist, though he believed the chiefs would be the most effective instrument in the fight for African rights. His close political ally was the Congress' first President-General, Dr John Llangalakhe Dube, who also studied in America. Dube founded a technical college (the Ohlange Institute), a girls' school and a newspaper. Seme and Dube, unlike Javabu, favoured a united black front to achieve equality, though like Jabavu they wanted a multi-racial society. Neither Seme nor Dube, however, conceived of a nationalist movement based on the African miners, of whom there were 195,000 in South Africa by 1910. Seme and Dube were as firmly wedded as Jabavu to ideas of elitist Christian and educated leadership. In any case, the miners were mostly on nine-month contracts, easily replaced and mainly from outside the country. It would take generations to organize them and overcome their disunity.

The politics of the intelligentsia in North Africa

North African nationalism goes back to ancient times, when the earliest inhabitants resisted Phoenician and Roman invaders. Modern Egyptian nationalism dates from Mehemet Ali's attempt to modernize the country in the early nineteenth century, but also takes in the pan-Islamic reformism of al-Afghani and Arabi's movement against the alien Turks and Europeans.

The British occupation of 1882 provided new grievances on which Egyptian nationalism could grow. The British promised to leave soon after restoring the country's finances, but stayed, and Egypt was condemned to forty years of colonial rule. Lord Cromer developed Egypt's agriculture, but he held back industrialization, political reform and the development of education, on which he spent only 1.5% of the budget between 1882 and 1901.

The Egyptian nationalist parties after 1882 were formed by the western-educated but Arabic-speaking intelligentsia. The Hizb al-Watani or Nationalist Party was led by the brilliant young lawyer Mustapha Kemal, who died at the age of 34. Its members were mainly representatives of the new middle class, or *effendiya* of *fallah* (peasant) origin. The more conservative nationalist grouping, dominant in the assembly until 1913, was the Hizb al-Umma (Party of the Nation), composed largely of aristocratic landowners. The most prominent figure was Saad Zaghlul, a former student of al-Afghani, who became Minister of Education as a move to appease those wanting constitutional changes before 1914, including increased powers for the legislative council and the general assembly. There was no resort to violent struggle until after the First World War in which Egypt was reduced to a mere British military base. Before 1914 Egypt enjoyed a relatively free press, and openly anti-European and pan-Islamic journals like *El-Moayyad*, founded in 1889 by Ali Youssef, could be printed and circulated. In contrast to the French in Algeria, in Egypt the British did not attempt to drive local nationalism underground. Thus Egyptian nationalism did not develop a militant form.

In Algeria the French ruthlessly suppressed all nationalist expression, and imprisoned or exiled even French-educated Muslims who pressed, not for independence, but for reforms. Those imprisoned included members of the 1912 Party of Young Algeria which advocated abolition of the indigenat, and the political and legal equality of Muslims with Europeans. In the long run, Algerian nationalism would have no alternative but armed rebellion. In Tunisia the French contained radical nationalism by allowing traditional rulers and western-educated young aristocrats to participate in councils and assemblies, and by favouring development projects, especially education. The more radical and truly nationalist Destour Party emerged only after the First World War.

Epilogue

At the time of Kenya's independence in 1963 some elders of the Embu community on the south-east slopes of Mount Kenya demanded the return of the shields and spears they had been forced to surrender to the British when their initial primary resistance was broken in 1906. This is only one illustration of the awareness of early resistance, which remained strong right through the colonial period to the era of restored independence. That this should be so is not surprising when for most African societies the colonial period was short, lasting for only two generations. The name of Samori was used by both Sekou Toure in Guinea and Houphouet Boigny in the Ivory Coast in the 1950s to win support from the masses. The leaders of the resistance to the imposition of colonial rule have thus often become the heroes of the new nations of post-colonial Africa.

Bibliography

The following books are recommended for further reading in addition to those listed in Volume 1.

AJAYI, J. F. A. — *Christian Missions in Nigeria 1841–1891*, Longman, 1965.

BLEY, H. — *South-West Africa under German rule*, Heinemann, 1971.

HARGREAVES, J. D. — *West Africa Partitioned, Vol I*, Macmillan, 1974.

HOLT, P. M. and DALY, M. W. (Eds) — *The History of the Sudan* (3rd Edition), Weidenfeld and Nicolson 1980.

ISAACMAN, A. F. — *The Tradition of Resistance in Mozambique*, Heinemann Educational Books, 1976.

ILIFFE, J. — *A Modern History of Tanganyika*, Cambridge, 1979.

ILIFFE, J. — *Tanganyika Under German Rule*, Cambridge University Press, 1969.

LEWIS, I. M. — *The Modern History of Somalia* (2nd Edition), Longman, 1979.

MATSON, A. T. — *Nandi Resistance to British Rule*, East African Publishing House, 1972.

MATSEBULA, J. S. M. — *A History of Swaziland*, Longman Southern Africa, 1972.

OLIVER, R. — *Sir Harry Johnston and the Scramble for Africa*, Chatto and Windus, 1957.

OGOT, B. A. (Ed) — *War and Society in Africa*, Cass, 1972.

PALMER, R. and PARSONS, N. (Eds) — *The Roots of Rural Poverty in Central and Southern Africa*, Heinemann Educational Books, 1977.

RANGER, T. O. — *Revolt in Southern Rhodesia*, Oxford University Press, 1960.

ROTBERG, R. I. — *The Rise of Nationalism in Central Africa*, Harvard, 1965.

RUBENSON, S. — *The Survival of Ethiopian Independence*, Heinemann Educational Books, 1976.

SORRENSON, M. P. K. — *Origins of European Settlement in Kenya*, Oxford University Press, 1968.

SUNDKLER, B. G. M. — *Bantu Prophets in South Africa* (2nd Edition), Oxford University Press, 1961.

SILLERY, A. — *Botswana: A Short Political History*, Methuen, 1974.

SLADE, R. — *King Leopold's Congo*, Oxford University Press, 1962.

TOUVAL, S. — *Somali Nationalism*, Harvard University Press, 1963.

Index

216